ROGER CASEMENT IN DEATH

ROGER CASEMENT
IN DEATH

OR

HAUNTING THE FREE STATE

W. J. McCORMACK

Published by the
UNIVERSITY COLLEGE DUBLIN PRESS
PREAS CHOLÁISTE OLLSCOILE BHAILE ÁTHA CLIATH
in conjunction with
THE RESEARCH CENTRE IN THE HISTORY OF THE BOOK
INSTITUTE OF ENGLISH STUDIES UNIVERSITY OF LONDON

2002

First published 2002 by
UNIVERSITY COLLEGE DUBLIN PRESS
Newman House 86 St Stephen's Green, Dublin 2, Ireland
www.ucdpress.ie

ISBN 1 900621 76 2 hardback
ISBN 1 900621 77 0 paperback

British Library Cataloguing in Publication Data
A catalogue record for this title is available from the British Library

Acknowledgements
Material quoted from the Casement Papers, the Curry Papers, the McCartan Papers,
the McGarrity Papers and the Maloney Papers, with some related material, is the
property of the National Library of Ireland and has been reproduced with the
permission of the Council of Trustees of the National Library of Ireland.

Typeset in Ireland in Caslon 540 and Bodoni Oldstyle
by Elaine Shiels, Bantry, Co. Cork
Text design by Lyn Davies
Printed in England by
MPG Books Ltd, Bodmin,
Cornwall

in memoriam

Francis Shaw sj
and
Liam de Paor

*

The images in this film, many of which were taken from rare archive footage, immdiately captivated me; but nonetheless, I fell asleep in the green velvet armchair I had pulled up to the television. As my waking consciousness ebbed away, I could still hear every word of the narrator's account of Casement, but was unable to grasp their meaning.

W. G. SEBALD *The Rings of Saturn* (1998)

Contents

Prefatory Note

This once short book began as a long essay. The objective had been to assess W. J. Maloney's *The Forged Casement Diaries* (1936) for plausibility. Roger Casement commands so many reputations today – humanitarian in the Third World, Irish patriot, British traitor – as to require critical attention, distinct from the work of biographers. To what extent did Maloney's account of what occurred in 1915–16, with regard to documents covertly associated with Sir Roger Casement, respond to analysis? I had no intention of moving away from my chosen text, not even to ask who the author was. I was concerned with 1936 a great deal more than 1916. My original intention is now principally embodied in chapter 3 of the present book.

Having come to some conclusions on that score, I found myself obliged to raise my head from the page to look left and right. The conclusions themselves demanded as much. On the one side stood the tragic figure of Casement, about whom a great deal has been written and a great deal more said. He remained consolingly familiar, unaltered in my mind by the strange book I had just examined in considerable detail. Now dead eighty-six years – twenty, when Maloney's book was published – he is still most typically represented to us through visual images, none of the biographies being currently available.

There are casual photographs, formal portraits, Sir John Lavery's covert sketch of the prisoner in the dock, Harry Kernoff's woodcut. A German image, the work of a lithographer named Fanto, played its part in the 1930s campaign, and attracted the Medusan admiration of Maud Gonne. These may be no more readily seen than the biography of Denis Gwynn or Roger Sawyer, yet Casement retains a high-recognition level in the eyes of the Irish public. Elsewhere, he awaits rediscovery. One way of reassessing the complex social and cultural experiences which the name Casement encapsulates is to investigate the manner in which English painting represented sexuality, classical antiquity and 'the orient' through images of enslavement.

The chapter in which this is attempted (see pp. 108–29 below) makes no claims to be exhaustive. Nor does it deny the importance of those several biographies. Among the more recent ones, B. L. Reid's (1976) seems to me the best, precisely because it is prepared to 'theorise' about the structure of

Roger Casement's psyche, however briefly. Since the days of Denis Gwynn (who was discreet though undeceived), Casement's biographers have broadly accepted the implication of truth behind the stories of scandalous diaries. His editors, on the other hand, have come from the school of deniers – until Roger Sawyer brought the two disciplines together. Though the biographies have added much to our knowledge of Casement, the essential relationship between him and his survivors remains tantalisingly visual. There is also the question of the metropolitan culture he officially served and increasingly sought to subvert: it too may prove more accessible through art history rather than political testimony. This strikes me as opening up a remarkable area of critical inquiry, but neither time nor space permits its development here. Casement remains in striking silhouette.

On the other side, as I turned I glimpsed a vacant space which – as I stared hard at it – filled with blankness. Utter blankness. This was Dr Maloney's visual relationship with me, one of his most attentive readers. In his book, profusely illustrated with portrait photographs obtained with great diligence, there was no picture of the author. True, the portrait-photographs were exclusively of villains – excluding Casement, that is. But one conclusion I had reached in scrutinising *The Forged Casement Diaries* was that its author did not suffer from modesty, false or otherwise. Who was Maloney?

The contrast between the biographer and his subject was startling. The temptation arose to pursue both, in a scamper of research which would have exhausted me without exhausting these additional topics. I have added little if anything to Casement's glory or infamy, because I have not been much concerned with what happened in 1903, or 1911. As for 1916, I have inevitably expanded upon a point here, or developed a cameo mugshot there, but essentially I remain concerned with what happened between – say – 1930 and 1936, when *The Forged Casement Diaries* was planned and executed, during the last days of the Irish Free State. For that reason, I have tried to add something to the almost nothing generally known of Dr Maloney. In advance of the forensic examination designed to put his Forgery Theory to the test, that seemed a legitimate extension of my original plan. I am aware that my perspective changes after chapter 7, apparently substituting a notion of history influenced by psychoanalysis for careful archival research. However, as confirmation of the Black Diaries' authenticity is reached, it becomes necessary to acknowledge their nature and content, and so allow Casement to reclaim our attention. In advance of some detailed editing work, one cannot avoid a modicum of speculation. I hope I have avoided Dr Maloney's tendency to disregard the evidence if it fails to support the speculation.

In summary form the argument contained in this book was presented to an Irish Studies seminar at the Institute of English Studies, in London University's Senate House in February 2002. I am grateful for the comments of all who spoke, especially Peter Hart, Siobhan Holland, Claire Hutton, Ben Levitas and John Maher. The previous year, a Literature and Politics seminar, which I taught at Goldsmiths College, endured some of these thoughts: I would in particular like to thank Ben Pitcher, Megan Roberts, Samantha Sen and Roshanara Voetzsch for the stimulation of their responses. In more secluded arenas Conor Carville, Mary Daly, Anthony Farrell, Mary King, Lucy MacDiarmid, Eunan O'Halpin, Roger Sawyer and Will Sulkin read drafts of the book at various stages. Ciaran Brady, Reinhard Doerries, Jeff Dudgeon, Helen Forde, Lisa Godson, David Rose and Lucinda Thomson discussed aspects of the argument, and they too greatly assisted me in avoiding error. Patrick and Hugh Casement were good enough to read through an interim typescript, and the latter responded with bracing comments on my bibliography. Dennis and Sylvia Tate gave me access to the Harry Kernoff woodcut, which strikes me as the most intriguing image of Casement which we have. Closer to home, Jane Desmarais provided an important detail at just the right moment.

As the National Library of Ireland plays a part in the history I have to relate, I want particularly to express my gratitude to its present-day administration, most notably the Director, Dr Brendan O'Donoghue, for his patience; the Keeper of Manuscripts, Dr Noel Kissane, for his canny good sense; and Mr Tom Desmond for his never failing helpfulness.

The staff of the Public Record Office (Kew and Myddleton Street), and the Wellcome Library of Medical History (London), were helpful beyond the call of duty. Material in the Bodley Library (Oxford), Cambridge University Library, the London School of Economics, and Rhodes House (Oxford) was expeditiously made available. Generous Scottish assistance was provided at every turn – by Simon Johnston (Royal College of Surgeons, Edinburgh), Jean Archibald (University of Edinburgh), Victoria Ingpen (Royal Society of Edinburgh) and Alison Gardiner (Lothian Health Services Archive). In Northern Ireland, Lesley Holmes of Belfast City Hall, Eileen Black of the Ulster Museum and Shan McAnena of Queen's University were helpful in tracing the career of Henrietta Rae. J. B. Lyons gave a draft of the typescript a clean bill of health, though it may have taken a turn for the worse since then.

While possible American sources for W. J. Maloney's career have not been thoroughly excavated, staff at the Lauinger Library (Georgetown University), the Falvey Memorial Library (University of Villanova), the Beinecke Library (Yale), Stanford University and the New York Public Library have assisted my distant inquiries meticulously. Back at Canada Water in east London, Eamon Dyas of News International came to the rescue when British Library resourcefulness failed me in one significant regard. Friendly competition between two TV production companies provided the impetus to bring this inquiry to a close. We have not heard the end of the matter.

On several occasions, Hugh Hartnett and Lucinda Thomson provided an entertaining dinner table round which the question of Casement was debated with vigour. In addition to my hosts, I should also like to thank Rosalinde Schut and James Hamilton for their contributions. Finally, an invitation to speak at the jubilee conference of the International Association of University Professors of English gave me the opportunity to reflect on the book's final shape in a peaceful atmosphere. At the risk of seeming to forge my date line, I therefore sign off –

W. J. Mc C
Roppeltsgasse, Bamberg
August 2001

Abbreviations

BOD. LIB.	Bodleian Library
BT	Board of Trade
FO	Foreign Office
HO	Home Office
IRA	Irish Republican Army
IRB	Irish Republican Brotherhood
IWM	Imperial War Museum
JNMD	*Journal of Nervous and Mental Disease*
LSE	London School of Economics and Political Science
NLI	National Library of Ireland
PRO	Public Records Office, London
RAMC	Royal Army Medical Corps
TSL	Type-signed letter
UCD	University College Dublin

ONE

'SIXTEEN' MEN THE ENGLISH SHOT?

Did you read that report by a man what's this his name is?
JAMES JOYCE, *Ulysses*

———

John Bull and Sheelagh? The relationship between Great Britain and Ireland has eluded definition. Metaphor, racial and religious stereotypes, class-analyses, theories of post-colonialism have all failed to pin it down. As seen on a map, the two islands have been compared to lovers, the one aggressive, the other disdainful. Before 1800, the two were sister-kingdoms – despite the 'gender' confusion. Ireland has successively been an Achilles heel, a Celtic Tiger, a flower in Blessed Mary's coronet, a granary, and a paean in the Erse. Meanwhile, the Grand Old Dame Britannia has now become the Sick Man of Europe. These tropes never satisfactorily account for the dynamic of attraction and repulsion which has characterised Anglo-Irish relations, at least since the sixteenth century. Occasionally, they are displaced by sudden eruptions or re-emergences of more concentrated material which defies linguistic tagging. One such occasion attaches to Sir Roger Casement (1864–1916).

There is a widespread, low-intensive belief that five diaries associated with Casement preserved in the Public Record Office at Kew are forged.[1] In Ireland it is an article of faith with some older patriots who hold that, at the time of Casement's trial for treason in 1916, the British authorities manufactured a record of frequent and promiscuous homosexual acts involving payments of money. The prisoner and – by extension – the nationalist cause he espoused were to be discredited by the underhand circulation of extracts from his private papers. Within a certain structure of thought, it follows that the article of faith should date back to inaugurating events, just as the doctrine of the Trinity is said to be implicit in the words of Christ. Thus it is held in this quarter that the diaries were always known to be phoney, like the gospel according to Judas (in whom Oscar Wilde saw the typical biographer). They weren't.

1   The documents are in PRO, HO 161/1–5

Religious analogies may seem strained, even in this largely irreligious age. In the 1890s, when Casement began to work for the Foreign Office, they were the common currency of Decadence and Imperialism alike, as the art of Victoria's final decades amply demonstrates. Old Testament narratives of the Israelite captivities – whether in Egypt or Babylon – provided a framework for representations of God's Own (European) People in their struggle against Darkness and Barbarism. The heroics of young virgins and faithful wives – Esther, Judith, Susanna – only made explicit the eroticism to which these larger themes became subject. The New Testament added a model for emulation in this cultural typology. More particularly, the generation of Irish separatist nationalists to which Casement belonged chose very deliberately to 'rise' in arms at Easter. Their rhetoric – the word is used without any pejorative implication – was richly endowed with theological terms. In advance of the insurrection, Pearse spoke of redemption and blood sacrifice. Afterwards, a nun described Casement as 'our glorious martyr, the John the Baptist of our Herod-ridden 20th Century'. A layman proclaimed that 'one more saint and martyr was added to Ireland's litany' with Casement's 'judicial murder'.[2]

Potentially 1932 was the year of transfiguration. The International Eucharistic Congress met in Dublin for a week in June, a vast display of Catholic piety and pageantry. Three months earlier de Valera had formed his first government, and the future of church-state relations was now unveiled before a respectful public. A timely memoir, *With de Valera in America*, was in press by the end of March, intended for publication as the Congress drew scores of thousands of visitors to the city. Its author, Patrick McCartan (1878–1963), was also proposing to print lithographic portraits of Roger Casement for sale to the faithful. His fellow doctor, W. J. Maloney (1882–1952), raised the possibility of issuing a diary he possessed, entitled 'A last Page' and written by Casement on the eve of sailing by U-boat to Ireland.[3] This too was to be issued 'in time for the Congress'. In practice it took them years to get the Casement project moving, though McCartan's book was published in the course of 1932.[4] The audacity of resurrecting Casement amid the massive

2   See B. L Reid, *The Lives of Roger Casement* (New Haven: Yale University Press, 1976), p. 451 n; Colm O Lochlainn, in a review of several books about Casement, *Irish Book Lover*, vol. 24 no. 6 (1936), p. 120.

3   Now preserved in NLI, MS 5,244 (134).

4   W. J. Maloney to Bulmer Hudson, 24 Mar. 1932 (NLI, MS 17,604 (1)). Maloney's headed stationery has already incorporated two additional initials into his name – W. J. M. A. Maloney.

demonstrations of Ireland's loyalty to Mother Church indicates the emotional and psychic intensity of the project. There were rival martyrs, of course: Louis Le Roux's biography of Patrick Pearse, published in the same year, climaxed with a solemn plea for canonisation.

The metamorphosis of Roger Casement was not accomplished solely in Catholic terms, nor even solely in religious terms. In a poem, which W. B. Yeats (1865–1939) began before the year of insurrection was over, the dead man was already loosened from politico-legal fact and readied for incorporation into a political mythology of 1916. 'Sixteen Dead Men' may exploit a numerological echo in the date of their execution, but its detail is manufactured. Only fourteen of these were court-martialled and shot in Dublin between 3 and 12 May.[5] Not all their names are equally remembered, and the process of uneven attention provides a context in which ideological and psychical 'splintering' can be appreciated. We are concerned with the chief exception – Casement – who was tried in the King's Bench Division before a jury and executed in Pentonville Jail by the common-hangman on 3 August 1916. He has been particularly remembered and, in the process, refashioned several times.

Yeats's appetite for tidiness in the annals of Irish martyrdom was a contributory factor in the longer conversion of death into ritual and metamorphosis. From the outset, Casement was to be 'changed utterly' and, if necessary, changed by sleight of hand. Succeeding decades saw the same process enacted in the decisions of state officials and bureaucrats. Twenty years after 'Sixteen Dead Men', Yeats responded to *The Forged Casement Diaries* with two new poems which further widened the distinction between history and myth. The one Sinn Féin leader to die on the gallows now bade fair be the super-hero of a new republicanism, less political, more cultic; less proletarian, more *übermenschlich*. At the same time – and here is the genius of the scheme – Casement consolidates a reputation for humanitarian universalism, as a near-saint.

It is not just the older generation of Irish nationalists who maintain this interpretation of Casement's fate. It has also attracted the support of some younger admirers of his work in defence of native peoples in Africa and South America. The most prominent of these is Angus Mitchell (born 1962) who published a transcript of what he terms Casement's *Amazon Journal* in 1997.

---

5   These were: Eamon Ceannt, Thomas Clarke, Con Colbert, James Connolly, Edward Daly, Sean Heuston, John MacBride, Sean MacDermott, Thomas MacDonagh, Michael Mallin, Michael O'Hanrahan, Patrick Pearse, Willie Pearse, and Joseph M. Plunkett. In Cork, Thomas Kent (or Ceannt) was executed (also by firing squad).

Mitchell devotes half of his introductory matter to the diaries controversy in the course of which he describes how 'a party of "forgery theorists" was born' in the 1930s with the publication in Dublin of a book by the American, Maloney. Mitchell himself is of this party, though less amusing and less abrasive than its founder. Given this latter-day endorsement, 'forgery theorists' will be the term used here (again without pejorative implications) for those who deny the basic authenticity of the five diaries preserved at Kew.[6]

A central plank in the Forgery Theorists' platform was for long what shall be termed the 'Normand Defence'. Its origins are analysed in the succeeding pages, and its inadequacies explored. For the moment, however, we should consider its mythic power. Basically, the 'Defence' argues that Casement translated (or transcribed) the diary of Armando Normand, a brutal manager of rubber-collection who worked for the Arana Brothers in the Putumayo district of South America. The curious intimacy of sadist and copyist is mirrored by the admission that Casement had sailed from London to South America with the boardroom butcher, Julio Cesar Arana, even sitting beside him at dinner on at least one occasion.[7] These 'near misses' become a trademark of the Casementalist trade. The 'Normand Defence' features in John Unterecker's agreeable – that is, uncritical – account of Yeats's friendship with McCartan, the Irish-American activist who played a large part in the posthumous melo-drama of Casement's reputation.[8] Meanwhile, Normand's diary remains elusive and uncannily pervasive. Inverted and then reassessed in terms of biblical typology, the untraceable document can be compared to the missing gospels or apocryphal gospels which lie just outside the Christian canon. Thus, while scholars postulate the existence of Q (a 'lost-gospel' source for Matthew and Luke) or debate the theological adequacy of Essene writings, Casementalists

6   Angus Mitchell, *The Amazon Journal of Roger Casement* (London: Anaconda; Dublin: Lilliput, 1997), p. 20.

7   The incident is said to have occurred in 1908, just after the Aranas had transferred their business into a London-registered company (The Peruvian Amazon Co.) and Casement was travelling out to take up his appointment as British consul at Rio de Janeiro. There is no suggestion that the two men had anything but the slightest shipboard acquaintance. See Howard and Ralph Wolf, *Rubber: A Story of Glory and Greed* (New York: Covici Friede, 1936), p. 90.

8   John Unterecker, *Yeats and Patrick McCartan: A Fenian Friendship* (Dublin: Dolmen, 1967), pp. 353–4. Though this book appeared in 1967, it complains on several occasions of the British authorities' refusal to allow examination of 'the presumably still-extant diaries' of Casement (p. 353, see also p. 354). Access has been allowed on a limited basis since the 1959 publication in Paris of transcript copies. No one with any experience of the Dolmen Press will blame Unterecker alone for this failure to update copy before publication.

use Normand's Black text as a means of redeeming Roger. Speculation about Normand (who is never observed in any other context) more closely resembles fiction than *The Brook Kerith*, George Moore's novel about Saint Paul, published in 1916. Indeed, a rattling three-generation American family saga is partly set in the Putumayo area in 1907, and Normand's career exploited in a chapter aptly called 'Descent to the Ninth Circle'.[9]

One finicking point about the 'Defence' might be noted by way of introducing the larger issue of Casement's motivation in 1910–11. An obscure American engineer, Walter Hardenburg (1886–1942), sometimes accompanied by a second traveller W. B. Perkins, had been working in South America where, to his horror, he came upon evidence of the most brutal exploitation. Journalistic articles in the magazine *Truth* prompted concern in London and, armed with the proofs of the American's book-in-progress, Casement was despatched to investigate.[10] By December 1912, *The Putumayo: The Devil's Paradise* was in print, containing Hardenburg's evidence and commentary, together with a summary version of Casement's official report. But wherever Hardenburg mentions the villain whose name attaches to the 'Defence' it is Norman (not Normand), and this is the case whether the American is translating material from South American papers (at least three different ones) or writing in his own person: Casement, however, gives the name as Normand. It is quite possible that Casement provides a greater degree of precision based on some familiarity with the name. On the other hand, he may be bamboozled by the near-palindrome of Armando/Normand and so adds an additional letter to Hardenburg's 'Norman'. The editor of *The Devil's Paradise* – C. Reginald Enock (1868–1970), an experienced traveller and author – goes to the trouble of preserving and indexing both versions of the name. Compared with Hardenburg, Casement is literally the inventor of Norman + d.[11]

9   Fred Mustard Stewart, *The Mannerings* (London: Allen, 1974).

10   The articles, signed 'Scrutator', appeared between 22 Sept. and 10 Nov. 1904, one of them using the sub-heading 'A British Owned Congo'. See also *The Morning Leader*, 23 Sept. 1904.

11   W. E. Hardenburg, *The Putumayo: The Devil's Paradise; Travels in the Peruvian Amazon Region and an Account of the Atrocities Committed Upon the Indians Therein . . . Together with Extracts from the Report of Sir Roger Casement Confirming the Occurrences* (London: Fisher Unwin, 1912). For Hardenburg on Norman [*sic*] see pp. 217, 221, 225, 233, 250. Casement's report is extracted and summarised on pp. 264–338. In *The River that God Forgot* (London: Collins, 1968), Richard Collier relies heavily on Hardenburg and surviving members of their family. He describes Normand [*sic*] as an insane Bolivian settled at Matanzas, 'a crazed twenty-two year old sadist' (p. 141), and quotes Julio Cesar Arana assuring the British parliamentary enquiry that Normand had been 'educated at an English public school' (p. 275).

Casement's oddities are rarely discussed. The religious – or rather mythopoeic – structure of beliefs concerning him is more augmented than analysed in the current debates. In these, the particular form of Christianity to which his career is typologically welded is Catholicism. Sponsors of Casement's sanctity have never been troubled by the official censorship imposed on the Jesuit, Fr Francis Shaw, when in 1966 he warned that the sin of blasphemy might contaminate 'blood sacrifice' interpretations of 1916.[12] Perhaps the most striking concordat between analysis and faith occurs on the title page of certain computer exercises conducted on writings attributed to Casement – the date of publication is specified through the Catholic Church's annual commemoration of the saints.[13] More often, the pattern of mythic invocation is diffuse and largely unconscious, happily mixing political, religious and sexual presuppositions. Just as Christ was wrongly accused of being a terrorist, so (it is contended) Casement was portrayed as a queer.

While the evidence in AD 32 was oral and evanescent, in the Irishman's case it was written and thus (potentially) permanent. But by whom was it written? What happened to it? At the time, Casement's close relatives naturally insisted that a forger had been at work, for they were a conventional family and homosexuality was a crime against state law and domestic order. This view was held by many but not all of his friends and associates. Indeed, Patrick Maume can cite one published source from 1917 in which Casement's homosexuality was recognised as political liability.[14] Very few (if any) members of this group actually saw evidence in 1916 or after. Those others who were shown material apparently incriminating Casement in this additional, highly charged offence have left contradictory accounts of what they saw. But neither John Redmond (1856–1918), leader of the Irish Party at Westminster, nor Michael Collins (1890–1922), military leader of the IRA and president of the IRB, declared that what they saw was bogus.

We shall hear more of the IRB, that is, the Irish Republican Brotherhood founded in 1858. From its secretive ranks came the central figures who had

---

12 Francis Shaw (1908–70) wrote 'The Canon of Irish History – A Challenge' to mark the fiftieth anniversary of the Easter Rebellion, but could not publish it until 1972. For a lengthy excerpt see Seamus Deane et al. (eds), *The Field Day Anthology of Irish Writing* (Derry: Field Day, 1991), vol. 3, pp. 590–5. Shaw contrasted Casement's horror of warfare with Patrick Pearse's conjuring of it.
13 See under Ó Maille in appendix III.
14 See Patrick Maume, *The Long Gestation: Irish Nationalist Life 1891–1918* (Dublin: Gill & Macmillan, 1999), p. 185. The objector was John Dillon Nugent.

determined on rising at Easter 1916, including Thomas Clarke and Patrick Pearse among those executed. Casement was never of their number, though some of his closest friends from the North were IRB men. Indeed, he should be associated with a small minority among the conspirators who opposed the launching of rebellion at that time – opposed, that is, on strategic grounds. Inevitable military defeat at first seemed briefly to vindicate these few, but the subsequent moral and political exploitation of defeat cast the naysayers into a curious light. For some, it was necessary to prove over and over again their full commitment to the Republic, whose proclamation they had sought to postpone. Like uneasy ghosts, they were compelled to return to the scene of their non-crime. Far from washing their hands of that blood sacrifice, they sought to wash their hands in it, retrospectively.

Now happily forgotten, a forgery lay buried at the crossroads or cross-purposes of 1916. Joseph Mary Plunkett (1887–1916) had gone to Germany in 1915 to assist (or displace) Casement in drumming up German support for an Irish insurrection. Back home in Dublin the following year, he forged the so-called Castle Document which purported to show that the British authorities were about to disarm nationalist volunteers and 'proclaim' Dublin: the objective of this fabrication was to persuade Eoin MacNeill (1867–1945), chief of staff of the Volunteers, to take more resolute military action. The day after Casement landed in Kerry, MacNeill discovered that the Document was bogus, and moved to cancel the Rising (as Casement also wished to do). Confusion among the rebels followed, as treachery and comradeship vied for supremacy in their higher ranks.

Similar tensions were persistent features of Casement's adult career. The son of an Indian Army officer who fought for Hungarian independence, an Irish-born official in the British colonial service, he achieved international renown for his report on barbarous conditions obtaining in the Belgian Congo (1904) and later for a similar exposure of sadistic brutality in the South American rubber industry. By this time, however, he had become a convert to Irish cultural nationalism and, in due course, to militant republicanism. In the autumn of 1914, he travelled to Berlin, via the United States and Norway, to raise German support for an Irish insurrection. On Good Friday 1916, he was arrested on the coast of County Kerry, transferred to London, and charged with high treason. Public opinion in Britain regarded him as the principal leader of what was termed the Sinn Féin rebellion, though Casement had travelled from Germany hoping to forestall it and, in any case, the rebellion was not the work of Sinn Féin.[15] His execution on 3 August was the final event in its suppression. Not until 1919 did conflict between armed Irish separatists and the British authorities break out, leading eventually to the Treaty of 1921. This phase of 'the Troubles' brought its own generation of heroes and martyrs, to augment that of Easter 1916. Amidst the growing company, a cult of Patrick Pearse was to prove the most enduring, with Michael Collins fated soon to divide the honours.

Scarcely aware that its foreign policy was coloured by Casement's German expedition, the new Irish Free State plunged into a civil war which did little to flatter republican separatism.[16] Some former zealots chose to accept state employment under the Treaty most notably, in the present context, the Belfast-born Quaker, Bulmer Hobson (1883–1969), who had been a close associate of Casement's. Hobson had been recruited to the IRB in 1904, the year of Casement's Congo Report, and four years later he moved south to Dublin. Hobson's choice was prophetic: northern republicanism was destined for disappointment, with Casement's reputation acting as a kind of cipher for more complex betrayals, compromises, and intractable problems. The dramatist, Sean O'Casey, regarded Hobson as a 'shit', and O'Casey rarely used dirty language.[17] Among the northern IRB leadership, there had been some distrust of Pearse, precisely arising from suspicions of his sexual orientation as a teacher of the young which, in the new southern (and predominantly Catholic) polity, were soon wrapped up in sacerdotal verbiage.[18]

After 1921, Casement began to fade into the background; the word 'handsome', ubiquitously deployed to connote some elusive characteristic, became his Cheshire cat smile, a dreadful posthumous condition for a man whose tragic condition even Yeats failed to appreciate. The partition of Ireland, confirmed in 1926, drew permanent borders isolating his beloved Antrim as

15   The early history of the Sinn Féin movement, a complex topic obscured for many by latter-day activities conducted under the same name, is authoritatively provided in Michael Laffan, *The Resurrection of Ireland: The Sinn Féin Party 1916–23* (Cambridge: Cambridge University Press, 1999).

16   On the origins of Irish–German relations in Casement's 1914–16 mission to Berlin, and J. M. Plunkett's visit of 1916, see Andreas Roth, *Mr Bewley in Berlin: Aspects of the Career of an Irish Diplomat 1933–1939* (Dublin: Four Courts, 2000), pp. 9–10.

17   David Krause (ed.), *The Letters of Sean O'Casey 1942–1954* (New York: Macmillan, 1980), p. 800. O'Casey, who left the IRB to devote himself to the Labour movement, believed that Hobson exploited his minority Protestant background to win favour and had been duly exploited in turn.

18   Confirmation of this suspicion was provided by Joseph McCullough, speaking about his father (Denis McCullough, 1883–1968) at an Irish Association meeting in Belfast, 23 Apr. 2001.

the only one of the 'Six Counties' to lack a frontier-link with the Free State. Ideologically and territorially, the dead Casement was a double loser in the 1920s. His reputation was preserved at the level of popular folklore rather than through official celebration. Gaelic football clubs were named after him.[19]

In the psychology of political commemoration, the relationship between Pearse and Casement is intriguing. There was no denying official perfidy in circulating – especially in America – evidence about Casement's sexual life. The blackguardism was blatant and personal, because it was unnecessary to the securing of a conviction. Seen in this light by fellow-nationalists, his purity was guaranteed by British insinuations to the contrary. Other issues were less easily accounted for, especially at home in Ireland. Prompted by the very elusiveness of that evidence after 1916, did something work to siphon off domestic anxiety about Pearse, anxiety which could never be (even privately) expressed? Casement was both saint and scapegoat. His utility to the cause he had served lay in sustained ambivalence. Thus memory and amnesia became the Siamese twin children of Irish revolution, inseparable and mutually exhausting.

During these years, a striking number of individuals who in 1916 or shortly afterwards had been shown material incriminating Casement in homosexuality passed away. Redmond died in 1918. So did Cecil Spring-Rice, the Anglo-Irish diplomat who circulated the damning (or damnable) material in Washington. In August 1922, Collins was assassinated in a republican ambush. John Quinn, a New York lawyer and patron of the arts to whom Ambassador Spring-Rice had strutted Casement's stuff, followed peacefully in 1924. F. E. Smith (Lord Birkenhead), the principal prosecutor in 1916, went to an even higher tribunal in 1930. Sir Arthur Conan Doyle, who had signed the petition for a reprieve and devised a defence on grounds of insanity, died the same year. While there were perhaps dozens still alive who had seen a diary, or a transcript of a diary, or a photograph of an extract in 1916 – not to mention yet others who had trafficked in such goods – twenty years were to take a heavy toll. With these deaths, access to important witnesses who had accepted the material as genuinely Casement's significantly declined.

19 I am grateful to Lisa Godson for her comments on the occurrence of Casement's name in newspapers and magazines in the 1920s. Eunan O'Halpin draws on his own family history to portray the attitudes of various groups of republican fellow-travellers with the Free State. See his *Defending Ireland: The Irish State and its Enemies Since 1922* (Oxford: Oxford University Press, 1999), pp. viii–ix.

Like Ernley Blackwell and Basil Thomson, Birkenhead has come down to us as an unlikeable fellow.[20] G. K. Chesterton mocked the self-propelled hypocrite – 'Are they clinging to their crosses, F. E. Smith . . .' in a poem called 'The Antichrist'. Though G. K. C. had no intention of assisting Casement when he mocked Smith/Birkenhead, the characterisation of his prosecutor conformed to the Irish view that the dead man belonged in a martyrology if not indeed a pantheon. After his death, Birkenhead was quickly the subject of a detailed restorative biography, appearing in two volumes from 1933 to 1935, the prelude period for Dr Maloney's restorative work on Casement. Written by a dutiful yet conscientious son, the life of Birkenhead commenced a reassesment of the 1916 trial which indirectly applied pressure on the Irish patriotic view of Casement.[21]

Nor should altering perspectives on the Great War be neglected. The jingoism which enveloped both trial and execution was quickly replaced by post-war depression and embitterment. Neither in Britain nor in Ireland (which lost 30,000 dead) did a land fit for heroes rise from the conflict. The bitterness dramatised in Sean O'Casey's partly expressionist play, *The Silver Tassie* (1928), was not peculiar to its Dublin setting. But in Dublin some people felt a little freer to reflect on the system which had called forth the war, called up the troops, and lied unconscionably to hide its incompetence. What lies had not been told, what forgeries left undone? To judge from police files released as late as June 2001, the physical location of 'the diary' which finally 'did for' Casement was difficult to establish in 1921.[22] Why the muddle, why the delay in releasing evidence of the muddle?

Two proposals of 1936 provide in contrasting ways a background for the refiguring of Casement's reputation with which I am centrally concerned. In London, the demolition of Pentonville Prison was considered, from which there arose the issue of re-interring its one political victim of note. A Repatriation Committee was established in London, with Sarah MacDermott in a leading

---

20   Emley Robertson Hay Blackwell (1868–1941) was legal adviser to the Home Office. Sir Basil Home Thomson (1861–1939) was assistant commissioner of Scotland Yard, head of the Special Branch, and author of several contradictory memoirs. They remain unchallenged as the villains of the Casement scandal.

21   See Frederick Smith, *Frederick Edwin Earl of Birkenhead*, 2 vols (London: Thornton Butterworth, 1933–35). Also, F. Smith *The Life of F. E. Smith, First Earl of Birkenhead*, revised and expanded ed. (London: Eyre & Spottiswoode, 1960).

22   See Stephen Gaselee (Librarian, Foreign Office) to New Scotland Yard (PRO, MEPO 2/10672).

role. Public meetings were held, duly attended by Special Branch officers. On Easter Sunday, over five hundred people gathered in Hyde Park to hear speakers including Hannah Sheehy Skeffington (who apologised for Tom Casement's absence due to ill health). The liberal English journalist, H. W. Nevinson, sent a letter of support. The meeting at Finsbury Town Hall, Clerkenwell, on 11 July 1936, with Fenner Brockway of the Independent Labour Party among the speakers, attracted only about fifty attendees. Still officially President of the Irish Free State, Eamon de Valera met a depution of the London Casement Committee in Leinster House, 29 July 1936. The British Special Branch in Holyhead duly noted the participation of Miss MacDermott, Mrs S. Cremin, and Mr Cliff-Murphy.[23]

Perhaps to head off the freelance activities of republican women whom de Valera found particularly troublesome, an official Irish government request had been made in the spring of 1936. The Prime Minister, Stanley Baldwin, publicly ruled out repatriation, in answers given in the House of Commons to the Scottish Communist, Willie Gallacher. De Valera's statement of some months later, regretting Britain's repeated refusal to allow Casement to return home in death, was widely reported in the London press. International dimensions were clearly discernible, even if the political wishes of official Dublin were not much different from those of Whitehall. The sleeping dog was allowed to lie on in Pentonville.

In Ireland, altered relations with other members of the Commonwealth were signalled in the drafting of a new constitution. Although the Free State had possessed a constitution, it scarcely impressed itself as an authorising text. If there was such a thing, the Proclamation of the Republic in 1916 was the thing, a text which (as Siobhan Holland has pointed out) was strikingly 'gendered' in addressing Ireland as woman. De Valera's folly-me-up authorising text, eschewing the word republic altogether, would commence with the Holy Trinity (a male monopoly), define woman's subordinate role in the family, and institutionalise a sexual politics in which the ambiguous figure of Casement would find no comfort. As authorising texts were debated – proclamations, democratic programmes, constitutions, even Soviets, and the rest – so a concern with forgeries manifests itself as an allegory of unease about authority and authorisation. Had 1916 been any less ambiguous than the legend of Casement?

23   PRO, MEPO 2/10675.

The process of arriving at a draft constitution in 1936 involved careful assessment of both Ulster's relationship with the southern state and the concept of republicanism as the ideal basis of the latter. The Irish Free State was about to be put to sleep, or – according to taste – woken from its slumberous lassitude into active republican virtue. The troublesome women – Hannah Sheehy Skeffington and Kathleen Lynn among them – had complaints to make about de Valera's proposal which touched on the underlying gender issues about Casement. His re-interment in Ireland might stimulate strong interpretations of all these political issues.[24] As if only to frustrate his admirers, Pentonville survived.

More specifically, shifts in Irish electoral politics in the early 1930s facilitated Casement's re-emergence from relative obscurity among the faithful dead. The Fianna Fáil party's electoral triumph in 1932 placed government in the hands of a Civil War republican who had been sentenced to death in 1916. Like Casement, Eamon de Valera had understood the importance of Irish America as a source of funding and as a platform for worldwide propaganda. Even before the new Constitution of 1937, Ireland was diversifying its external relations through, for example, the Treaty of Westminster and (more broadly) the League of Nations. Countries other than Britain began to play a role in its economic and even (to a limited extent) its cultural life. Naturally, Catholic Europe featured in this latter development: a Librairie Française opened at 19 Nassau Street, Dublin, in the 1930s, and an Italian Institute fostered cultural dialogue with a state at once more undeniably Roman in its religion than Ireland and more assertively political in its attitude to culture.

Additionally, from the late 1920s, German industrial expertise was at work. One small-scale instance is peculiarly relevant to this inquiry – the interest of the printer Colm O Lochlainn (1892–1972) in type designs and other aspects of his craft as they were nurtured in the homeland of Gutenberg. O Lochlainn had been close to the IRB leadership in 1916, and his social thinking was influenced by the liberalism of *Rerum Novarum*, the papal encyclical issued a year after his birth. His company, which traded as The Three Candles Press,

24 See a letter of 31 Jan. 1922 in Curry Papers (NLI, MS 17,031) for Maloney's early dedication to the cause of repatriation: 'We shall move Sir Rogers remains from Pentonville to the most sacred spot in Ireland, where it shall be in a place of pilgrimage . . .'. On later official Irish efforts towards repatriation, see reports in *The Times* on 6 Mar., 12 Mar., 4 June (all 1936). When fifteen files of Metropolitan Police records were released to the PRO in June 2001, one (MEPO 2/10675) dealing with activities in 1936–7 remained embargoed. It was released for public access in February 2002.

employed a young Dubliner of German extraction, through whom it developed links with the print trades of Leipzig and other major German centres.[25]

With Hitler's electoral triumph in 1933, books and travelling scholarships joined type design and afforestation in the portfolio of Teutonic largesse. While the new, and partly covert, approach should not be exaggerated, it conditioned and modified a context in which Casement might be reassessed. After all, German–Irish common interests had been at the heart of his approach to the national question in 1914–16. Working in Nazi Berlin the great American journalist, William Shirer, listened to a radio play based on Casement's life.[26] The sentiment was reciprocated. On its front page for 22 December 1936, the *Irish Press* passively acknowledged Adolf Hitler as the Santa Claus of Germany, without a quote mark to mitigate Goebbels's Yuletide broadcast.

25 Chalmers Trench, 'The Three Candles Press in the Thirties', *Long Room*, no. 41 (1996), pp. 35–42.
26 William L. Shirer, 'Will Hitler Take Ireland?' *The Nation*, 31 Jan, 1942, p. 134. The article appeared in 'Ireland and America: A Special Supplement on Ireland's Position in the Battle of the Atlantic'.

TWO

THE VIEW FROM RADICAL HAMPSTEAD

Ireland is governed by police inspectors, gombeen men,
and priests, not by Secretaries of State.
BERNARD SHAW, *in the Daily News* (1916)

—

While principally concerned with the 1930s and the activities of Dr Maloney, we shall have to reach back for a moment to recover some details of twenty years earlier, recently made available through the release of Metropolitan Police papers to the PRO. This is not simply a matter of excavating the arguments advanced to explain (away) the 'degenerate diary' found among Casement's private effects; a larger London context can be articulated to counterbalance the Irish frame of reference which has predominated to date.

One English friend of Casement's – the journalist and anti-slaver, Henry Woodd Nevinson (1856–1941) – having been shown the original of the Putumayo report by Casement himself, wrote a satirical letter to the press but his editor thought it too violent. In it he had proposed with Swiftian delicacy a sporting expedition to hunt 'Normand and the rest' in Peru rather than exterminate African giraffes. Just as Casement had a London circle – perhaps several, non-intersecting ones – so too Normand should in due course be weighed up as an ex-Londoner (see chapter 8 below). But for the moment, we have paused on Nevinson's modest proposal. This had been advanced before Casement acted on his pro-German view of Irish prospects and while he still moved in a circle which could accommodate varieties of dissent from British orthodoxies. When the crisis of 1916 arose, Nevinson attended the court hearings and provided every manner of psychological support. Yet he does not seem to have had the material for a Normand Defence. Nor, in his subsequent voluminous loyal references to his dead friend, did he adopt this Defence. In his private journal, he had responded to news of the Dublin insurrection by

thinking a great deal about Casement – 'so noble, so splendid in every way except in the commonest common sense of cattle'.[1]

London journalism constituted a useful and convivial company for a man whose visits to the imperial capital had combined relaxation from arduous duty with briefings at headquarters. Before the decisive commitment to Irish nationalism in 1913, Casement treated London as 'home', though he never had long-term accommodation there. Even before he became an Irish republican, he was – to use Wolfe Tone's phrase – 'a man of no property' who came from the propertied classes. In London, at the centre of the known and owned universe, the word 'from' in that phrase stang like an accusation. In 1908, the Belfast-born Robert Wilson Lynd (1879–1949) had become assistant literary editor of the *Daily News*. The following year, Lynd married Sylvia Dryhurst (1888–1952), who later pursued a modest literary career as novelist, poet, and anthologist. The couple went to live in Hampstead, just a few doors away from Mrs Lynd's parents, Alfred Robert Dryhurst, and his Dublin-born wife (*née* Norah Florence Robinson). By 1911, Casement was in the habit of visiting both households on Devonshire Hill.[2]

A. R. Dryhurst (died 1949) was a public administrator, rising to be assistant-secretary of the British Museum, and retiring in 1924. His one traceable contribution to scholarship is a small monograph on the Italian painter, Raphael, published in 1905 and issued in a second edition in December 1909. Dryhurst plays little or no part in the Casement story, except to underscore a pattern of connubial partnership in which the wife takes the more active political role. The Dryhursts' one traceable collaboration in intellectual matters was a joint translation of the Belgian Ernest Nys's *Researches in the History of Economics* which appeared in 1899.

Nannie Dryhurst, though resistant to latter-day enquiry, was a member of Peter Kropotkin's London circle. In 1909, she published a translation of *The Great French Revolution 1789–93*. Though translators pledge no greater loyalty to their authors than lawyers do to their clients, Kropotkin (1842–1921) was a formidable figure with whom to associate. A Russian prince by birth, a noted geographer by vocation, and a political anarchist of considerable influence, he had made London his home in the 1890s. The Dryhursts' association with him is consistent with their daughter's meeting Lynd, who was a lifelong

---

1   BOD. LIB., MSS Eng Misc 619/3 f. 87 (entry of 26 Apr. 1916 or very shortly after).
2   For example, see entries for 28 Jan., 28 May, 10 June and 15 July in PRO, HO 164/5 (ledger for 1911).

exponent of James Connolly's version of Irish socialism and whom Casement had known in Ulster.

The heyday of anarchism had passed, its literary requiem ironically sounded by Joseph Conrad in *The Secret Agent* (1907). The new theme, not always distinctly audible, was anti-imperialism. Britain's undignified conflict with the Boers of South Africa had given rise to much disquiet. Elsewhere on the dark continent, the great powers were grabbing what they could or intensifying the exploitation of what they already held. In literary terms, the new concerns had been reflected in Conrad's *Heart of Darkness* (1902), in which Casement's Congo featured even before Casement had completed his official report for the Foreign Office.

In 1907, Mrs Dryhurst spoke at an international conference in The Hague on the subjugation of Georgia within the Czar's empire. The published report of a similar conference on nations and subject races, held in London in 1910, was effectively edited by her. Speakers addressed the problems of individual regions or countries, including Nevinson (on Morocco), William Gibson and George Gavan Duffy (on Ireland). Sir Charles Dilke, J. H. Harris, Keir Hardie and E. D. Morel spoke on contemporary slavery. Her son-in-law contributed a preface. The mercurial Dilke, an erstwhile republican who thought bananas detrimental to Anglo-Saxon good health, commended Casement's work.[3] The *dramatis personae* was a veritable Casement fan club, though a careful reading of the book reveals the broader context in which his individual achievements were received.

The tendency to celebrate him as an Irish hero, and as an Irish humanitarian, has likewise tended to obscure his position vis-à-vis the larger world of British *fin-de-siècle* and Edwardian culture. In the political terms of 1907, what is lost is his role in the campaigns of an entire generation drawn from across the United Kingdom. They were Liberals-Wanna-be-Something-Better. Dryhurst was clearly a central figure, for she is listed as honorary secretary of the movement, with an official address at 40, Outer Temple, The Strand. She

3   Dilke's career indicated limitations to the consistent 'doing-good' of such radicals. In 1868, he had held that 'the gradual extinction of the inferior races is not only a law of nature, but a blessing to mankind'. An opponent of Gladstonian Home Rule for Ireland, by the 1890s he had come to a limited tolerance of remoter native peoples who might enjoy 'equality under paternal despotism'. See Sven Lindqvist, *A History of Bombing* (London: Granta, 2001), sect. 45, where Dilke's *Greater Britain* of 1868 is quoted. See also Robert J. C. Young, *Postcolonialism: An Historical Introduction* (Oxford: Blackwell, 2001), pp. 35–8. Dilke died in 1911.

and Lynd constituted what might loosely be called the Irish 'Left' of these gatherings: in some contrast Gibson would turn up 'in the picturesque national Irish dress of saffron kilt' with mantle flung across his shoulders the better to commence his address in Gaelic, descending through French to mere English.[4] Casement, though he knew little or no Gaelic, was closer to Gibson than to Kropotkin.

The intellectual backdrop to these domestic and suburban developments is dominated by the Fabian Society (founded in 1884) and the Labour Party (1906). While the cast is in turn dominated by G. B. Shaw and the Webbs, the radical scene accommodated many individuals of lesser fame. Sidney Haldane Olivier (1859–1943) was a man of diverse interests and achievements. A colonial official like Casement, he had been secretary of the Fabians from 1886 to 1889, became governor of Jamaica in 1907, and then returned home as permanent secretary of the Board of Agriculture (1913–17). A lifelong friend of Shaw, his socialist-liberal views survived high office, for in 1927 he published *The Anatomy of African Misery*, and reissued his *White Capital and Coloured Labour* (2nd edn, 1929). These works pursued Casement's 'third-world' themes, though not Casement's own political objectives.

But before Olivier makes his small contribution to the drama of Casement's trial, the Hampstead circle of the Dryhursts and Lynds deserves a further moment's attention. One gathering point was Wildwood Farm, where Mrs Charlotte Wilson presided and her husband kept to the margins. She had edited the tiny but influential magazine *Freedom* (founded 1886) and contributed *Anarchism and Outrage* (1893) to the Freedom pamphlets series. But Kropotkin's was now an idiom of the past. At Wildwood of the new century, the Shaws, the Webbs, the Dryhursts and Oliviers congregated to discuss radical-practical solutions to the world, before drifting on to the Heath where cultivated nature gave relief. The 'Hampstead Historic' meetings brought together old anarchists – Mrs Dryhurst and Mrs Wilson both classed themselves as such – and figures like Olivier who were concerned with agriculture and environmental politics. As the most trenchant critic of the rubber industry, Roger Casement spoke against political imperialism and the intensive

---

4   *Nationalities and Subject Races: Report of a Conference Held at Caxton Hall, Westminster, June 28–30 1910* (London: King, n.d.), pp. 85, 87. William Gibson (1868–1942) was the eldest son of Edward, 1st Baron Ashbourne, sometime Lord Chancellor of Ireland who sat in several Tory cabinets; he married Marianne de Monbrison, member of an old French Protestant family, both converted to Catholicism.

farming of natural resources. By 1913, he had joined the Irish Volunteers as the direct expression of feelings which had turned him away from the larger world towards his own corner of the British Empire.

It is well known that a powerful motive in this reorientation was literature. Yeats and his associates, first through the Celtic Twilight and then through the Abbey Theatre, had argued the spiritual superiority of Connemara over Hampstead. Within that broad perspective, Ireland was to be recognised as a subject nation, not as a component part of the United Kingdom. Politically, this was an unremarkable development, quite in keeping with a tradition of Irish nationalism, and representative of a more recent nationalism evident also in Italy, Norway, Finland, Hungary and elsewhere. Psychologically, however, cultural nationalism offered some individuals an opportunity for re-casting themselves as outcasts or victims, seeking survival through marginalisation. Victimage could thus be accounted as a spiritual good in itself, and the renunciation of power converted into a celebration of impotence.

The contrast between Yeats and Casement in this regard hardly needs to be detailed. Nevertheless, London continued to provide coterie-forums in which transformations of the greatest import for the new century took place. Celebrating Sligo, Yeats moved backwards and forwards between the two islands, recruiting English supporters to his side, such as Edward Gordon Craig (1872–1966), and clashing with his former mentor William Morris. Casement too pursued a double agenda, a far less creative one: increasingly devoted to the Glens of Antrim, their tiny farms and quaint manners, he committed himself also to the German Empire. He could not, or would not, keep Glenarm out of the Arms Race.

The aesthetics of these ominous rearrangements can be observed precisely where the worlds of Mrs Dryhurst and W.B.Y. interconnect. They were both Dubliners by birth and may have had some acquaintance before May 1900 when she was involved with Edward Gordon Craig in a production of *Dido and Aeneas* for the Purcell Operatic Society.[5] Yeats attended a revival the following year, and sought out Craig to learn how his austere yet sensuous stage arrangements might be adapted to Irish purposes. Margaret Olivier, in a late memoir of her husband, describes an occasion of about the same

5   See Ronald Schuchard, '"An Attendant Lord": H. W. Nevinson's Friendship with W. B. Yeats', *Yeats Annual*, no. 7 (1990), pp. 90–130 where (p. 97) the details of the Purcell occasion are spelled out, and where Nevinson's part in the Casement defence is also explored (though without any reference to Mrs Dryhurst).

date on which Yeats and Morris argued furiously about Zola's naturalism. Representation, in the political and aesthetic senses, was a point of conflict. It did not automatically follow that those who worked for subject nations regarded democracy as the *beau ideal*.

The dangerous intersection of literature and politics was not a meeting of one-way country lanes, picturesque or famine-purged. Anarchism and its attendant ideologies split left- and right-wards. Literary modernism produced T. S. Eliot and Bertold Brecht. London was home to both avant-garde and reactionary movements, and its suburban intelligentsia entertained dialogue between revolutionary futures and equally unreal pasts. Casementalists who see their hero all but exclusively in Irish terms fail to recognise the Welsh poet, Edward Thomas (killed in action 1917), or the Scottish traveller Cunningham Graham (trained horses for the army), as his fellow-Londoners. This failure contributes to the tragedy of Casement's reputation, for it neglects to observe the behaviour of the Dryhursts, Oliviers and others.

In one sense, London was exactly the right place for Casement to nurture his highly conflicted objectives – British justice for Peruvian slaves, German arms for Irish voters impatient with parliamentary give and take. The imperial capital had watched a succession of Hibernian adventurers invade its political and cultural institutions – Lord Castlereagh, the Duke of Wellington, Daniel O'Connell, Arthur Conan Doyle, C. S. Parnell, Arthur Sullivan, Oscar Wilde, Bernard Shaw. . . . Not all of these had been to the manor born, not all had avoided tragedy. But London was a debating society in which Irish accents and Irish arguments were familiar. These now contributed to a drastic shift in the tone of contemporary literature as reflected in magazines like *The Egoist*, which serialised James Joyce's *Portrait of the Artist as a Young Man*. Joyce and D. H. Lawrence graphically illustrated the distance between emergent fiction and the assumptions of Georgian England. When Nevinson – on leave from the war front which he covered as a journalist – dined with Letitia Fairfield on Good Friday 1916, they little knew that their friend Casement was being transported under arrest from County Kerry to the Tower of London. The table talk was 'of modern writers whom [Nevinson] did not even know by name'.[6]

6   BOD. LIB., MSS Eng. Misc. 619/3. Josephine Letitia Denny Fairfield (1885–1978), an Irish medical doctor and barrister-at-law, maintained her interest in Casement right through to the 1960s when she arranged for a short forensic examination of the 1911 diary. When Roger McHugh published his article in *Threshold* (Belfast, 1960), Fairfield responded in the next number. As she was a convert to Catholicism whom the Pope honoured in 1966, she upsets any notion of pious unanimity on the question.

Even before that calamitous landing from a U-boat, Casement's difficulty had been peculiarly one of timing. Long before Edward VII died (1910), the pre-war Indian summer was waning. Culturally, the Victorian synthesis of realism and moral fervour had collapsed in the 1890s, not least because of the dramatic experiments of Wilde and Shaw. More material explanations were avoided, or attributed to alien forces. Germany had hugely outstripped Britain in industrial power. As if in parodic anticipation of this triumph, the clamorously divergent ideas of Marx, Wagner, Freud and Nietzsche had invaded the thoughtful Englander's library. On the streets, Labour was demanding to be heard. Indeed, in 1916 Sinn Féin vied with Glasgow strikers for journalistic denunciation. Conspiracy theorists might want to consider if the government did not choose to play up the Casement trial in London as a way of avoiding confrontation with militant trades unionism. It may be advisable to reclassify his execution as a British event, rather than insist on it as an Irish martyrdom.

When he returned from South America in 1910, it had proved difficult to convince the Foreign Office to move to end brutality in the rubber industry. The area in question was not British; in fact it was debatable whether Brazil, Peru or even Colombia was the sovereign government of the wide tract of jungle territory where murder, torture, and sexual depravity were employed to enslave a population wholly without rights. In contrast, the commercial interests were British, in part at least, and could be expected to resist interference in their profitable activities. Boardrooms do not encourage righteous campaigners. The report itself posed problems, given the disturbing nature of the evidence and the emotional commitment of the chief enquirer. Casement began work in the second week of January 1911, quickly disposed of a shorthand typist (male), and continued till late March with the task of writing up the report longhand.[7] Casement's writing procedures are of signficance when one comes to consider the question of forgery in relation to his diaries for (broadly) the same period.

The approved version of his report retained the highly charged language which distinguished him from career-diplomats. Casement's determination to convince his superiors drew him into areas of judgment which, strictly speaking, were the responsibility of others. He spoke to friends and associates quite freely about the atrocities he had uncovered, and mobilised unofficial support to overcome the resistance of vested interests. So much was natural in a driven crusader, less so in a regular consular official. The Dryhurst circle had

7   Roger Sawyer, *Casement: The Flawed Hero* (London: Routledge, 1984), p. 95.

its part to play in the wider campaign as did the wider world of artistic London. The painter, William Rothenstein (1872–1945), proposed a double portrait of two Peruvian boys Casement had brought to the imperial capital for their own protection. This required trips to Hampstead for sittings (supervised by Casement's sister, Nina) not to mention bribes in the form of sweets and ice cream. One such visit was made on 15 July 1911, just a month before Casement set out on his last South American voyage. Rothenstein's picture was unfinished, but the project formed the basis for a useful journalistic feature.[8]

Thereafter, London saw very little of him. After the second and final South American journey, he holidayed in Barbados, and spent some time in the United States. When he returned, his purpose was simply to answer calls from the Foreign Office. Early 1912 saw him successively in Belfast, Germany, and Falmouth. There was a spell of FO duty while the Putumayo report was published, but he managed to spend part of August, all of September, and part of October in Ireland. His homeland, not Britain, exercised the dominant attractive influence, while exhaustion and ill health were also taking their toll. Though Casement had been knighted in June 1911 for his work in South America, he retired on pension two years later. All too quickly, his commitment to Ireland demanded travel to the United States, thence to Germany – and the scaffold.

In February 1914, Nannie Dryhurst wrote on behalf of the Nationalities and Subject Races Committee begging Casement to chair a conference at the Westminster Palace Hotel. At this point, her errant friend was still in America. A year later, while he was visiting Irish prisoners of war at Limburg, Casement took delivery of a second letter. How she succeeded in communicating with a man who had gone beyond the pale remains a mystery – there are many! He had apparently conveyed two messages to her through Alice Stopford Green, and Mrs Dryhurst in turn was proposing an American route for their correspondence. The intermediary was to be Editha Phelps with an address at a library in Chicago. No names or locations were to be committed to paper for, in wartime, 'the examination of letters both going & coming to this country is very close'. These fragmentary lines testify to the affection he was still held in, but also to the double jeopardy he had embraced in trusting Imperial Germany.[9]

8   See Roger Sawyer's comments in *BBC History*, vol. 2 no. 8 (Aug. 2001). For Rothenstein's comments see his *Men and Memories* 1900–1922 (London: Faber, 1934), vol. 2, pp. 170–1.
9   See N. F. Dryhurst to R. Casement, 6 Feb. 1914 and 29 Apr. 1915 (NLI, MSS 13,073/2/i and 13,073/46/vii).

'Casement's Last Adventure', as a comrade-in-arms termed it, washed him up on the south-west coast of Ireland on Good Friday 1916.[10] Contrary to his wishes, the planned insurrection went ahead in Dublin on Easter Monday. It was all over in a week. The British authorities had more problems on their hands than the so-called Sinn Féin Rebellion. Losses at sea were mounting; the battle of Verdun was imminent. Strikes in the munitions factories demonstrated the power of Red Clydeside and the danger to the war-effort posed by internationalist socialism. On the day that Eamon de Valera (1882–1975) was condemned to death in Dublin, Jimmy Maxton (1885–1946) was jailed for calling a strike in Glasgow. Commutation of de Valera's sentence acknowledged the fact of his American birth, as Britain sought to involve the United States actively in the war. By the time of Casement's execution (3 August), Jutland had been ambiguously won, and the dreadful Somme endlessly fought. The worst day of casualties since the war began led to a works stoppage in Belfast, drawing attention to the delicate linkage between Ulster loyalism in the ranks and disgruntlement in the factories and shipyards. The English coast was bombarded on 4 August, the first enemy action on British soil since the eighteenth century. Not a political context in which ethical scruple gripped the national mind.

So the blackguarding of Casement went ahead. Strictly limited circulation of the diaries, in various shapes and forms, was calculated to counter Irish-American opposition to the war and likewise to demoralise campaigners at home who had been calling for clemency. At least three distinct agencies were involved in London – the Foreign Office, Scotland Yard, and Naval Intelligence. Their targets included significant individuals such as the Archbishop of Canterbury and the leader of the Irish Party, newspapers like the *Daily Express*, and clubroom gossips who could be relied upon to embroider whatever threads of scandal they snatched at. The general imputation was of sexual deviancy to the point of depravity, the specific locations and times of offence varying from one circulation to another.

The trial had taken place between 26 and 29 June in the High Court. Casement's principal London supporters were Bernard Shaw and Arthur

---

10 Cf. *Casement's Last Adventure*, by Captain Robert Monteith, First Battalion, Dublin Regiment, Irish Republican Army (Chicago: privately printed, 1932). Like McCartan's *With de Valera in America*, Monteith's remarkably lavish publication was designed to impress in the context of the Eucharistic Congress. Despite this timing, the author repeatedly invokes a Connollyite 'Workers' Republic' politics. For some comment on its textual history, see appendix III below.

Conan Doyle, with Yeats active at a discreet distance. Indeed, all three of these eminent literary figures felt a need to express their solidarity with the prisoner by means of special pleading. In each case, reason was on their side. Yeats had access to the Prime Minister (Herbert Asquith) which he thought could best be exploited privately. Shaw also declined to sign the open petition for clemency, on the grounds that his notoriety might repel others. Conan Doyle had argued a defence on grounds of insanity. Viewed collectively, these attitudes revealed the extent to which the pre-war London in which Casement had moved no longer united in sympathy for the outcast.

A petition was drawn up, with notable support from men with literary reputations. These included William Archer, Arnold Bennett, Hall Caine, G. K. Chesterton, Arthur Conan Doyle, John Drinkwater, John Galsworthy, Jerome K. Jerome, John Masefield, and Israel Zangwil. But Joseph Conrad was a puzzling absentee, for he had known Casement in the Congo. Churchmen were not to the fore, despite Casement's belief that missionary activity (Catholic and Protestant) should be encouraged in the Putumayo: the Bishop of Winchester was the only Anglican prelate to sign up, with the President of the Baptist Union as his most distinguished nonconformist supporter. No notable Catholic cleric lent this name to the petition, Irish or British. Scientists and the Left outnumbered the Christian soldiers. Women were virtually invisible on the list, Beatrice Webb being the exception.

Women were of course prominent behind the scenes, especially the historian Alice Stopford (Mrs J. R. Green). Mrs Voynich of the Queens Road (later best-ever-selling author of *The Gadfly*) sent flowers: she was born Ethel Lilian Boole (1867–1947), daughter of the Irish mathematician whose algebra is used on the Internet. Family supporters were exclusively female – Mrs Nina Newman (sister) and the Bannisters (cousins), especially Gertrude. The Casement males were dispersed in Australia and South Africa. Not all of this support was helpful. Another cousin, May Casement, had written to the prisoner on 31 May in affectionate and sympathetic terms, recalling their happier youth in Grannie's care. Kent Police reported that she had been fifteen months under Dr Worthington, having previously spent time in a Scottish lunatic asylum. She was 'still mentally deficient'.[11]

Miss Casement's pathetic condition may have encouraged Conan Doyle in formulating his 'guilty but insane' defence which was nevertheless rejected

---

11 PRO, MEPO 2/10670. May Casement's address was 5, Woodford Villas, Birchingham.

by the prisoner's advisers. Evidence of a 'family weakness' could have provided a basis for the argument, without having to depend exclusively on Casement's recent and embarrassing activities in Germany. Embarrassment – whether or not Conan Doyle and Shaw knew of the dangers – might not be restricted to the field of politics and gunrunning. A leading American journalist told Nannie Dryhurst 'that a month ago [i.e. beginning of June] every American and English journalist had been shown certain documents'. Scandalised by the import of these, and by the publicity given them in the *Daily Express*, she nonetheless accepted them as 'undeniably . . . in his handwriting and found among his papers'.[12]

Turning to Sidney Olivier as a more respectable mediator with the authorities, Mrs Dryhurst outlined what will later become the Normand Defence. Of the 'depraved' passages cited by the newspapers, she declared 'I believe these . . . are notes of the evidence Roger Casement took down in Putumayo . . . He told us . . . he had found unspeakable horrors had been committed upon the unfortunate natives there. And the evidence was such that he could not employ a woman secretary to take it down: the work he translated from the Spanish or Portuguese himself.'[13]

Olivier communicated this explanation to Scotland Yard on 5 July, his letter being answered two days later by Basil Thomson whom Olivier does not appear to have known personally. Olivier was prepared to declare that he had known Casement well when he was serving the Colonial Office. Between 1907 and 1913, Olivier had been out of England, so that he could not have been privy to Casement's revelations after his return from the Putumayo in 1910 (and again in 1911). Nannie Dryhurst was not only a long-term supporter of the Georgian cause and subject races generally, she had embraced Sinn Féin also.[14] With her reputation as a member of Kropotkin's circle, she can hardly have escaped wartime surveillance of some kind. Thomson, who informed Olivier that 'the diaries [*sic*, plural] describe acts committed in

12 Copy of N. F. Dryhurst to S. Olivier, 2 July 1916, preserved in police files (PRO, MEPO 2/10672).
13 Dryhurst to Olivier, 7 July 1916 (PRO, MEPO 2/10672). She does not name Normand (or anyone else). However, Letitia Fairfield claimed that 'the preposterous Normand story' was originally suggested by Ben Allen who, in turn, must be a candidate for the role of 'leading American journalist' whom Mrs Dryhurst cited; see Fairfield's letter to the editor of *Threshold* (Belfast), vol. 4 no. 2 (autumn/winter 1960), p. 92.
14 In his private journal for 11 May 1916, Nevinson noted Mrs Dryhurst's particular concern with the fate of Thomas MacDonagh: she was 'Hopeful pleas of insanity will be put forward for Casement' (BOD. LIB., MSS Eng. Misc 619/4 f. 12).

London and Ireland as well as S. America', was not interested in defences of Casement provided by a fellow-Irish rebel.[15]

Thomson was undoubtedly lying when he assured Olivier that 'no journalist American or otherwise has seen the diaries'. The *Daily Express* was proof positive of this, unless Thomson was relying on a duplicitous use of words. Appeals for clemency fell on ears deafened by the murmur of 'degeneracy', 'perversion', and 'unnatural practices'. Casement was executed on 3 August 1916 at Pentonville Jail, with a more than usually ghoulish crowd of ill wishers gathered outside. The war proceeded, peace finally came, and then the Irish 'Troubles' of 1919–22. Basil Thomson was convicted of public indecency (heterosexual) in 1925.

In James Joyce's *Ulysses* (1922), Casement is invoked but cannot be named by a nearly nameless public house gossip. Ironically, it is the ferociously xenophobic Citizen who recalls Casement's name and stamps Irish identity upon him. The new Irish state coming into existence while Joyce's novel was emerging would not improve on this performance. Casement's supporters were now fragmented, with English liberals disengaging from Irish concerns, and Irish republicans splitting into 'left' and 'right' factions.

When Joyce (for purely testamentary reasons) married in London in 1931, the wedding reception was held in Robert Lynd's Hampstead house. Lynd's daughter, Moira, was an avowed Communist. Mrs Dryhurst had died the previous October. As a conscientious objector in 1916 and atheistical logician, Bertrand Russell, who invoked Casement's wartime execution in *Freedom and Organisation* (1934), was not an ally who appealed to the mythopoeic pro-Nazis of diehard Irish republicanism, Sean Russell being no close kinsman. What W. H. Auden called 'the low dishonest decade' was under way even in Dublin Castle, and with it a revolution – or rather, *putsch* – in Irish public attitudes towards Casement. In some distinction from the bier-hall variety, it was a book-*putsch*.

---

15   B. Thomson to S. Olivier, 7 July 1916 (PRO, MEPO 2/10672).

THREE

THE 'FORGED' CASEMENT DIARIES
(1936)
A CHAPTER OF BOOK HISTORY

A publicist, now-a-days, is a man who bores the community with . . .
the illegalities of his private life.
OSCAR WILDE, *in 'Pen, Pencil and Poison – A Study in Green'* (1891)

—

CASEMENT BEFORE MALONEY

After his execution, Hampstead did not inconvenience itself on Casement's behalf. English liberal interest rapidly waned, not least because the Irish Free State was soon in a position to vindicate him in whatever manner it might choose. Ten years passed. Before 1930, a very few books had appeared which sought to clarify Casement's motivation and movements in the years leading up to his death. Published outside the mainstream of opinion-forming media – one in Munich though in English, another in German, a third privately in Chicago – these were the work of individuals who had known the man in some limited regard. The Irish Free State had been host to none of these. A change of perspective was imminent.

In 1932 Dr Patrick McCartan, who had known Casement personally and who would play a leading role in the Great Forgery Theory, published *With de Valera in America* under the Brentano imprint in New York and, for local consumption, through the Dublin bookseller, Fitzpatrick. His tributes to the journalistic skill of W. J. Maloney were lavish, but these celebrated an episode in the history of Irish America without hinting at any future contributions from his medical colleague. As far as either of them was concerned with Casement, the initiative appeared to have passed into other hands. With *The Life and Death of Roger Casement* (1930), Denis Gwynn (1893–1972) had been the first to attempt a comprehensive biography, though only two paragraphs covered the early life and social background.[1] This was not the only feature of the book which would subsequently appear odd: it also passed over the issue of forgery with what now seems remarkable insouciance.

What Gwynn had to say on this topic was autobiographical, but not directly so. In the summer of 1917, he was employed in the Ministry of Information, having been invalided home from France. A colleague, George Herbert Mair (1887–1926), admitted that he had been responsible for having Casement's diary copied for circulation in various forms a year earlier. What Gwynn concluded in his 1930 biography was that a diary had undoubtedly existed in 1916 – whether it had been genuinely Casement's was 'at least doubtful'.[2] He had sought access to this material, without success. So he got on with the task of recounting Casement's services to humanity as an investigator of atrocities committed in the Belgian Congo and the Putumayo region of South America. The consul's conversion to Irish nationalism was treated as a logical extension of this 'anti-colonial' crusade which, of course, he had pursued at the behest of the greatest colonial power then active.

Whether out of delicacy or ignorance, Gwynn did not further identify Mair. Some alert readers in Irish literary circles knew who – if not exactly what – he was. A graduate of Aberdeen University and Oxford, briefly a theatre reviewer for the *Manchester Guardian*, Mair had edited Thomas Wilson's *Arte of Rhetorique* (1560) while still at Oxford, and two years later published *English Literature: Modern* in the Home University Library series, a work still being reprinted in the late 1960s. One reason why Mair's popular handbook survived so well lay in his keen appreciation of new drama – including the plays of J. M. Synge (1871–1909). And in the same year – 1911 – Mair married Molly Allgood (1887–1952), Synge's youthful fiancée: an infant daughter died in February 1916 as the hunt for Casement was hotting up.

This accounts for 'who' Mair was; the 'what' is less easily traced. His career took him into 'intelligence' and war work in France for which he was honoured.[3] Quite what his gallous deeds had been no one has ever established.

1   In fact, a short biography had appeared as early as 1923 from a town close to Casement's beloved Antrim Glens: Robert McCahan, *The Life of Sir Roger David Casement, Knt, CMG* (Coleraine: Northern Constitution, 1923). The topic of Casement's diaries is discussed in one paragraph, with the writer concluding that they 'may be fictitious so far as we know', p. 36.

2   Denis Gwynn, *The Life and Death of Roger Casement* (London: Cape, 1930), p. 18.

3   In the opinion of Elizabeth Coxhead, he was engaged in 'often dangerous secret service work', *Daughters of Erin* (London: Secker, 1965), p. 207. Mair was awarded the Military Cross, being gazetted (that is, publicly listed as such) on 2 Dec. 1918, almost a month after hostilities had

Nor was he beyond criticism. In November 1915, Sir Arthur Markham MP raised the issue of Mair's odd role as a journalist working for *The Daily Chronicle* and as a press censor paid (it seems) £500 per annum from the secret service budget. Markham went to some length to establish his own friendship with John Buchan, to show that he could tell a derring-doer from a double dealer. Five years later, when the war was well over, Mair was obliged to write to *The Times* denying authorship of a book entitled *Mirrors of Downing Street*.[4] Yet, according to the same paper at the time of his death, Mair's greatest role was as director of the Press Section within the United Kingdom's delegation at the Paris peace talks. His masterly summary of the Versailles Treaty took thirty-six unbroken hours of mental hard labour.

In connection with state policy and language, it is worth revisiting the introduction Mair wrote to Wilson's account of sixteenth-century rhetoric. Early in its third section, he argued that Wilson (?1525–81) could hardly be termed an Elizabethan, despite serving as Secretary of State under the Virgin Queen: he was of an older fashion. Yet Mair is oddly impelled to conclude this argument by declaring that the term 'fits best the high sense of glory and achievement which sprang upon the nation after the destruction of Spain and lasted till the inexplicable apparition of unsought melancholy which saddened the reign of James'.[5]

Certainly the man who had Casement's 'diary' copied for the purposes of war-propaganda was intrigued by Tudor statecraft. The fast-forward to the 'inexplicable apparition' of a later melancholy had its own rationale. From an early age, Mair was prone to alcoholism, a disease in which man and wife contended for distinction and extinction. He died in abject circumstances in January 1926, another of the lost witnesses or near witnesses to the Casement business and its own melancholy statecraft.[6] Though he had 'worked for the

3   *cont.* ceased. He was not decorated until 13 Apr. 1921. King Carol made him a Commander of the Crown of Romania in December 1921, for services rendered during the late war (*The Times*, 8 Dec. 1921, p. 13). The issue of W. J. Maloney's MC will be discussed later. In neither case was there a report in *The Times*.

4   See a report of the House of Commons exchange in *The Times*, 1 Dec. 1915, p. 12; for the letter, written from Geneva, see *The Times*, 13 Dec. 1920, p. 8.

5   Mair's text has been re-edited for an electronic edition by Judy Boss (University of Oregon, 1998).

6   On Mair (1887–1926), see W. J. Mc Cormack, *Fool of the Family: A Life of J. M. Synge* (London: Weidenfeld & Nicolson; New York: New York University Press, 2000), pp. 403–4. See also the obituary in *The Times*, 4 Jan. 1926, p. 14, and details of his will on 28 Aug. 1926 (p. 13).

Home Office and the Foreign Office jointly in a confidential capacity', he was surrounded at Golders Green crematorium by mourners from the Fourth Estate – no political grandees, no mandarin civil servants, indeed his widow stayed away just as she had stayed away from Synge's funeral.[7]

Later in the same year, one of Casement's most faithful English defenders, the journalist Clement Shorter (1857–1926), also died. This acceleration of deaths, culminating with Birkenhead's in 1930, can only have encouraged writing about Casement. The risk of libel was reduced, and the need to augment living memory underlined. The twentieth anniversary of the trial and execution saw at least three full-scale books into print, together with a good deal of commemorative journalism. Gwynn's book was republished in a popular series, and Geoffrey Parmiter (died 2000) added his own substantial account of the life.

The son of Stephen Gwynn, nationalist MP and author, Gwynn had not been deterred 'by the lack of enthusiasm shown for his undertaking by Casement's surviving relatives' – an attitude among them which may have been connected to the younger Gwynn's own embrace of Catholicism. Parmiter, we are told, benefited from 'originals and documents' contributed by the same relatives.[8] This does not tally with the view of at least one more recent biographer, who suggests that the Parrys (Casement's cousin and her husband) did not think Parmiter the right person for the task of recording their kinsman's life.[9] But of the three publications in 1936, William Joseph Maloney's *The Forged Casement Diaries* was by far the most daring.

MALONEY EX MACHINA

Part of the daring lay in the author's unfamiliarity to the Irish public. The demonstration of Casement's martyrdom did not come from the pen of a renowned scholar or celebrated politician. The delicate nature of the issues

7   Among the mourners on 6 Jan. were Edith Shackleton and Norah Heald, who will resurface in Yeats's political life; see *The Times*, 7 Jan. 1926, p. 15.

8   Colm O Lochlainn in *Irish Book Lover*, vol. 24 no. 6 (1936), p. 120. See also the preface to Geoffrey de W. Parmiter, *Roger Casement* (London: Barker, 1936), p. xvi. In practice, Parmiter had used the facilities and materials of NLI; in other words, his biography of Casement was the first product of archival engineering arranged by Maloney and his managers, including the earliest publicly traceable versions of the Normand Defence; see Parmiter to R. I. Best, 31 Aug. 1935 (NLI, MS 13,078 (8)).

9   Roger Sawyer to the present writer, 22 June 2001.

involved curiously disenfranchised any such local authorities, who might be suspected of self-interest in vindicating a dead comrade. That Maloney was quite unknown to readers in Dublin constituted a major aspect of his success (such as it was). He provided an external standard of veracity, combined with passionate concern. Medical doctors have often succeeded in Irish politics for similar reasons.

He also exuded the zeal of the convert. The example of a British Army officer 'going over' to Sinn Féin in revulsion at the horrors of the Great War was one Irish readers were familiar with – both Robert Barton and Erskine Childers had undergone that transformation as had (at a lower level) Tom Barry and Liam O'Flaherty. At a more abstract level, the idea of an honest man coming out from among the imperial lines and identifying himself with the indignant minority had great emotional appeal. Despite giving his life for the republican cause, Childers was always believed by a few to be a British agent. Might not the same question arise in less dramatic cases? Maloney's identity both requires and resists close questioning.

Contrary to the assertions of latter-day commentators, Maloney was not Irish but Scottish by origin. Born in 1882, the future theorist came of a family which probably had been Irish one or two generations earlier. Having qualified as a doctor in his native Edinburgh, Maloney moved to the United States in 1911. Two years later, he made a distinguished marriage. In August 1914 he returned home to enlist, and served in the Royal Army Medical Corps. Wounded at Gallipoli in June 1915, he was discharged after prolonged hospitalisation. The official date of his being 'invalided with honour' was 4 August 1916, the day after Casement's execution. At the time, the army deemed him permanently incapacitated, and for the rest of his life he could only travel with great difficulty. According to an autobiographical interpolation in *The Forged Casement Diaries*, on 13 August 1916, he 'returned home to the United States. As the ship docked, a reporter from the *New York Herald*, full of the Casement story, came to [him]. Photographic specimen pages of the diary . . . had been brought to the *Herald* office'.[10] This is a claim which will require further investigation.

10 W. J. Maloney, *The Forged Casement Diaries* (Dublin: Talbot Press, 1936), p. 25. In an endnote, Maloney adds that the following day he protested to the *Herald*'s editor about any contemplated use of these photographs but his action was 'uncalled for'. This seems an extraordinary bout of activity in a man sent 'home' to New York by the British Army on the grounds of permanent disability.

The psychic splintering which characterises aspects of Irish commemoration finds its reflection in Maloney's career. Back in America, we are told, he
made enough money in journalism to set himself up as a consultant neurologist.[11]
In 1925, he scored a remarkable, if temporary, success in persuading the
dramatist Eugene O'Neill to give up alcohol. *The Forged Casement Diaries*
appeared at the end of 1936, from the decidedly provincial Talbot Press of
Dublin. One or two medical publications excepted, all of Maloney's not
inconsiderable output was issued from obscure presses in which the practice
of self-publication may be suspected where it isn't openly admitted. Given
that Gwynn's London publishers had succeeded in finding an American co-
publisher for his biography of Casement, it is striking that Maloney could not
follow the same path. The reluctance of London firms to issue a ringing
indictment of the British Foreign Office – and raise the question of German
support for Irish independence – can be exaggerated; more crucially, one is
entitled to query why no New York company took up the cause. Was there
some sub-conscious desire among the Forgery Theorists that the resurrection
should ideally take place at home in Ireland?

TEXT AND CONTEXT

There is no reason to believe that the author of *The Forged Casement Diaries*
ever had access to material circulated in 1916. At the time, he had been
struggling to survive the efforts of two empires to have him killed: the empire
which he and Casement had served, and the Reich which Casement sought to
mobilise on behalf of an Irish republic. Two years later, when Maloney had
begun pamphleteering on behalf of Irish independence, the campaign to
discredit Casement was largely forgotten; America had entered the war and,
soon, the war was over. The issue in 1918 was President Wilson's evolving
attitude towards Ireland, in which Casement played no part. One could hardly
expect, some fifteen years later again, that Maloney might recover evidence
closely guarded by those who had touted it round Washington. Primary
sources simply were not available. Indeed, it was questionable as to whether

---

11 F. N. L. Poynter in his 'Editor's Note' prefacing W. J. Maloney, *George and John Armstrong of
Castleton: Two Eighteenth-Century Medical Pioneers* (London: Livingstone, 1954). Up to this point,
I have drawn on Poynter for biographical data, also on American medical directories; but see
chapter 9 for a more extensive treatment.

any *primary* evidence had ever existed. The method of analysis Maloney was obliged to adopt focused instead on the revelations of witnesses and – to a degree – of those implicated in the blackening campaign. Let us first examine his approach to Sir Wyndham Childs (1876–1946).

A professional soldier, whose career later took him through the War Office and the Metropolitan Police (he was Assistant Commissioner from 1921 to 1928), Childs was in some ways a minor actor in the drama. In his retirement, he published a book of reminiscences in which he devoted two pages to the Casement business of Easter 1916. Appearing in 1930, *Episodes and Reflections* directly fed into the evidence gathering which Maloney and his IRB friends decided upon. When *The Forged Casement Diaries* eventually saw the December light of day in 1936, Childs was cited to exemplify the confusion among British conspirators as to where the suspect diary had been originally found. Here was material for scriptural disputation. Childs, Maloney averred, claimed that it had been discovered on or near Casement's person on Good Friday 1916, on Banna Strand.

In fact, Childs never made any such ludicrous claim. In his book, he did indeed describe the items seized by the police – a collapsible boat, an Irish flag etc. – but the one sentence he devoted to the diary is to be found in a different paragraph, where it is unambiguously detached from the personal possessions of Casement at the moment of his arrest. Maloney's misrepresentation of Childs's evidence may have proceeded from haste rather than guile, but it is complicated by his suppression of the Major-General's retrospective opinion of the campaign to circulate excerpts from Casement's diary. 'Much has been written about this document, both in America and in this country [i.e. Britain], and much has been disclosed which, in my judgment, should never have been mentioned or so much as insinuated.'[12] Childs will re-emerge in the aftermath of Maloney's appearing in print, and indeed his reminiscences shed light on an incident of 1922 – the assassination of Sir Henry Wilson – which flits in and out of the background conjured by Maloney's managers.

Maloney's treatment of Denis Gwynn is no more precise, though the interest lies in the historian's potential as a seeming ally rather than in his former service to the British war effort. At no point did Gwynn claim to have seen either original or copy of a diary. But this does not prevent Maloney from citing Gwynn as a witness. Within a single page, he claims that 'Gwynn

12 Wyndham Childs, *Episodes and Reflections* (London: Cassell, 1930), p. 113. See Eunan O'Halpin, *Head of the Civil Service: A Study of Sir Warren Fisher* (London: Routledge, 1989), pp. 91–5, 132–3.

describes the diary as a record of indecent experiences in the Putumayo, Paris and London . . . [and] Gwynn corroborates the Paris entries'.[13] Additionally, Maloney invokes Gwynn to prove that G. H. Mair *copied* the diary, though the historian had carefully written how the latter had declared 'it was he who had been responsible for having the diary copied. He claimed [*sic*] to have read it, and I remember that he referred to one passage describing an incident in London. I regret now that I made no further inquiries'.[14]

Internal evidence strongly suggests that Maloney's book got under way in 1931–2 following New York publication of Gwynn's biography, under the altered title, *Traitor or Patriot*. Maloney persists in alluding to this latter item as a London publication which he misnames *Traitor and* [*sic*] *Patriot*, a not insignificant error. Gwynn's American title – chosen perhaps for a more paradox-delighting readership – is echoed in the first heading of Maloney's preface, 'Imperial Attitude to Subject Traitor-Patriots'. Oddly enough, Angus Mitchell in 1997 also alludes to the American (second) edition of Gwynn's biography, giving (like Maloney) a London imprint. Forgery theorists stick together.

The echo of Gwynn's American title in the preface to Maloney's book is only one of many indicators of his mental patterns. More substantial evidence of the American doctor's impetuosity can be traced in the seventh chapter of *The Forged Casement Diaries*. He begins by summarising press despatches from London in 1916 about atrocities allegedly committed in Dublin during Easter week: these included impromptu shooting of her followers by Constance Gore-Booth (a commander with the Irish Citizen Army), together with 'numerous cases of unarmed persons killed by the rebels'. Maloney then quickly switches to deal with British propaganda on American soil. Quoting an article by Alfred Noyes in the evening edition of the *Philadelphia Public Ledger* (31 August 1916), he details the newspaper's headings and subheadings, e.g. 'Revelations of Casement's Diary . . . Sinn Fein Outrages'. Soon he is referring to 'the Casement atrocity diary'.[15]

There follow rather tedious retrospects on Casement's earlier life until, nearly half way through chapter 10, 'the atrocity diary' resurfaces. This is not just a matter of reiterated argument – the phrase itself is repeated some

---

13 Maloney, *Forged Casement Diaries*, p. 176.
14 Gwynn, *Life and Death*, p. 20.
15 Maloney, *Forged Casement Diaries*, pp. 102–3, 107. For no apparent reason, Maloney annotates the last phrase with a reference to Mrs Alice Roosevelt Longworth's memoirs, published in 1933.

twenty times, and in increasingly formulaic ways as if it had become a mantra. Admittedly, some of this repetition results from the author's heavily ironic insistence that the 'atrocity diary' had not been legally 'found' – this last pedantic detail seems to have been borrowed from John Quinn. But the very notion of 'Casement's atrocity diary' stems from Maloney's own confusion of two distinct elements in Noyes's propaganda. He ends up appearing more the victim of British cunning than its critic.

In reaching this interim conclusion, one should note an intrusive comment on popular credulity which Maloney makes as the 'atrocity diary' commences its serial reproduction in his text. 'The world that hailed the "Angel of Mons" might question the propriety but not the truth of the Casement diary.'[16] This is a bold attempt to encapsulate the susceptibility of people to fantasies in time of stress and looming defeat. But Maloney's particular example only serves to remind informed readers that he boasted service in that dreadful battle, and won the Mons Star for his pains. The external narrative is disrupted by an eruption of personal reference all the more poignant because its origin in traumatic experience is not acknowledged. (See pp. 137–42 below for more on Mons.) Again, the savage critic has become moiled in the wickedness or folly he seeks to denounce.

Though enough has been said to explode Maloney as a serious academic writer, there remains the question of his moral authority. His style aspires at times to the *saeve indignatio* of Jonathan Swift who, in his pamphleteering, was not above distortions of fact. The difference between the two rests, of course, in the greater control exercised by the Dean of Saint Patrick's. While Swift remains notorious for the obsessive and neurotic character of his imagery, a dialectic of argument is maintained even when tactical deviations and digressions occur. Part of Maloney's motivation may be traced to the battlefields of Flanders and Asia Minor, or to deep-seated anxieties using those surface referents for cover. His individual and specific concern is constantly inundated with material of great moral power – the denunciation of official dishonesty – but which actually detracts from the business in hand. No one can doubt his outrage at allegations that the German Army had been recycling corpses to obtain glycerine for munitions, nor his contempt for a related forgery of documents to back up the claim. Here the battle-tested soldier's code of honour

16 *Ibid.*, p. 147. The 'angel of Mons' was seen by thousands of demoralised British troops on Sunday 23 Aug. 1914, hovering over the battlefield and urging them on. In some accounts, the apparition took the form of a medieval archer.

is manifest. But this in itself does nothing to discredit documentation circulated about Casement – unless one believes to be false *everything* the British authorities did and do. Five chapters expounding something very close to the latter view had certainly put G. B. Shaw off.

As early as 1934, Shaw had been informed of Maloney's project; indeed by November he had read the manuscript and found it wanting. He cautioned Gertrude Parry (loyal to a fault) against any reliance on its publication clearing the dead man's name. 'It is a monument of zealous industry; but it does not clear the ground: it rather overcrowds it.' He then advised Maloney against publication, a view already reached by whatever American firms to which the typescript had been sent.[17] There is no evidence that Casement's surviving relatives greatly assisted Maloney, though polite contact was established through Bulmer Hobson. There is also a telling omission which may forever evade inquiry. What is odd in both the generalised indignation of *The Forged Casement Diaries* and its specific account of the man is the absence of the word homosexual(ity). The greatest weakness of Maloney's argument is his inability to articulate – even in this very basic sense – the charge laid against his hero. His moral integrity appears so absolute that it could not even name the 'immorality' under discussion. Yet this integrity proceeded less from innocence than from a considerably disturbed psychic organisation.

In his compositional method, one could trace the spasmodic manner in which Maloney responded to the outer world. Influences are retained in the order of their occurrence rather than in any intellectual or logical coherence. Thus Geoffrey Parmiter – whose biography of Casement appeared earlier in 1936 than Maloney's own book – crops up in a footnote on the final text-page. Within this rigid structure, Maloney moves rapidly backwards and forwards to record incidents in Casement's life, and occasionally drops into autobiographical mode. The reader is told of the invalided doctor greeted on arrival in New York with news of the campaign to vilify Casement, but is left uninformed of a pamphlet Maloney wrote shortly afterwards in which this vilification is never mentioned and the Allied cause implicitly supported.

As if in mechanical reaction against such restraint, the New York address of Sir William Wiseman suddenly erupts into chapter 7. As an intelligence chief, Wiseman (1885–1962) has certainly been a major if remote figure in Britain's American-based officialdom: his intrusion into Maloney's text is unprepared

17   G. B. Shaw to Gertrude Parry, 19 Nov. 1924, in Bernard Shaw, *Collected Letters, 1926–1950* (London: Max Reinhardt, 1988), pp. 387–9.

for, reinscribing the site at which a bogus letter to Lloyd George had been allegedly found in 1919. Though the reader can't be expected to know, this alludes to an earlier anonymous publication of Maloney's. These subconscious gestures in his signed text constitute a sort of fragmentary statement-of-the-self. The person we may slowly and painfully reconstruct from a dozen or so such details is – quite understandably – a damaged one. Whether literally or otherwise, the author is in shell shock; his moral authority lies precisely in a lack of authority or (to be more exact) in a congruence of responsibility and victimage. Such a psychic condition attunes naturally to Casement's, but the result is neither scholarship, nor forensic science, nor a case proven.

The manner in which Maloney's arguments proceed along the trajectory of his own reading is reflected simply enough in his preferred title for the book, *The Forged Casement Diary* [*sic*]. Initially he focused on the notion of a single document. While this might seem strangely naïve in a seasoned anti-British campaigner, it also suggests Maloney's insensitive ear for English idiom. 'To keep a diary' does not mean simply to write up one bound volume; when we say that Samuel Pepys kept a diary for nine years, we acknowledge its multiple volumes. When Maloney assumes that Basil Thomson contradicts himself in sometimes referring to Casement's diary and sometimes to his diaries, he reveals his own constricted apprehension of the words, a factor perhaps complicated by war-damage. The quality of Maloney's mental processes is questionable, at moments such as these.

It is only when he learned of Michael Collins's and Eamonn Duggan's being shown two (physically distinct) diaries late in 1921,[18] and Duggan's leaving a written account of their appearance, that he abandons the first theory without, however, removing it from his evolving text. Accordingly, the title is modified, without further adjustment. And the implications of there having been more than one Casement diary in the hands of the British authorities are serious, for they raise the possibility that persons shown incriminating material were not necessarily shown the same material. Ben S. Allen, the one witness whom Maloney could call a personal friend, ventured such a notion but he was ignored.[19] Characteristically, the Forgery Theorist persisted with a reductive

18 This incident occurred at the time of the Treaty negotiations in London. Birkenhead offered to let Collins see Casement diaries in the House of Lords; Collins took Duggan with him, and the two men were left alone to examine the documents. See Duggan's statement in NLI, MS 17,601 (6).
19 See Ben S. Allen to W. Maloney, 2 Dec. 1932 (NLI, MS 17,601 (1)). Declining to condemn Reginald Hall out of hand for his use of Casement's private writing, Allen wrote, 'if he alone had

analysis, finally concluding that there was a two-part diary, fabricated by two different hands.[20]

This naïveté is additionally illustrated through his treatment of what I term the Normand Defence. Variously attributed to Ben S. Allen, Bulmer Hobson, P. S. O'Hegarty (1879–1955), and Geoffrey Parmiter, the theory explained the existence of an obscene diary evidently in Casement's handwriting. Armando Normand was an official of the rubber company whose practices the former consul was investigating. Of obscure background, but partly educated in England, Normand inflicted unspeakable cruelties on native Indian labourers, on women, and even children. In the words of Roger Sawyer, recent biographer of Casement and anti-slavery activist, 'it was claimed that Casement had had in his possession a perverted diary of Normand's . . . which he sent to the Foreign Office as evidence'.[21] We now know that Mrs Dryhurst had ventured a similar explanation as early as July 1916, though her circle does not appear to have had contact with Maloney at any time.

In his fourteenth chapter, Maloney took up this Defence, quoting Hobson and O'Hegarty to the effect that Casement had told them about Normand's diary which

recorded in his own hand details of the most abominable and unnatural crimes . . . [Casement] said that he had sent the diary to the Foreign Office . . . With the Normand diary at his disposal the artist constructing the draft forgery had no lack of indecency to hinder him in the completion of his task . . . and as this translation of Normand's diary was in Casement's handwriting, all that was needed was the changing of its dates so as to make them correspond to those of Casement's Putumayo investigation, and then its choicest entries were ready to be incorporated in the model document.[22]

19 *cont.* used it . . . I might join in condemning him'. While the surface meaning relates to wartime propaganda in general, there is an implication that other British officials were using related material. Rivalry between branches of the security forces may have played an unintended part in obscuring the extent of the material at their disposal. See chapter 6 below for a fuller account of Allen.

20 Maloney, *Forged Casement Diaries*, p. 183.

21 Roger Sawyer, *Casement: The Flawed Hero* (London: Routledge, 1984), p. 90. In his report of 17 Mar. 1911, Casement referred to Normand as being 'Peruvian or Bolivian' and went on to note that he took twenty per cent of the gross rubber output in his section. 'Everyone of these criminals kept a large staff of unfortunate Indian women for immoral purposes'.

22 Maloney, *Forged Casement Diaries*, p. 199.

There are many objections to this theory which derive from material made available since 1936. But, even at the time of writing, it was shaky. First Maloney posits Casement's possession of Normand's actual diary which he sent to the FO; then he refers to a translation of this, in Casement's handwriting, though Casement was acknowledged by all authorities to be a poor linguist with – in H. S. Dickey's view (see chapter 7) – deplorable Spanish and Portuguese for a man intent on serious business in South America. Quite how the doctored material was to have been 'incorporated' into the final forgery remains unexplained. If Maloney had consulted Casement's published report on conditions in the Putumayo region, he would have known of Normand's sadistic behaviour. But if he had applied his medical intelligence to the same sources, he would also have realised that Normand was unmistakably (and violently) heterosexual. On both counts, Normand's diary (if such ever existed) could not be used as evidence of Casement's passive homosexuality.[23]

In mitigation of these defects, Maloney invokes the statements made by Hobson and O'Hegarty. Each separately recounted how Casement had spoken at length to them of Normand's crimes and vices, and each deposited his statement in the National Library of Ireland. These documents, however, should be read in the context of Hobson's comprehensive control over the production of *The Forged Casement Diaries*. Everything, from the postponement of a full biography (perhaps in three volumes) to the choice of illustrations for a book focused on destroying memories of Casement's apparent homosexuality, was transmitted through him. By 1936, Hobson (sometime a printer's apprentice) was ensconced in Dublin Castle, looking after the Stamps Office; O'Hegarty (a bibliophile) was accommodated in a different branch of the Irish Civil Service. In these contexts, the war-damaged New York doctor is managed by former members of the IRB in Dublin. Mediating between the two cities was the American-based 'Fenian', Patrick McCartan, who arranged for the financing of the publication and its careful distributing *gratis* to – amongst others – W. B. Yeats and Francis Stuart.

The great poet's public response to *The Forged Casement Diaries* took the form of two distinctly ungreat ballad poems. Compared to his figuring of Parnell as tragic hero, Yeats's 'Roger Casement' is strikingly deficient in sublimity. His calculated naïveté was suspended in private correspondence,

---

23 This explanation may have fed into Maloney's later notion of an 'atrocity diary' which he conjured from separate elements in Alfred Noyes's American journalism, a further instance of disturbed mental processes in the construction of a Forgery Theory; on Noyes, see chapter 5 below.

though it is curious that the topic of Casement's sexuality as raised by Maloney's book featured in his letters to two people, both of whom were women with whom he had a sexual relationship. In the case of Dorothy Wellesley, matters were complicated by her lesbianism. Before the publication of his poems, Yeats told her plainly that 'the Casement evidence [*sic*] was not true' though nothing about Casement's sexuality had featured as evidence at either trial or appeal.[24] As with his casual attitude to counting the firing squad's victims, the great poet carried legal inexactitude into his Casement ballad, alleging perjury where there had been no statement one way or the other. Later he reported to Wellesley that in Dublin

> Public opinion is excited & there is a demand for a production of the documents & their submission to some impartial tribunal. It would be a great relief to me if they were so submitted & proved genuine. If Casement were a homo-sexual what matter! But if the British Government can with impugnity forge evidence to prove him so no unpopular man with a cause will ever be safe.[25]

In keeping with the official ambivalence about Casement in the Irish Free State, no impartial tribunal eventuated. Eamon de Valera's refusal to demand one was crucial in ensuring that nothing forensic happened in the 1930s nor in the succeeding three decades. As a consequence, Maloney's great efforts resulted in little beyond moral victory among the faithful. In such company few noted the failure of his book to examine the contradictions which it unearthed. Having abandoned the one-diary forgery theory for an expanded version which accommodated what Collins and Duggan had seen in 1921, he was content to heap sarcasm on the irreconcilable descriptions provided by witnesses. This was gratifying because it suggested in the enemy a degree of incompetence as well as a monstrous capacity for blackguardism. It never occurred to Maloney that John Redmond might have been shown a different diary from the one of which John Quinn saw photographs, nor that the British authorities might have in their possession three or even four such diaries. Discrepancies were interpreted as evidence of forgery as such, rather than evidence of more material than was ever admitted by the sponsors of the

24 W. B. Yeats to Dorothy Wellesley, 4 Dec. 1936; quoted in John Unterecker, *Yeats and Patrick McCartan: A Fenian Friendship* (Dublin: Dolmen, 1967), p. 379.
25 W. B. Yeats to Dorothy Wellesley, 18 Feb, [1937], in *Letters on Poetry from W. B. Yeats to Dorothy Wellesley* (London: Oxford University Press, 1964), p. 124.

campaign to vilify Casement. In an odd way, the claim that the authorities had 'a diary' was accepted literally, whereas a more vigilant suspicion might have wondered if they had (found or manufactured) quite a few more than one.

Not for the last time, one is perturbed by admissions preserved in the various archives Maloney built up in the National Library of Ireland. At an early stage of his approaches to Eamonn Duggan, he was depressed by the small number of surviving witnesses, a factor which later assisted in creating an aura of unfalsifiability in the eventual book. It seemed that he must rely on Duggan and on Casement's surviving brother with whom Collins had been in correspondence. The brother, a witness in no meaningful sense, declined to perform as required. Undaunted, Maloney confided to Hobson that 'anything we gather from Duggan will be so inserted in the text as to be inferentially what Collins saw'. The skills of a propagandist are not however matched by a comparable shrewdness of judgment. His one reservation about using the National Library as repository for pre-edited archives was that it might fall to the old enemy. 'England will, unless more political wisdom is shown, recapture the Free State.'[26]

With the illicit publication of three diaries in 1959, and their subsequent release, the presumption of one-or-at-the-most-two documents was exploded. Five items now constitute the Black Diaries corpus in the Public Record Office. This expansion in the number and nature of the material contested by Maloney's successors complicates the issue of forgery versus authenticity, for it opens up the possibility that there may have been both authentic *and* forged material circulated to vilify Casement. Nor has Maloney's tally of discrepancies been wholly explained away. The American journalist, Benjamin Shannon Allen of Associated Press, told Maloney he had been shown 'a rolled manu-script' repeatedly by Captain Reginald Hall in 1916. 'The paper was buff in colour, with blue lines and with the sheets ragged at the top as if they had been torn from what, in my school days, we called a composition book'.[27] There are good grounds for interrogating Maloney's relationship with Allen –

26 W. J. Maloney to B. Hobson, 8 Oct. 1932 (NLI, MS 17,604 (1)).

27 From a letter (no date given), Ben S. Allen to W. Maloney, quoted in part in Maloney, *Forged Casement Diaries*, p. 174. But see pp. 91–7 below for a discussion of two letters dated Oct. and Dec. 1932, from Allen to Maloney. H. Montgomery Hyde argued that the 1903 diary preserved in Kew had originally included the torn pages described by Allen, but the description does not match the item now readily available for inspection. See Hyde, *Famous Trials, 9: Roger Casement* (London: Penguin, 1963), pp. 173–4.

see chapter 6 below. Nevertheless, it remains incontrovertible that nothing at Kew matches Allen's rolled manuscript. And the diaries preserved in the PRO and elsewhere do not add up to a sequence of annual records, with the result that any inquiry into the alleged forgery of surviving documents should address the difficult issue of suppressed, lost or destroyed documentation. Even today, the British authorities have yet to explain what happened to the buff-coloured manuscript. As it is not among the Black Diaries, where is it?

NO ZOLA

Despite abandoning his hero after 1936, Maloney has acquired a modest cultic reputation in Irish second-hand bookshops which remains unscrutinised. In his adopted city, he was less fortunate. In what is perhaps the most acute and detailed biography of Casement, the New Yorker B. L. Reid is unequivocal in rejecting the forgery theory, but he does so on grounds other than a close examination of the book which set up the theory.[28] The high standing of *The Forged Casement Diaries* among those who still pursue the issue derives in no small part from the book's impact upon W. B. Yeats and, at a lower level of poetic achievement, upon Alfred Noyes.[29] (A repentant Englishman is always welcome.) As the latter had been moved by Yeats's ballad (in turn inspired by Maloney's rhetoric) to 'come clean' about what he had done to besmirch Casement's name, it seemed that within a few months, the New York doctor had overturned a verdict and exposed the forgers. To draw an analogy from the French 1890s, he was Émile Zola to Casement's Dreyfus.[30]

There is some evidence that Maloney was so regarded. Noyes, in his last contribution to the controversy, invokes Zola in connection with one episode in Casement's downfall.[31] Herbert O. Mackey, chief forgery theorist of the 1960s, borrowed the novelist's famous title for a pamphlet, *I Accuse: A Monstrous Fraud Which Deceived Two Continents* (Dublin, n.d.). The analogy is of course

---

28 B. L. Reid, *The Lives of Roger Casement* (New Haven, London: Yale University Press, 1976).

29 Yeats published one of his ballads in the daily *Irish Press*, and Noyes (who had worked for the Foreign Office) replied in a letter published in the same paper on 12 Feb. 1937. For the ballads see *Yeats's Poems*, ed. A. N. Jeffares (London: Macmillan, 1989), pp. 423–5.

30 The *Catholic World* reviewed Maloney's book in tandem with an account of the Dreyfus case written by members of the Dreyfus family.

31 Alfred Noyes, *The Accusing Ghost; or, Justice for Casement* (London: Gollancz, 1957, p. 121).

entirely false. For a start, Alfred Dreyfus had been convicted of treason specifically on the basis of forged evidence: the two went together, the treason, the *bordereau*. In contrast, Casement did little to deny his actions, but denied the right of any country save Ireland to claim his allegiance; forgery never affected these courtroom proceedings. Whereas Dreyfus had been going about his proper peacetime business as a French army officer when the accusation fell upon him, Casement had been arrested as he debouched from an enemy submarine in mid-war.

In addition, Zola had issued *J'accuse* while the issues were still lively. He spoke from a well-informed familiarity with French society, its commonplace anti-Semitism and its network of corruption. He was, it hardly need be said, the master of diagnostic fiction, an analyst of passion and prejudice. Maloney, on the other hand, was writing nearly twenty years after the death of his subject, from a remote base in New York. An inexperienced writer on topics outside medicine and propaganda, he laid claim to no historical training or skill. 'An infant in Irish affairs', was how he described himself to the Irish-American leader, Joe McGarrity.[32] In other respects, his affinity was with Casement rather than Zola. Like the former consul, Maloney in 1915 found his life imperilled by Britain's global strategy – he was an officer pawn, Casement a knight in check. If one was efficiently turned off in the solitude of Pentonville, the other endured the shambles of Gallipoli. Both men had served the empire bravely; only one of them survived to tell the tale. At a subliminal depth, *The Forged Casement Diaries* is a work of personal score settling, even autobiography. This description does not reduce Casement's achievement as a humanitarian.

It had been this factor, rather than sympathy with his extreme nationalism, which rallied Conan Doyle, Bernard Shaw and other London-based intellectuals to Casement's side in 1916. For his retrospective saviour twenty years later, the Talbot Press was a last resort, possessing only the merit of a Dublin imprint. The consequence was to identify Maloney as Irish-American, even Irish, whereas his background was quite different. Maloney's reputation, therefore, stands on a certain paradox. Apart from some carefully stage-managed reviews, his book excited little response. To be sure, Yeats wrote two indifferent ballads, but in private, he thought the diaries might well be genuine. There was the lesser achievement of Noyes's confession, but that was not a confession to forgery, merely to blackguardism. Shaw, after publication,

---

32   W. J. Maloney to J. McGarrity, undated, probably early 1930s (NLI, MS 17,462).

remained as unmoved as he had been when first he saw the doctor's manuscript. Yet despite this unsatisfactory outcome, Maloney clearly decided to let the Casement issue look after itself. Perhaps this was the decision of one who knew when to cut his losses, but hardly the response of a Saint Paul.[33]

The personality of the man is not much in evidence in the book – apart, that is, from the furious sarcasm which informs his comment on British official morals. To get a different perspective on Maloney and his attitudes, one might return to a publication of 1918 seemingly irrelevant to the present inquiry, *Locomotor Ataxia*. The subtitle of this substantial medical tome declared it to be 'an introduction to the study and treatment of nervous diseases', whereas it was in fact devoted almost exclusively to the diagnosis and treatment of syphilis, with reference to the decay of bodily movement and co-ordination. In the preface, Maloney explained how the war had interrupted his research, made all the right acknowledgments to professional superiors, and proceeded to summarise his own method which

> is based on the thesis that perfect thinking is essential to perfect moving; and perfect moving is the outward sign of perfect thinking. Training in perfect thinking is, therefore, training in perfect moving; and training in perfect moving is training in perfect thinking.

While this may be no more than yo-yo writing, others might detect omens of recent alternative medicines. Certainly, this outlook was compatible with the mythopoeic version of 1916. But Maloney had targets as well as theories, and his wrath fell especially on 'those who foster the Emanuel movement and ... the earnest members of that faith which is disguised as science and called Christian'. Quite why the followers of Mrs Baker Eddy should have been attacked remains obscure, unless the *Christian Science Monitor*'s role in the press coverage of Casement justified this digression. The animus was not simply that of a scientist opposing claptrap. Maloney deplored 'this material and impious age', complained in evangelical fashion that 'the Jordan flows unheeded and the waters of Bethesda rise unwatched'.[34] While remembering his own war experiences and consequent disability, we might suspect a crank labouring at his claptrap.

33 The most thoughtful successor to Maloney was Roger McHugh, whose 'Casement: The Public Record Office Manuscripts' appeared in the Belfast-based theatre journal, *Threshold* (1960), pp. 28–57.
34 W. J. M. A. Maloney, *Locomotor Ataxia* (New York: Appleton, 1918), p. ix.

FOUR

MANAGING DR MALONEY

Draw round, beloved and bitter men,
Draw round and raise a shout.
W. B. YEATS, *'The Ghost of Roger Casement'* (1936)

EVIDENCE IN THE ARCHIVES

The preservation in the National Library of Ireland of what is usually termed the Maloney Papers is itself a phenomenon worthy of scholarly attention. These link with other major collections, such as the papers of Joseph McGarrity (1874–1940) and Patrick McCartan, to provide a broad background against which to study the non-print history of *The Forged Casement Diaries*. As in most major archives, what NLI terms – for example – 'The Hatch Papers' does not contain the entire archive of John Hatch, let alone his family or circle. Thus the McCartan Papers constitute a large but necessarily incomplete collection of letters and other manuscript materials associated with the American-based veteran: other papers of his will be found in other libraries and archives. The major holding of Joseph McGarrity's papers is to be found at Villanova University, Philadelphia.[1]

In relation to Dr Maloney, what NLI holds under several different headings is essentially a single but dispersed dossier narrating the publication of *The Forged Casement Diaries*. It was apparently Maloney himself who conceived the device of depositing material in the Library, with a view ultimately to

---

1 These consist of two distinct groups: Group One (originally six boxes, with some recent additions) were accessed in 1940 at the time of McGarrity's death. This material is mainly personal, and has been augmented by donations from his daughter Elizabeth de Feo (born 1914). Group Two (six boxes) was presented by the heirs of McGarrity's eldest daughter, Mary Shore, *c.* 1999. The McGarrity Papers at NLI were probably routed through his political organisation in Philadelphia, rather than through his family, and reached Dublin after the Second World War. I am grateful to Bente Polites of Villanova University Library for this information.

establishing that the allegations about Casement's sexuality had been based on forged evidence.[2] In 1933, P. S. O'Hegarty was in touch with an English bookseller, about the possible purchase by the NLI of a dossier of letters connected with Conan Doyle's petition in 1916, while also identifying Maloney as a possible intermediary/ purchaser.[3] To Gertrude Parry, Maloney wrote in 1933 'we should make it the finest in the world of its kind. No other National Library will have such a complete record of its greatest national heroes.'[4] Aside from the highly selective manner in which Maloney donated material, his use of the library probably strikes people today as presumptuous, even improper. Within twenty years or so of the Irish state's establishment, the issue doubtless appeared in a different light. National honour was at stake, though one can detect in the Librarian's receipt issued for a portion of this deposit a good deal of professional caution.[5]

From the point of view of historians working on the book trade, it is nonetheless a remarkable and valuable dossier, including a typescript as prepared for (and perhaps actually used by) the printer and a set of the galley proofs, lightly annotated. In addition, there is correspondence about illustrations and the cost of these, financial subventions, possible prefaces by third parties, accounts, lists of reviewing outlets, serialisation, the distribution of complimentary copies, etc. But it does not touch on any other aspects of Maloney's life and work – there is nothing on his medical career, and only the most incidental comment on his family.

A sensible point at which to begin a survey of this material would appear to be the earliest document on file. To judge from the catalogues, this is a typed letter from Maloney to George Gavan Duffy (1882–1951), Casement's solicitor, dated 9 September 1916, some five weeks after the execution.[6] On closer examination, however, this turns out to be a copy of a letter to Gavan Duffy, not the original. On closer examination still, it turns out to be a copy of a letter – not from Maloney – but from John Quinn, the New York lawyer who had known Casement and who had been shown incriminating evidence just a

2   After his wife's death, Maloney also devised a Margaret Sarah McKim Maloney Memorial Collection in the New York Public Library, and a collation of its holdings with those of the NLI would further extend the analysis of archival engineering.

3   See NLI, MS 17,602.

4   W. J. Maloney to G. Parry, 28 July 1933 (NLI, MS 13075/2/iii).

5   NLI, MS 18,415. The librarian was Richard Irvine Best (1872–1959), a Celtic scholar of high repute who features in Joyce's *Ulysses*.

6   NLI, MS 17,603.

few months or weeks earlier. Yet despite this irrefutable identification of its authorship, the copy is actually signed by Maloney as though he were its author. Despite also this, its text was quoted in Maloney's book as Quinn's letter.[7] The mind briefly boggles as to how such an archival mare's nest came about. Was it through a clumsy attempt at fabrication on Maloney's part, designed to establish that he had been on the case as early as September 1916 (when he was, we are to presume, near-prostrate, permanently incapacitated by those Gallipoli wounds)? Alternatively, was it the misleading (but unintended) consequence of Maloney's desire to authenticate the copy as one which he much later transmitted to a third party, carelessly putting his own signature where the actual author's would have appeared on the original? This cultured pearl is to be found among the McGarrity Papers.

A different perspective on this very early period of Maloney's career as a propagandist is to be found among miscellaneous press cuttings assembled by McCartan. Some day these may assist a biographer, keen to go beyond the preliminary sketch outlined here (chapters 9 and 10 below). According to one cutting dateable to late 1916, which specified the Royal Army Medical Corps as his 'regiment', the wounded doctor was proposing to volunteer for renewed active service. However unlikely this outcome must now seem, the reference does little to suggest Maloney's later detestation of British war methods. For the period of the blackguardly circulation of material vilifying Casement, the only primary evidence we have of Maloney's attitude indicates loyalty to the Allied cause.

By 1917, however, he is busy as a journalist using the pseudonym W. J. McNeece (or McNeice) which combined his own first initials with his mother's maiden name. A shift in his politics is clearly discernible. In 1918, he wrote in *America* on Sinn Féin and France, signing himself, Jean Mayle.[8] We owe these fragments of obscure journalism to McCartan who assembled them years later; his first contact with Maloney appears to have been established in 1919, that is, when the Irish war of independence got under way. By 1921, the year which ended with the Treaty, McCartan was no longer addressing his correspondent formally as Dr Maloney but, instead, inquiring about Mrs Maloney's radium treatment for cancer and generally indicating a close relationship between two men who shared medicine as a profession. Maloney was by no

7   W. J. Maloney, *The Forged Casement Diaries* (Dublin: Talbot Press, 1936), p. 27.
8   NLI, MS 17,685 (1). This is the implication of McCartan's arrangement, though other evidence suggests there was a Jean Mayle.

means exclusively concerned with Irish affairs, for we find in *America* of
11 June 1921 an article on America in Haiti, signed by William McNeice.[9]

In January 1922, McCartan voted in favour of the Treaty but when civil
war broke out shortly afterwards he took no part in the fighting, despite his
considerable reputation as an IRA volunteer. Prior to the bitterest conflict at
home, the year saw the assassination in London of Field-Marshal Sir Henry
Wilson (1864–1922), a native of Longford and an intransigent opponent of
Sinn Féin in all its manifestations. Two men were duly executed for the
crime, for which the IRA denied any responsibility, a circumstance which will
later impinge on the reception of *The Forged Casement Diaries*. In the opinion
of Assistant Commissioner Childs, one of the convicted assassins was 'a poet,
a musician and a deep thinker'.[10] McCartan's inactivity during the Civil War
led in time to a situation in which republicans regarded him as a supporter of
the Free State while Free-staters suspected him of die-hardism. His decision
to settle in the United States – which he had visited as an envoy of the Dáil
and as an escort to de Valera – eased his anomalous political position in
Ireland. His movements backward and forward across the Atlantic sometimes
brought him into direct contact with Maloney and sometimes generated a
correspondence now usefully preserved. Maloney gradually became attached
to Joe McGarrity, who ran the *Irish Press* of Philadelphia.

Maloney's transition from an invalid eager for more action in the British
Army to a propagandist for Irish independence is difficult to trace in detail.
The published pamphlets of October 1918 onwards are evidence of his industry
for his adopted cause. Nor is it difficult to see talent in his propaganda. For the
New York Evening Post he could neatly expose military cynicism, writing that
'The Irish were officially patronised as valuable missile troops and were given
the chance to make good the wastage of war in their ranks.'[11] 'Make good' is
worthy of Swift denouncing Marlborough. Nothing so pithy will be found in
The Forged Casement Diaries. Far from being a universally accepted convert,
however, Maloney was denounced by John Devoy (1842–1928) as 'the cleverest
and most subtle agent of the British Government who ever did England's
work among Irishmen'.[12] Devoy had been the patriarch of Irish America for

9   P. McCartan to W. J. Maloney, 14 Nov. 1921 (NLI, MS 17,675 (2)), also refers to McCartan's
plans for a Medical Research Institute under the Dáil.
10   Wyndham Childs, *Episodes and Reflections* (London: Cassell, 1930), pp. 188–90.
11   *New York Evening Post*, 2 May 1917, p. 11.
12   Quoted in *The Times*, 17 Oct. 1929, p. 15; see also *New York Sun*, 16 Oct. 1929. The denunciation was issued several years earlier.

decades, but the events of 1919–22 upset his pre-eminence by thrusting forward home-based leaders of de Valera's quality.

Publication of an article *circa* March 1922 in the *Evening Bulletin* (Philadelphia) about a Casement diary may perhaps be attributed to Maloney. Certainly he was in correspondence with Charles Curry in the course of the year about Casement's German papers.[13] Charles Emerson Curry (died 1935) was an American physicist based in Munich whom Casement had met in 1915 through the Limerick-born American consul, Thomas St John Gaffney. The two struck up a close relationship, and when Casement finally left for Berlin he wrote 'A Last Word for my true friend Charles Curry', a last word which ran to forty-five foolscap pages.[14] Clearly Curry had been important in Casement's isolated German years. He became (perhaps, by self-appointment) Casement's literary executor in Germany, and in 1922 he published *Sir Roger Casement's Diaries: His Mission to Germany and the Findlay Affair*. In the present context, the most significant record of the Curry relationship is Casement's admission made on 26 March 1916 that 'if he were taken alive the English would not grant him the dignity of a trial for High Treason that might make an Irish martyr of him; rather they would try to "humiliate & degrade" him by a charge of "something baser," would find "some dastardly means" to strike him "by a coward's blow".'[15] Here the object of Maloney's theory comes close to jeopardising it some twenty years in advance.

Whatever the extent of Maloney's assistance to Curry in the preparation of his book, the New York doctor had pressing domestic concerns of his own. In late summer 1922, he and Mrs Maloney were in London, where she was receiving treatment in Harley Street or thereabouts. On 5 August, he wrote to McCartan from 47 Wimpole Street reporting that his wife was physically improving but 'her mental state is not too good. She cannot let me out of her sight, and as she is not well enough to travel I am just waiting till I can get her built up for the homeward voyage.'[16] He also commented on the opinion, attributed to Michael Collins, that the civil war in Ireland had been work of Irish Americans. Less than three weeks later, Collins was dead. It seems

13 NLI, MSS 17,031 and 17,602.

14 B. L. Reid, *The Lives of Roger Casement* (New Haven: Yale University Press, 1976), pp. 303, 333. The original is in the NLI, MS 17,026.

15 *Ibid.*, p. 342, quoting NLI, MS 5244.

16 Maloney to McCartan, 5 Aug. 1922 (NLI, MS 17,642). The London address cited was that of two medical practitioners.

reasonable to deduce from this letter that Maloney did not visit Ireland in the course of his transatlantic visit.

It is not until late the following year that Casement emerges as a theme in the McCartan/Maloney correspondence. Something of a flurry occurs in the early winter of 1923 with McCartan admitting on 15 November 'Have got none of the Casement stuff for you yet'. Eleven days later he informed his correspondent plainly 'The British Gov. has Casement's diaries & photographs of the Putumayo but won't give them up.' The absence of any insistence on these diaries being forged may be explicable in the contest of a correspondence between two future Forgery Theorists. Certainly, the crusade was under way. By the beginning of December Bulmer Hobson, already installed in the Government Stationery Office, 'is doing the Casement stuff for you'.[17] There is, however, no reference to forgeries or to theories based on their supposed existence, no reference to allegations of illicit sexuality.

THE GHOST OF OSCAR WILDE

Unease nevertheless stirred. In February 1924, Hobson confided to McCartan he ought – as he had intended – to write a book about Casement 'but that period was to me too intense a personal tragedy. I have spent most of the intervening years trying to forget it. This was not fair to Roger but I could only continue to live here by assuming an indifference that I was far from feeling.'[18] The tragic theme may well derive from the guilt which one who opposed the Rebellion might well feel in serving a state based on that inaugurating moment. Later in the year, however, a wholly unrelated publication brought the topic of homosexuality into view. Communications with the late Oscar Wilde (1854–1900) had resulted in 'psychic messages' which created a stir in 1924.[19] Even the hard-headed McCartan was impressed. By 1 September, he had given the matter some thought. Then 'you go off wondering if Oscar Wilde did write the stuff. Doesn't matter. The stuff attributed to him is good but I hear one of the Jesuits were [*sic*] told off to investigate the handwriting &

17 NLI, MS 17675 (4).
18 Hobson to McCartan, typed copy, 13 Feb. 1924 (NLI, MS 17675 (5)).
19 Hesther Travers Smith, *Psychic Messages from Oscar Wilde* (London: Werner Laurie, 1924).

reports that it is Wilde's. Think myself that it is possible. I am convinced one can get in touch with spirits but don't know if they are good or bad.' [20]

Psychic writing had transformed Yeats's negotiations with the occult when he was introduced to the practice by his wife – on their honeymoon. Spiritualism generally had enjoyed a post-war boom as bereaved wives and parents tried to communicate with their dead kin, whose bodies lay in the regimented cemeteries of Belgium and France. Conan Doyle published *The New Revelation* (April 1918) even before the guns fell silent, and his *History of Spiritualism* (1926) proved to be his last book. Roger Casement had uncannily close affinities with all of these people. He and Wilde had been persecuted for their sexuality – actual or perceived. In 1909 Doyle had taken up the cause of oppressed workers in the Belgian Congo and later based a character in *The Lost World* on Casement's adventures. Doyle and Yeats had both assisted in his defence and the search for a reprieve. Now Wilde, the first of them to die, was writing from beyond the grave. Who next?

More mundane disturbances also threatened. There had been near mutiny in the Free State army in March, resulting in a purge of men linked to the IRB. The political ramifications included the resignation of Joseph McGrath (1887–1966), and a shift towards more conservative rule. These were people with whom McCartan had much in common. On the lighter side, efforts to revive the ancient Tailteann Games as Ireland's Olympics met with modest success, though the associated literary competitions brought G. K. Chesterton to Dublin and Yeats quoted Mussolini with relish on the trampling down of liberty. In America, Maloney was pursuing the ghost of Roger Casement, with specific reference to the German diary but also with a view to writing that full biography. By late autumn he had recruited McCartan to his side. In early November the Ulsterman had received and read 'the Casement Diary' and promised to submit it to the Talbot Press. 'After reading it', McCartan remarked with palpable unease, 'I felt inclined to give it to P. S. O'Hegarty and ask him to write his opinion . . . for I think he is not so pro-German as I am . . . It is obvious that this part of his [i. e. Casement's] diary was written under great mental strain – amounting almost to a serious malady.'[21]

20 McCartan to Hobson, typed copy, 1 Sept. 1924 (NLI, MS 17675 (5)). Mediums such as Smith normally did not reproduce the handwriting of their 'contacts' in the other world, but wrote in their terrestrial script. This was an exceptional case.

21 McCartan to Maloney, typed copy, 7 Nov. 1924 (NLI, MS 17,675). Patrick Sarsfield O'Hegarty (1879–1955) is treated in chapter 5 below.

Nothing came of any approach to the Talbot Press. Those closest to Casement were least enthusiastic for a revival of detailed interest. Hobson's reservations have already been voiced. In the family, the dead man's cousin, Gertrude Bannister (now Mrs Sydney Parry) was particularly apprehensive. Before the year ended McCartan was able to report her anxieties and some of the steps she had taken in search of reassurance. She is 'haunted by one fear – the Diary which the English claim to hold. She does not know whether it is a forgery or a genuine diary.' Through friends she had consulted the new Labour Prime Minister in London, Ramsay MacDonald. He 'advised that it was better in Casement's interests to let it lie where it is as some formalities had to be gone through before getting it out of Gov. keeping. It would thus MacDonald claimed be brought to the attention of the public.'[22] Nobody wanted that.

In November 1923, McCartan had been content to remark that the British Goverment had diaries of Casement's and photographs from the Putumayo. In the succeeding year, he had read the German diary as published by Curry and Maloney, and gave his off-the-record professional view that it had been (in part at least) written under great mental strain. By November 1924, the bothersome material is reduced to a single diary which the English *claim* to hold. Hesitancy is detectable among the Theorists. Though MacDonald did not remain long in power, the arrival of a wholly new party in Downing Street and Whitehall quite altered the prospects of the British Government 'giving up' whatever it was they held. The old Liberals had been eclipsed by Labour, of whom radical action might be expected or feared. What Mrs Parry sought was a private surrender of any documents to her or to other members of Casement's family, envisaging a bonfire north of the Irish border. Maloney might have had other ideas – of an official release of the diary or diaries. McCartan's advice to him was now less steady than heretofore. He downplayed Mrs Parry's fears, while conceding that they must be respected. He added 'Of course there will be nothing in your stuff as I presume you won't touch that filth'. And again, 'If I were her Id let them do their worst even though I knew the diary stuff were true. We know all about poor Oscar Wilde but who thinks now of his sins?'[23]

It is difficult to conclude that Patrick McCartan was wholly convinced the material circulated to break the clemency petition in 1916 was forged. It is

---

22   McCartan to Maloney, typed copy, 3 Dec. 1924 (NLI, MS 17,675 (5)).
23   *Ibid.*

equally difficult to conclude that he regarded Casement as having been conventionally heterosexual. Repeated sympathetic references to Wilde are significant, as are the para-medical opinions. 'Filth', however, offensively strikes a defensive note. Unfortunately, the collection of latter-day typed copies of the correspondence between McCartan and Maloney dries up at the end of 1924 – probably because they were in closer communication in America – and the story is taken up at the beginning of the low dishonest decade.[24]

IN THE EARLY 1930S

Although little evidence of its progress has been uncovered, it is clear that the large-scale biographical undertaking had been under way for some time. In June 1932, Maloney told Joe McGarrity that 'In all the years of moving [,] the Casement documents have been arranged and thrown into confusion many times. I am now having them sorted by an expert.'[25] To judge from the archive in NLI, Maloney's crucial partnership now involved McGarrity rather than McCartan – but we should remember that Maloney (aided locally by Hobson) was largely responsible for designing the archive. Certainly, relations between the two involved family links. Maloney stood as sponsor when one of McGarrity's daughters was baptised, and on one occasion he offered medical support. Loans appear to have been cheerfully exchanged from time to time.

The issue of deliberate archival engineering is a delicate one. Nothing improper occurs when a writer deposits his files – even his active files – in a public library. Vanity may be suspected, but nothing worse. In the case of a New York resident handicapped in his movements, a secure Dublin location (some day to serve as an office, perhaps) must have seemed desirable. Yet, in systematically depositing material with NLI in the early 1930s, Maloney implicitly added the dignity of the institution to the project upon which he was engaged. The Librarian, R. I. Best's receipt establishes that statements

---

24 The inclusion of this correspondence *in typed copy form only* is another curious feature of the NLI archive as constructed by the theorists.

25 W. J. Maloney to J. McGarrity, 23 June 1932 (NLI, MS 17,462). See also MS 17,604 (1) where Maloney informs Hobson that he has 'practically ready for publication a short book of between 40,000 and 50,000 words on Casement's life before he became a Consul ... also practically completed a much larger work on Casement in America' (8 Sept. 1931).

about Casement's diaries made by Bulmer Hobson and P. S. O'Hegarty, together with a letter from Ben S. Allen, had been accessed by the beginning of April 1933.[26] From other sources, we know that a statement by Michael F. Doyle, Casement's American counsel in 1916, had been deposited even earlier.

Certainly, contact had been made between Hobson and Maloney eighteen months earlier, if not before. Within the McGarrity Papers, one finds about thirty letters from Maloney to Hobson, written between September 1931 and February 1937, broadly focused on the Casement issue. Initially, these are quite formal in their mode of address, demonstrating the important role McCartan had previously played in recruiting Hobson to Maloney's cause in the mid-1920s. At the outset of the direct correspondence, the doctor confessed, 'I am a poor investigator'. Finally, having a received a copy of *The Forged Casement Diaries* in November 1936, he wrote to thank Hobson 'for the very wonderful book you have turned out'.[27] Between these two less than assertive claims to be sole author of the work in question, scores of documents chronicle the emergence of the book bearing Maloney's name.

Not all of the documentation flatters *The Forged Casement Diaries*. There is, for example, evidence or testimony grudgingly provided at the insistence of the inquirer. As we shall see, Ben S. Allen was not spontaneous in his contribution to the NLI archive. Even in Dublin, there was resistance. In September 1932, Hobson was able to report success in fulfilling Maloney's instructions to contact Eamonn Duggan: 'after a talk I asked him to write a statement which I could send to you. Reluctantly he did so.'[28] The hand-written and undated statement ran to six sheets of Dáil Éireann stationery, in which the former Minister stated baldly of the material he had seen with Collins in 1921 – 'I believe it was his [i.e. Casement's] diary.' This is not a sentence Maloney chose to publish. More embarrassing had been Duggan's account of how Irish influence had been brought to bear on the reviled Lord Birkenhead to prevent the London publication of Casement material in the 1920s, 'At the request of certain people here [i.e., in Dublin] who didn't wish the memory of Casement or any one associated with 1916 reviled, Birkenhead went to the publishers . . . with the result that the book was not published.'[29] This too was a sentence Maloney chose not to publish.

26   NLI, MS 17,462 – the date is 3 Apr. 1933.

27   Maloney to Hobson, 8 Sept. 1931 and 24 Nov. 1936 (NLI, MS 17604 (1)).

28   22 Sept. 1932 (NLI, MS 17,604 (2)).

29   NLI, MS 17,601 (6).

Having successfully tracked down his only American witness (Allen), Maloney turned to more intimate associates of Casement's. In the course of 1933, two of his defending lawyers, Gavan Duffy and the Welshman T. Artemis Jones, entered into correspondence which eventually featured in the published book. Their position, of course, might have been regarded as predictable – or even compromised by their very involvement in the defence. While lawyers cannot generally be supposed to have personal commitments, High Treason was a very special offence and forgery (in effect by the prosecution) an even more special allegation. Impartiality was not a virtue in Maloney's scheme of things. He was more interested in testimony than evidence. Early in the new year, P. S. O'Hegarty wrote a statement in which the Normand Defence acquires a degree of precision. According to the Secretary of the Department of Posts and Telegraphs, Casement 'had captured this man's private diary, in which were recorded in his own hand details of the most abominable and unnatural crimes. He said that he had sent the Diary to the Foreign Office, and had kept a copy of it. I cannot clearly recollect now whether the Diary went in with his Report or subsequent to it, or whether it was the Diary which went in or the copy.'[30]

These lesser uncertainties were not finally admitted into Maloney's text, any more than O'Hegarty's frank acknowledgement that his views were based on a single evening's conversation with Casement in London during the winter of 1912, that is, twenty years earlier. The following month, Bulmer Hobson made his statement, and in March Oliver St John Gogarty provided a brief account of Collins's evidence. Hobson, like O'Hegarty, cited Casement's own alleged account of the Normand diary, but neither man claimed to have been shown any document by Casement though by their accounts he retained either the original diary or a copy. Gogarty's letter to Maloney said little or nothing.[31] One may wonder why Hobson and O'Hegarty had not invoked the Normand Theory in 1916 when they might just possibly have saved their friend's life, and additionally wonder why in 1933 they did not refer back to that period and their anguish in knowing the true origins of the documents then blackening his name.

The accumulation of personal statements was not Maloney's only *modus operandi* in 1933. Wary of British gunboats in Kildare Street bent on sinking

---

30 Handwritten statement of Patrick Sarsfield O'Hegarty, dated 4 Jan. 1933 (NLI, MS 17,601 (11)).
31 Statement by Bulmer Hobson, dated 17 Feb. 1933 (NLI, MS 17601 (8)); O. St J. Gogarty to W. Maloney, 11 Mar. 1933 (NLI, MS 17601 (7)).

the National Library, he contemplated a dedicated Casement Museum to be housed in the hero's rather humble birthplace. Reviving a notion raised with Charles Curry as early as January 1922, an endowed lectureship was also considered, as a means of annually commemorating Casement just as other saints had their days. A Casement Prize was devised for the Irish Academy of Letters, money raised to finance it, and W. B. Yeats duly informed but only after Maloney had first shown him 'the proof of the forgery'.[32] This preliminary annunciation took place in America. Yeats, however, had nothing for the expanding archive, despite privileged access to the Theory, and despite his early affiliation to the IRB. He will not feature in Maloney's project until after the publication of *The Forged Casement Diaries*.

If the greatest living poet in the English language was not for turning, other more obscure recruits were at work. A commercial research assistant was taken on board, a Mr O'Keefe, who searched for references (presumably in the press) to Casement's alleged indecency.[33] However, as the letter in which this detail was transmitted to Joe McGarrity also pinpointed someone named Patchin as 'the chief Chicago medium of the Casement stories from London when he was the Chicago Tribune's correspondent', it may be that O'Keefe was at least as committed to tracking down the traducers of 1916 as he was to locating material for academic analysis in 1933. Objectivity was not an objective.

By the autumn of 1934, Mrs Parry was sufficiently concerned about the effect of Maloney's work to consult G. B. Shaw. A manuscript or typescript was evidently in circulation among American publishers, though another significant absence in the Maloney Papers in NLI is a file of rejection slips from such firms. There is very little evidence of attempts to place the book with any publisher other than the firm which eventually issued it. And that firm – the

32 W. Maloney to J. McGarrity, 24 Jan. 1933 (NLI, MS 17,642). The Casement Award (£50) was given to Brinsley McNamara (1934), F. R. Higgins (1935), Rutherford Mayne (1937), Austin Clarke (1938), Paul Vincent Carroll (1939), and C. Day Lewis (1940). No award was made in 1936, at a time when the Academy was having difficulties in sustaining its various schemes to encourage literature, and the Managers were preoccupied with Maloney's publication; the Casement Award lapsed after 1940. See John Unterecker, *Yeats and Patrick McCartan: A Fenian Friendship* (Dublin: Dolmen, 1967), p. 437. (N.B. The pagination of this pamphlet derives from the serial second *Dolmen Yeats Papers* of which it is one part and so gives an exaggerated indication of its length.)
33 W. Maloney to J. McGarrity, 17 Jan 1933 (NLI, MS 17462). In an undated letter, E. J. O'Keefe reported 'I have found no photographs of Casement diary', though he probably refers to pictures published in newspapers rather than the actual material circulated in 1916: see NLI, MS 17,602.

Talbot Press of Dublin – initially turned the project down unambiguously, in keeping with its decision of 1924.

The letter from W. J. Lyon to Bulmer Hobson is preserved in all its unhelpful simplicity. Dated 21 November 1935, it states baldly that Maloney's book 'is not a publishing proposition for the Talbot Press'. However, in an immediately adjacent NLI file is an estimate from the printing firm, Alex Thom, dated 25 November and addressed to Hobson at his Dublin Castle office. Whether in swift response to the Talbot Press's decision, or in tandem with the original enquiry, the former IRB man had established the basic costs of having Maloney's book published. (The Talbot Press was not renowned for elaborate design or vigorous promotion campaigns; they offered for sale what others printed.) And, in the same file, attached to Lyon's letter is an undated memo in Hobson's hand, detailing two agreements:

1   we pay £150. The publisher to issue & account to us for 50% of the proceeds of sale. We to get all free copies we want.

2   (re. illustrations) Publisher to insert illustrations from blocks supplied & we to pay 4/- per copy for those we want.[34]

Here, in essence, is the plan to publish *The Forged Casement Diaries*. Questions immediately arise, the first being – who is 'we'?

One answer to the question is opened up by consideration of other activities commemorating Casement which were afoot in late 1935. Two letters, difficult to date, establish that Maloney had paid $1,200 for a German portrait, the price to include the stone from which the lithograph had been made. Characteristically, he is vague as to the date of this transaction – 'just after the Treaty was signed'. The motivation, however, clearly involves a wish to suppress damaging allegations – 'I bought it not because I liked it, but because Gaffney, who was hawking it round on behalf of the artist, persuaded me that the Germans felt we believed the worst of C'. Gaffney, who was a minor American diplomat of uncertain loyalties, advised that Patrick McCartan could sell on the portrait, and thus it came into the hands of Colm O Lochlainn. In December 1935 the Three Candles Press issued a limited edition of the Fanto image on handmade Japanese paper.[35]

34 NLI, MS 17604 (6–7).
35 See typescript letter, 9F.3 in NLI, MS 17,604, and Gaffney to Maloney (undated) in MS 17,596. For an account of the 1935 print, see Chalmers Trench, 'The Three Candles Press in the Thirties', *Long Room*, no. 41 (1996), p. 40. According to Maloney, he paid $1,000 for the portrait

O Lochlainn and McCartan had much in common, both having been active in the Volunteer movement, both being to one degree or another republican intellectuals. Given Maloney's physical disabilities, there is nothing untoward in his book being advanced by a group of friends closer to the point of publication. Nevertheless, the correspondence just quoted strongly suggests that Maloney was fit enough to be in Germany some time in the 1920s, when inflation would have forced the lithographer to part with his stone for hard US cash, and again in the early 1930s. Now, in 1935, indifference at the Talbot Press was offset by the de-luxe publication of Fanto's image by the Three Candles. The long delayed book was still possible. Indeed, foreign support might be relied upon. Maloney thought the Italian consul in Dublin 'would put out the Casement Affair in a French edition at Paris, and in a German edition in Vienna within a month. It is the propaganda Italy is now looking for.'[36]

Nothing appears to have come of these international schemes. 'We' is simply Hobson, assisted by O'Hegarty, encouraged by McCartan, and enabled by the purse of Joe McGrath. Each had particular talents to bring to the task. Hobson had administrative experience in handling commissions and dealing with commercial firms. O'Hegarty was a bibliophile, who relished proof-correcting and such chores. McCartan had an overview of Irish-American opinion which informed the shaping of the book; he travelled to Dublin in 1936 to oversee publication of his protégé.[37] More material witnesses were also on hand. Remembered principally for the Irish Hospitals Sweepstake, McGrath was one of the wealthiest men in de Valeran Ireland, agent for Siemens-Schuckert, the German industrial giant who had undertaken to harness the River Shannon for electro-generation. No author should be without such a team of supporters.

Seen in another light, these names read like a short list of IRB survivors, attaching themselves to the anomalous figure of the Scottish doctor and Military Cross holder, William Joseph [Marie Alois] Maloney, of New York. They are making their way in the world by various means, by attachment to the new (if hardly ideal) Free State as bureaucrats, or by professional advance,

---

35 *cont.* and only $200 for the stone. This would suggest that the portrait was not itself a lithograph, and that Fanto sold the stone (from which he could have made images in some number) in desperate circumstances – post-war German inflation.

36 W. J. Maloney to B. Hobson, 25 Sept. 1935 (NLI, MS 17604 (1)). The diplomat in question was Romano Lodi Fé.

37 See Unterecker, *Yeats and Patrick McCartan*, p. 377.

or by a deft substitution of business for politics. But they find themselves compelled to look back – Orpheus like – at a beloved past which they cannot rescue from hellish innuendo. In this latter perspective, they exemplify post-revolutionary angst not wholly dissimilar to the Trotskyist or Weberian paradigms of contrasting European contexts. Casement in this interpretation is less the subject of their concern than a vehicle for larger, more inchoate anxieties.

The preservation of a detailed reconstructable chronicle of book production for *The Forged Casement Diaries* exemplifies an attitude towards re-reading the past. Its minutiae are invested with significance, not in relation to juridical vindication of a wronged individual but as the authentification of stages of a process or narrative of legitimation, rites of passage purging the recent but now fading past of dangerous contradictions and compromises, and projecting residual guilt onto a suitably external agency. This potent psychological mechanism worked as if to undo Yeats's poignant lines written 'In Memory of Eva Gore-Booth and Con Markiewicz':

> We the great gazebo built,
> They convicted us of guilt.

IN PRODUCTION, 1936

Though the material for such a chronology is scattered through a number of different files, a relatively complete record can be constructed.

9 JANUARY   McCartan reports that Maloney's preferred title for the book is *The Forged Casement Diary* [*sic*], indicating that the implications of Collins and Duggan having seen two diaries in 1921 have not yet been fully absorbed into the theory. But this emphasis was not simply reductive. McCartan and Maloney 'agreed that more [people] will read the headlines of the reviews than will read the book'. On this basis, they 'will be at once convinced it is a forgery'. There is, however, still a distinction made between publication in America and in Ireland. When Maloney called the book *The Casement Affair*, 'he was thinking of the American public & that title was suggested by the "Dryfus? [*sic*] Affair" – the Jewish French officer you remember. He wants 3 copies of proofs so that he may submit a copy

to publishers here [i.e. in America]. In Ireland he says we can come out bold & call it a forgery.'[38]

10 FEBRUARY   Galley proofs sent by the printer to Hobson.[39]

3 MARCH   McCartan hopes that O'Hegarty will write a preface which de Valera will then agree to sign.[40]

20 MARCH   Hobson's informal accounts (scribbled on sheets of official stationery from Dublin Castle) record the purchase of Parmiter's biography of Casement for 15/-, some five weeks after the printers have issued galley proofs.[41]

24 MARCH   A letter from London News Agency Photos: Hobson had sought illustrations for 'a book dealing with the period of the European War'.[42]

18 APRIL   The Talbot Press refers to an agreement of 6 December 1935, and adds four further clauses (which apparently are accepted). Just three weeks elapse between the Press's rejection of the book and the agreement to publish it.[43]

1 MAY   O'Hegarty's notes about the galley proofs carry this date.[44]

5 MAY   Page proofs issued.[45]

19 JUNE   Proofs of 'Index, Chronological Table and List of Illustrations' issued.[46]

17 JULY   Maloney consoles Hobson in the wake of de Valera's refusal to write a preface.[47]

38 NLI, MS 17,604 (3).
39 NLI, MS 17,604 (6).
40 NLI, MS 17,604 (3).
41 NLI, MS 17,604 (9).
42 NLI, MS 17,604 (7).
43 NLI, MS 17,604 (6).
44 NLI, MS 17,604 (4).
45 NLI, MS 17,604 (6).
46 Ibid.
47 NLI, MS 17,604 (1).

29 JULY   As 'Dr McCartan has not succeeded in getting an American publisher', the print run is settled at 1,000 copies.[48]

8 SEPTEMBER   Hobson is asked to meet An Seabhach (*nom-de-plume* of Senator Pádraig Ó Siochfhradha, 1883–1964) of the Talbot Press to discuss the book. Next day, the two discuss possible libel actions, especially in relation to the treatment of G. H. Mair and James Tuohy, an American journalist. With Mair certainly dead by this date, anxiety about the risk of prosecution arises at a remarkably late date – some four months after second proofs have been issued.[49]

13 OCTOBER   Typed copy of a letter (almost certainly from Hobson) to Joe McGrath establishes that the latter paid £150 towards publication costs.[50]

27 OCTOBER   Finished books available from the printer; fifty copies already despatched to McCartan.[51]

30 OCTOBER   Denis Gwynn writes to Hobson (from Burns Oates, a London-based Catholic firm of publishers) about *The Forged Casement Diaries*: 'cannot say I feel happy about the probable result of publishing it . . . [Augustine] Birrell told me a few years before he died that he could not have the slightest doubt that the Diary was genuine.'[52]

1 DECEMBER   The book is advertised by Talbot Press in the *Irish Independent* (and on 9 December in the *Irish Press*).

1 JANUARY 1937   Bill from Talbot Press sent to Hobson, at his private address.[53]

This last detail draws attention to the persistent blurring of distinctions between private and public roles which characterised the managing of

---

48 NLI, MS 17,604 (6).   49 *Ibid.*
50 NLI, MS 17,604 (4).   51 NLI, MS 17,604 (6).
52 NLI, MS 17,604 (4). The English essayist and lawyer Birrell (1850–1933) had been responsible for the establishment of the National University of Ireland (1908) while Chief Secretary for Ireland (1907–16). His good-natured but indolent administration failed to detect the serious threat of insurrection, and he was obliged to resign after the Easter Rising.
53 NLI, MS 17,604 (6).

Maloney. Hobson had conducted most of the correspondence from Dublin Castle, giving the impression that publication of *The Forged Casement Diaries* carried official approval. Other minor deceptions were practised to disguise the nature of the project. When, for example, the London agency was asked to supply illustrations from the period of the Great War, the address from which this request emanated went a long way towards indicating the kind of book planned. The agency, of course, was unaware that Dublin Castle had no hand in the project which, in the event, dealt with a rather smaller topic than the War. In the 1930s, rules about what a civil servant did in his spare time may have been no more rigid than codes of practice about the use of official stationery. By contrast, we live today in a box-ticking bureaucracy. But the distinction between the public and the private realms ran deeper than mere bookkeeping.

One potential witness who failed to perform as requested was George Gavan Duffy who, as Casement's solicitor, was best qualified to comment on the private-public distinction. At the time of 1916 trial, Gavan Duffy had been forced to resign from the legal firm of which he was a partner, in order to defend Casement. When the Treaty was being signed in December 1921, he was the last to append his name.[54] Courageous and cautious, in January 1933 he regretted Maloney's decision to deposit a particular statement in NLI, because he (Gavan Duffy) was not in a position to confirm it despite being so invoked.[55] On the whole, he took a view quite different from the project managers, recommending to Maloney that the forgery theory be relegated to an appendix in the larger biography. As B. L. Reid noted years later, he seems 'carefully to have avoided a real repudiation of the diaries'.[56] In December of 1936, Gavan Duffy was promoted to be a High Court judge.

Just as the early stages of the Maloney project had been accompanied by O Lochlainn's publication of the Fanto lithograph, so the culmination of the

54   See Frank Pakenham, *Peace by Ordeal*, revised edn (London: New English Library, 1967), p. 243.

55   The document in question related to Michael Francis Doyle, the American lawyer, who joined Casement's defence team in 1916. At the end of the previous year, Doyle had acted for Gaffney, the Irish-born American Consul-General in Munich when Gaffney was forced to resign by the US State Department. (See *Answer of the Hon. T. St John Gaffney* [1916], which was published from Doyle's Philadelphia office.) Among those who testified in Gaffney's support was Mrs Irene B. Sheridan, widow of General Philip 'the only good Indian is a dead Indian' Sheridan, who had resided at Munich at the beginning of the war. Gaffney's *Breaking the Silence: England, Ireland, Wilson and the War* (New York: Liveright, 1930) contains an account of Casement's last days in Germany.

56   Reid, *Lives of Roger Casement*, pp. 471–2. See NLI, MSS 5,388 and 5,588.

managers' effort also had its visual complements. The venerable image of Robert Johnston, at ninety-seven the 'oldest living Fenian' and father of the poet Ethna Carberry, was published to emphasise Casement's friendship with that generation. More recent generations were also mobilised, to combine historical politics, poetry, and modern techniques of persuasion. There was, for example, John McDonagh, a brother of the executed poet, who produced plays for the state radio-station's Athlone wavelength. In November 1936, he changed roles to feature as the author of *On Banna Strand*, described as a 'new play' about Casement. Presented as part of a programme in Dublin's Mansion House to commemorate Fenians executed in 1867 – 'the Manchester Martyrs'[57] – it demonstated that, even if Casement's solicitor declined to support the cause, one could always rely on the dead.

57   *Irish Press* (Dublin), 23 Nov. 1936, p. 5.

FIVE

BALLADS AND BLACKMAIL

PUBLIC AND PRIVATE RESPONSES

—

YEATS AND HIS CIRCLES

Two major reactions to this modest exercise in publishing can be traced. The first has W. B. Yeats for its epicentre, the second 'resurrects' the assassination of Sir Henry Wilson. The Nobel prizewinner played no major part in seeing Maloney's book into print. As early as May 1933, he did suggest to McCartan that Shaw might write a preface; Shaw's attitude has already been noted.[1] Yeats may have had a hand in persuading his old friend, the poet and painter, George William Russell (AE) (1867–1935) to write something now preserved in NLI with miscellaneous papers of Hobson's. The piece in question was not used, perhaps because its warm commendation of Casement moved into uncharted territory:

> He was not without that element of fantasy which is deep rooted in Irish character. He told me of a story he intended to write, of an Ireland that through some distur- bance on earth was parted from Europe and had drifted a thousand miles westward. The book was to be an imagination of the reconcilement of the two Irelands in their common peril . . . I never had the faintest tingling of suspicion of that

1 John Unterecker, *Yeats and Patrick McCartan: A Fenian Friendship* (Dublin: Dolmen, 1967), p. 354. Unterecker was misled by a phrase in a letter of Yeats's: 'I have just got a book published by the Talbot Press' (p. 377), where a comma after 'book' would have removed ambiguity, or where the substitution of 'received' for 'got' would have had the same effect. It is symptomatic of Yeats critics that they should opt for strong readings of his pronouncements in ideological contexts they approve of, ignoring (as in this case) the poet's evasive behaviour. Read with eyes untinted by rosa alchemica, Yeats's comments indicate that he was shifting responsibility for Maloney to the Shaws as fast as possible, not even pausing to read whatever came his way. See Unterecker, pp. 357–8, 'When I saw Mrs Shaw a couple of weeks ago she asked me about the Casement book and was very eager about it. I notice that Shaw does what she wants so I hope Maloney will go there.' Yeats to Patrick McCartan, 12 July 1933. This clearly refers to a stage in the full biographical project rather than the study of forgery.

corrupted psyche which was spread by hint and rumour after his death. I do not believe that legend of the lying wartime propagandists. I knew of another legend of like evil character spread about another Irish patriot with the tale of a diary showing unspeakable depravity, and I was able to track it down to its root in indecent fabrication. He remains in my imagination the gallant adventurer. I cannot be judge of the wisdom of the last year of his life . . .[2]

This, though positive on the forgery issue with regard to Casement, unhelpfully raised questions about another fraud imposed on the patriotic archive. Could this have implicated Darrell Figgis (1882–1925) who had run guns with Casement and Erskine Childers (1870–1922), written a study of Russell, and committed suicide in London? (His death, by the way, had nothing to do with Casemental matters.) If Figgis (or whoever) had been the victim of black-guardism through 'indecent fabrication' perhaps the perpetrators might in 1935 yet be identified. Perhaps they were not English. Best to avoid any parallels to the Casement business as might rebound back into the patriotic Hall of Fame. When Russell died in 1935, his son was becoming a prominent US-based literary agent, active in the market where Maloney's book was failing to find a publisher.

No preface finally appeared in *The Forged Casement Diaries*, and we can be certain that Shaw and de Valera refused to supply one. According to Yeats's communications with McCartan, Shaw thought G. K. Chesterton might oblige, but nothing came of that, either. (Chesterton died in 1936 as the project was reaching its climax.) One name strikingly missing from these searches for a preface is that of Robert Lynd, who had rallied to Casement in 1916 and who wielded considerable influence as a regular contributor to the *New Statesman*. Lynd had remained a socialist, an advocate of James Connolly's politics, and so an unlikely ally for Maloney and his Germanophile allies. An even more notable absentee was Sean O'Casey whose opinion of Casement (but not Hobson) was very high.

In all of this, the absence of any contribution by Yeats himself is even more striking, for all that he had been in correspondence with the project manager

---

2   NLI, MS 17,604 (9). See also MS 13,075/2/iii where Maloney tells Gertrude Parry in a letter of 1 May 1932, 'AE has sent me a delightful preface' – this for part of the full-scale biography. Alan Denson suggested years ago that AE had written something for a book about Casement projected (but not written) by H. W. Nevinson; see Denson (ed.), *Letters from AE* (New York: Abelard-Schuman, 1961), p. 90n. Maloney confided to Hobson, 8 Sept. 1931, that his multi-volume life would contain introductions by Padraic Colum, AE, and Hobson himself (see NLI, MS 17,604 (1)).

when testimony was gathered into NLI. Just before he left on an Italian government sponsored visit to Rome, Yeats in late 1934 received what Unterecker
calls 'the manuscript of Maloney's book on the Casement diaries'.[3] But the
poet had other things to do between May 1933 and late 1936 when he finally
received a copy of Maloney's book. Indeed, he 'did no more than look at the
chapter headings before I sent Maloney's Mss. to Mrs. Shaw'.[4] The period was
one of remarkable fertility and activity for Yeats, issuing in such sonorous texts
as 'Parnell's Funeral' and 'Supernatural Songs' together with what is politely
called his flirtation with fascism. Though this political background is more
articulate in the poetry, Yeats's drama – in particular *Resurrection* (1931) and
The Words Upon the Window-pane (1934) – deserve close attention. Both of
these plays raise [*sic*] the issue of physical return by the dead, in forms hardly
to be approved by theologians. In the poetry, Parnell's heart is regarded as
sacramental food for the nation; in the drama, Swift's voice offers a diagnosis
of revolutionary decay through modernity. If Yeats cannily avoided a direct
involvement in Maloney's Casement project, he was committed to more
sublime work in a related context. He also embarked on a regime of sexual
regeneration involving surgery and leading to numerous affairs.

   Publicly, these were difficult times for Yeats. The Irish Academy of Letters,
founded with Shaw in 1932, quickly came under attack from right-wing
Catholic spokesmen. As elsewhere in Europe, authoritarian influences were
gaining ground in Ireland. Yeats was not averse to an anti-democratic *Zeitgeist*,
though he found the populist and Catholic side of Irish fascism disturbing.
This did not prevent him from writing songs for the Blueshirts, and later
approving Nazi legislation. In the local context, however, he was caught
between attraction and revulsion, passion and cunning. The Casement business provided an opportunity for a temporary reconciliation between these
powerful forces. It also distanced him from Shaw, never a natural ally though
on occasion a useful one.

   The Academy needed funds, and Yeats knew how lucrative an American
tour could be. During the winter of 1932–3, he spent almost four months in

3   This is implausible as it stands, first as to anyone entrusting a manuscript rather than a
typescript copy, and second as to there being by this date a finished book focused on the diaries.
See Unterecker, *Yeats and Patrick McCartan*, p. 371.
4   Yeats to McCartan [1 October 1934] quoted in Unterecker, *Yeats and Patrick McCartan*, p. 371.
If we take Yeats's plural 'mss' at face value, the reference may be to Maloney's multi-volume
biography of Casement rather than the narrower study eventually published as *The Forged
Casement Diaries*.

the United States, visiting both New York and Boston. It is likely that he met the Great Forgery Theorist during this period and was shown 'the proof'. In a letter of November 1936 to Ethel Mannin he speaks of 'a Dr Maloney I knew in New York', a phrase which nicely suggests in its use of the perfect tense a relationship consigned to the past.[5] Yeats displayed no desire to renew the acquaintance, and was content to deal with McCartan, an effective fundraiser.

THE DOLPHIN DINNER

A year brought great changes, at home and abroad. The Japanese invaded China, with massive loss of life. James Maxton set out for Barcelona to investigate the imprisonment of left-wingers in republican Barcelona. Chamberlain replaced Baldwin as British Prime Minister while Germany and Italy withdrew from non-intervention committees. World war shuddered in the loins of Europe. As for Ireland, de Valera's new Constitution was approved by the electorate on 1 July. With *The Forged Casement Diaries* published, serialised, and largely forgotten, a few of the interested parties broke the surface of their own discretion. Michael Francis Doyle appeared in Dublin to represent the USA at an international Catholic Conference, follower-up to the Eucharistic Congress of five years earlier; from this he took time off to present de Valera with a facsimile Declaration of Independence, a nice Philadelphian salute to Ireland's new constitution.[6] Casement's second coming missed its moment.

Yeats's Academy hosted a dinner for McCartan on 17 August 1937 in the Dolphin Hotel, near the Dublin quays, with F. R. Higgins presiding and Denis McCullough (of the old IRB) as principal speaker. The attendance included the Gogartys, man and wife, but not (apparently) either Mrs Yeats

5   W. B. Yeats to E. Mannin, 15 Nov. [1936], in Allan Wade (ed.), *The Letters of W. B. Yeats* (London: Hart-Davis, 1954), p. 867. Existing biographies of Yeats are silent on Maloney, and it would be unwise to speculate in advance of Roy Foster's second volume (due 2003). However, from 'An Evening in New York with W. B. Yeats' by John Quinn one can infer that the poet had not made the doctor's acquaintance during his 1920 visit nor was the latter a point of reference for the lawyer-patron. Equally significant is the non-appearance of Casement as a burning issue in the Yeats–Quinn conversations. See Richard Londraville's edited transcription in *Yeats Annual*, no. 6 (1988), pp. 166–85.

6   For Doyle's visit, see *Irish Press* (Dublin), 12 Aug. 1937, p. 1 etc. At this time, or some other, Casement's American lawyer acquired part-ownership of the celebrated Kerry beauty-spot, having solved the riddle posed by Bing Crosby in the croon, 'How Can I Buy Killarney?'

or Mrs McCartan. The Ulster-born humorist Lynn Doyle was present, adding words of timely social criticism to the nationalist sentiments of McCullough who deplored cinema and other innovations. Dublin's lord mayor rebuked McCartan for a slur on the good name of Irish publicans (never mind the republicans).

There was no sign of Maloney and no mention of Casement, the great object of the honoured guest's machinations less than a year earlier.[7] The Dolphin dinner was also oddly marked by Yeats, the host's receiving a generous cheque from the guest. If this had an ulterior motive, nothing resulted. Maloney's elevation to the rank of Academician had been suggested – vainly, for Yeats made no effort to argue his case.[8] As an extensive report in *The Irish Times* indicates, he was now preoccupied with a different scandal of Hiberno-English relations – London's retention of Hugh Lane's Impressionist pictures – which was promising to inspire great poetry – 'The Municipal Gallery Re-visited'.[9]

JUSTICE FOR ALFRED NOYES

Yeats was fond of invoking the great names of the dead: in the business of Casement's ghost, he was obliged to treat with lesser living figures – the largely forgotten English poet, Alfred Noyes (1880–1959), for example. So the year 1937 had begun inauspiciously, and the eclipse of Casement as a rallying point for malcontents took its time. Yeats's poem inspired by Maloney's book – supposedly to the tune, 'The Glen of Aherlow' – appeared on 2 February 1937. Its six stanzas read:

> I say that Roger Casement
> Did what he had to do,
> He died upon the gallows,
> But that is nothing new.

7   For an account of the speeches, see *Irish Press* (Dublin), 18 Aug. 1937, p. 7. Both the *Irish Press* and the *Evening Herald* published a photograph of the dinner party, identifying many but not all of the notables present. The balding man, seated below the photographer's right arm and looking towards the camera, might be Maloney though there is no reference to his presence. The *Irish Press* caption refers to a 'Mdm Kostal', otherwise unidentified.

8   See Unterecker, *Yeats and Patrick McCartan*, pp. 392–4 for Maloney's Academy candidature.

9   *The Irish Times*, 18 Aug. 1937, pp. 7–8, esp. p. 8.

Afraid they might be beaten
Before the bench of Time,
They turned a trick by forgery
And blackened his good name;

A perjurer stood ready
To prove their forgery true;
They gave it out to all the world –
And that is something new.

For Spring-Rice had to whisper it,
Being their Ambassador,
And then the speakers got it,
And writers by the score.

Come Alfred Noyes and all the troup [*sic*]
That cried it far and wide,
Come from the forger and his desk,
Desert the perjurer's side;

Come speak your bit in public
That some amends be made
To that most gallant gentleman
That is in the [*sic*] quick-lime laid.

Poetic licence would be the kindest explanation. Behind the stodgy imitation ballad-metre and the clumsy argument, it is possible to discern a grain of dimly conscious mockery, as if Yeats were matching his style to Maloney's. And in private, he expressed the wish that some tribunal of inquiry might prove the diaries genuine. The poet was gyrating between opposites. A second poem, 'The Ghost of Roger Casement', originally drew heavily on Thomas Gray's 'Elegy Written in a Country Churchyard' (1751) and consequently associated Casement with mute, inglorious *English* heroes. This was hardly Fenian solidarity. In correspondence, Yeats went out of his way to insist that he and Shaw pursued the same objectives of truth and justice, unmindful of popular opinion. On the streets of Dublin, however, the impact was immediate and obliging. On 2 February, Mrs Yeats 'was surprised at the defference [*sic*] everybody showed in buses & shop [*sic*]'. The Casement ballad had won back national approval for a poet whose Academy and Abbey Theatre had been under populist attack.

But not universal approval. Yeats's old lover, Maud Gonne, wrote a radio review of the controversy, including the poems and the poet's acknowledgement of Alfred Noyes's generous statement. Her script, preserved in NLI in the McGarrity Papers, gives no indication of when or where it was broadcast, though it is possible an American station was involved. It opens:

> On the paper jacket covering Dr Maloney's book 'The Forged Casement Diaries' published by the Talbot Press, the life like portrait of Casement by the german [*sic*] artist held me gazing into Fitzpatrick's bookshop in O'Connell Street a long time in spite of a too playful and unkind wind. The haunting sadness in those wise beautiful eyes drew me there again next day to gaze again, until I felt I must possess a copy of that portrait. I hadn't the necessary 7/6 in my purse, but I went into the shop and Mr Fitzpatrick kindly let me carry the volume home and then send the money later.[10]

As Mr Fitzpatrick had featured on the title page of McCartan's autobiography four years earlier – and, it seems, on no other title page – we can deduce a republican sympathy in the window display. Gonne's bathos sits uneasily with her deliberate identification (in 1937) of Germany as the source of the portrait. And it is the portrait which inspires her, not the prospect of a forensic analysis in prose. No such excess of feeling marked her attitude to 'our own poet' who was 'over generous and hasty, I think, when he withdrew his poem and accepted Mr Alfred Noyes' profuse apologies and wordy praise of Casement. From his lips that posthumas [*sic*] praise of Casement made me shudder and anyone reading carefully will see that it is not a complete withdrawal and repudiation of the forgery.' This last point was a shrewd one and, as she supported a tribunal of inquiry, there can be no doubt of her own convictions.

Maud Gonne had targeted a far lesser poet than her erstwhile lover, a premodernist remembered only for 'The Highwayman', a piece of narrative verse once familiar among school children. Yeats fixed upon the same figure, issuing his challenge to Noyes, whom Maloney had identified as the principal forgery trafficker in America, together with Cecil Spring-Rice regrettably

10 NLI, MS 17, 462. The typescript is endorsed by McGarrity, who asked for it to be returned to him.

dead. As Spring-Rice also had claims to very minor literary achievement – 'I Vow to Thee My Country' – the dispute was neatly set up between the Nobel prizewinner and two nonentities. But Noyes, to Yeats's apparent surprise, took up the challenge in a lengthy letter published in the *Irish Press* of 12 February. With reference to his own acceptance of the diaries' authenticity in 1916, he said of the Normand Defence – 'the explanatory suggestion now made by Dr. Maloney that Casement had transcribed, with his own hand, the diary of a Peruvian criminal was not then forthcoming'.

Noyes then proceeded with a lengthy defence of Spring-Rice's integrity, and moved to deal with 'one or two mistakes' (natural enough in the circumstances) in Maloney's book which in turn had misled Yeats:

> My only reference to Casement was in the one paragraph (about twelve lines) of an article which was written shortly after a typed copy of the 'diary' had been shown to me in circumstances which then seemed to preclude all doubt of its authenticity. The article containing this paragraph was issued through a Press Bureau, and it appeared in the 'Philadelphia Public Ledger' some weeks after Casement's death. Headlines, prefatory editorial notes, and the machinery of publicity (for which I was not responsible) gave my dozen lines about Casement a disproportionate prominence, which naturally misled Dr. Maloney as to the real extent of my allusions to the matter. It will be noted that, in his own book, though he refers to me again and again, all his quotations are repetitions from that paragraph of twelve lines . . . His references to my 'two hundred lectures' in American give the impression that these also were about Casement. They were on entirely different subjects . . .[11]

Noyes then embarked on a critique of the Normand Defence no less rigorous than it was understated. He questioned whether the copying of a man's diary – even that of a criminal and for the purpose of prosecuting him – was a credible incident in the life of Roger Casement. He referred to Maloney's theory as 'the strikingly *un*Irish explanation *that Casement had transcribed another man's diary, for use by the British Government against that other man's character* [original emphasis]'. This was not an ethical argument on Noyes's part, for the grossness of the crimes might outweigh considerations of gentlemanly fair play. It was closer to an invocation of professional utilitarianism – that is, evidence thus obtained would have had little value in any prosecution of Normand, as Casement well knew.

11   *Irish Press* (Dublin), 12 Feb. 1937, p. 8.

Such a conclusion scarcely does justice to Noyes's unexpected liveliness in answering Yeats's challenge. His responses to the Defence, which was crucial to both Yeats and Maloney's dramatisation of their hero, are better read as a psychological confrontation with Casement himself. Or, to be more exact, Noyes indirectly addresses himself to the ghost of a man he had never met, whose (alleged) diary he had briefly seen, and whose reputation he had damaged (though not to the extent nor with the motivation alleged by Maloney). From this rhetorical position, he mildly suggests that it is implausible to credit a man of Casement's social position with underhand behaviour of the kind suggested by Maloney on the authority of Hobson and O'Hegarty, who had oddly neglected to publicise the matter themselves.

This was fine, this was in many ways a mockery of Yeats's own procedures. But Noyes went on to open up uncomfortable ethical questions about the diary or diaries:

> those who had seen a copy of it might wonder whether the transcription of so loathesome a thing at such length – it ran to many pages – was a very much better explanation from Casement's point of view than the former suggestion that it was the work of a temporarily disordered mind.[12]

Maybe Noyes was a prude. But, as Maud Gonne noted, he had not abjured the Authenticity Theory. Instead he proposed that Yeats and some English historian (such as G. P. Gooch) should sit on a committee of inquiry. Yeats's flamboyant acknowledgement of Noyes's 'noble letter', together with his rewriting of the ballad to exonerate the English poet, ignored the more penetrating details of Noyes's response. If there was remorse in the latter, there was also a measure of determined intelligence.

Noyes is known among Forgery Theorists as the author of *The Accusing Ghost; Or, Justice for Casement* published in 1957. This slim volume does little to amplify what the author had written in *Two Worlds for Memory* (1953), though the later book contains a great deal of quoted matter to swell out its size.[13] *Two Worlds* includes valuable material from the controversy which ran in the *Irish Press* after the publication of Maloney's work in serial form, including 'letters . . . from irreconcilables, who simply put their fingers in their ears and refused to

---

12 *Ibid.*, p. 9.

13 Roger Sawyer takes a more positive view of Noyes and *The Accusing Ghost*, listing the book among those which have 'dealt entirely, or almost entirely, with the forgery issue'. See Sawyer, *Roger Casement's Diaries* (London: Pimlico, 1997), pp. 264–5.

listen to any rebuttal of their own wild charges'. Noyes's objection to use of the diary arose because he had come to appreciate that it had not been introduced into the trial or legally established by any other means.[14]

THE 'IRISH PRESS'

The publication of 'Roger Casement' in the *Irish Press* has been studied in terms exclusively of Yeats's response to Maloney's forgery thesis and Noyes's subsequent act of contrition. Some day, a historian of newspapers should examine the episode as an instance of journalistic practice intersecting actively with literary and ideological change.[15] One might, for example, examine the compositor's or sub-editor's role in laying out the page on which Yeats's ballad was printed. An article immediately below recalled the execution in 1777 of the Revd William Dodd – for forgery – under the heading *It Happened To-day*. In a column to the right, Seamus Ó Searchaigh, secretary of Coláiste Uladh at Cloghaneely in Donegal, publicly corrected a detail in Maloney's book.

But the Yeatsian declaration of 2 February 1937 occurred within a larger communicative framework than the compositor's page. On 12 January, the paper had concluded its serialisation of Ernie O'Malley's fine Troubles auto-biography, *On Another Man's Wound*, published earlier in book form in Cork. Next day, serialisation of *The Forged Casement Diaries* began.[16] To prepare readers, McCartan contributed a two-part 'Sketch of the Career of Dr W. J. Maloney' which not only celebrated 'The Man Who Exposed the Casement Forgeries' but also complicated his already muddled biography. On Saturday 30 January,

14   Alfred Noyes, *Two Worlds for Memory* (London: Sheen & Ward, 1953), pp. 123–37, quoting p. 131. Noyes revealed (p. 113) that he had been recruited to the News Department (later the Ministry of Information) by Hugh Montgomery, and shown a typescript of the Casement material by Stephen Gaselee (p. 124).

15   The opportunity is missed in Mark O'Brien, *De Valera, Fianna Fáil and the* Irish Press*: The Truth in the News* (Dublin: Irish Academic Press, 2001).

16   The text (without Maloney's erratic footnotes) appeared in twenty-three instalments, concluding on Monday 8 Feb. In some ways, it is preferable to the book, in that it is more fully illustrated, the illustrations are integrated in a manner which photogravure plates could not be, and the use of newly devised sub-section headings provides a shorthand guide to the narrative. This allows for the remarkable presentation of 'Casement the Parnellite', a metamorphosis which complicates the Theory's citation of the Pigott forgeries which implicated Parnell in violence. By 20 Jan. the serial was appearing on the small-ads page behind the sports section.

a front-page article announced Yeats's forthcoming challenge to Noyes, setting up 'Roger Casement' as a dynamic literary *coup*.

Certainly, the dispute was not limited to the two poets. Appreciations of Maloney's service to Irish national self-respect were printed on 3 February (p. 9), with contributions from a number of eminent figures. These were the Fianna Fáil politician Seán T. O'Kelly (1882–1966), P. J. Little (1884–1963) who was de Valera's Parliamentary Secretary, Professor Eoin MacNeill (1867–1945) who had been Chief of Staff in the Irish Volunteers and yet (like Casement) had opposed the Easter Rising on tactical grounds, and finally Liam Gogan (1891–1979), a poet in Gaelic. Of these Gogan was the least influential and the most symptomatic. Characteristically, Yeats appropriated the tributes to himself, dropping Gogan as unworthy of him.

Described as a close friend of Casement – he was only twenty-five in 1916 – Gogan had been involved in buying German arms for the Rising. Employed by the National Museum since pre-independence days, he was promoted Keeper of the Art and Industry division in 1936. Throughout the 1930s and indeed much of the 1940s, the museum's Director was the Austrian Adolf Mahr (1887–1951), the Nazi party's top secret agent in Ireland. It is therefore of more than casual interest that Gogan should recommend Maloney's work be brought to the attention of Wilhelmstrasse. Not given to false modesty, he used the appearance of Yeats's poem to recall his own composition of two pieces dedicated to Casement – dutifully reprinted in the *Irish Press* on 4 February. Gogan's most symptomatic gesture was to describe his dead friend as 'a Protestant saint!' Lest this should alarm the faithful, the paper carried an article 'Casement's Conversion' [to Catholicism] on 5 February.

The process of commemoration deepened with the republication, on 9 February, of Casement's Speech from the Dock, a form of martyrological literature dating back to Robert Emmet's trial in 1803. On 15 February, an article signed M. C. (Mollie Childers, widow of Erskine Childers) recalled Casement's friendship with the historian Alice Stopford Green. Women featured in the prompt endorsement of Maloney's thesis, with letters from Maud Gonne MacBride and Hanna Sheehy Skeffington (22 February) and Alice Milligan (27 February). George Noble Plunkett (1851–1948, father of the executed 1916 leader, Joseph Mary Plunkett) chimed in with Gonne and Skeffington. But the argument was never allowed to become a one-sided address to the jury of *Irish Press* readers. De Valera's newspaper facilitated comment from the far side of the Irish Sea.

Sir Wyndham Childs, writing from the Marlborough Club in London's Pall Mall, corrected several errors in Maloney's treatment of his memoirs (6 February). Consistent with his opinion of 1934, G. B. Shaw wrote to deplore the excesses of Maloney's industry (11 February) in a letter Yeats described as 'vegetarian, sexless'.[17] Shaw was more publicly rebuked by Diarmuid Murphy of University College Galway five days later. Francis Stuart (1902–2000) also took Shaw to task; and Stuart's fellow novelist, the republican socialist Peadar O'Donnell (1893–1986), embraced the Normand Defence (15 February) while lambasting Noyes. Later, Máire Comerford obligingly rewrote an article by Dr Dickey for inclusion in the *Irish Press*.

The most (the only) original contribution came from the independent Dáil Deputy, Frank McDermott (1886–1975) who mocked the government's refusal to request clarification from Britain as to the existence of diaries. His letter (19 February) was accompanied by an *Irish Press* editorial rebuking him in turn. Pointedly recording the de Valera family's ownership of the newspaper in which he now argued the toss with the Taoiseach, McDermott insisted on logical and ethical distinctions of little appeal to controversialists of the day:

> It might, or might not, have been desirable to revive the story of the Casement Diary (of which not one Irishman in a thousand had heard before Dr. Maloney's book was given publicity in this country) and to press the matter through to a decisive test. An agitation, however, which after accusing the British Government of base and deliberate forgery stops short of pressing the matter to a test can only be described as mischevous [*sic*]. . . I do not mean to imply that even if the Diary was authentic, the British Government were justified in using it as they did during the war, but their conduct in the circumstances would not have been beyond all forgiveness and their enemies were no more chivalrous than they.[18]

Unyielding to domestic sceptics on the issue of Casement's purity, the *Irish Press* bought off the wrath of Shaw by reprinting (24 February) his *Manchester Guardian* letter of 1916. And there *Irish Press* interest in Casement's reputation rested. The last word was twenty years old, by now historical rather than political.

Or, rather, the lasting words were archival. One of the remarkable features of the NLI files is the preservation of the original letters of Stuart and others

---

17 W. B. Yeats to D. Wellesley, 18 Feb. [1937], in Kathleen Raine (ed.), *Letters on Poetry from W. B. Yeats to Dorothy Wellesley* (London: Oxford University Press, 1940), p. 128.

18 *Irish Press* (Dublin), 19 Feb. 1937, p. 16.

in MS 5,460 from which we learn that Stuart defended Casement on the headed notepaper of the Shelbourne Hotel. From its roof in 1916, British troops had fired on Citizen Army rebels who had – miming the Western Front – entrenched themselves in Saint Stephen's Green. The gathering in of documentation indicates the extent to which the *Irish Press* facilitated the Hobson–McCartan management of Maloney's project, handing over correspondence for NLI. The newspaper's ultimate proprietor, Eamon de Valera, remained invisible: this was a storm without a taoiseach.

Such reviews as appeared were respectful, one or two of them effusive. Francis Stuart obliged on the Athlone wavelength, in what was virtually a pre-publication complement to the stage-play by the station's drama producer.[19] An element of 'puffing' – that is, reviews organised by publisher or author – can be detected. Sean O'Faolain, who had received a complimentary copy of the book at McCartan's direction, was set up to write a notice for *The Listener*, published by the BBC. What he wrote he described as milk-and-water, suggesting in advance that it shoud be 'pulled'. In the event, his review did not appear. A former government minister Ernest Blythe (1889–1975) noted the book in the *Irish Independent*, and he (like Hobson) had begun his political career as a Protestant recruit to the IRB. Colm O Lochlainn praised Maloney's dedication in *The Irish Book Lover*, which O Lochlainn himself published.[20]

P. S. O'HEGARTY – A BIBLIOGRAPHICAL NOTE

The most intriguing review appeared in *The Dublin Magazine*, a journal of international repute run by the minor poet, Seamus O'Sullivan and his wife, the painter Estella Solomons. O'Hegarty, who had carefully read the proofs of *The Forged Casement Diaries*, wrote a page-long notice for the January–March 1937 issue. Central to his account is the evidence of Ben S. Allen who is quoted as follows, 'My own theory is that it was a diary copied by Sir Roger during the Putumayo investigation.' O'Hegarty now embellishes the Normand Defence with categorical statements to the effect that Casement had sent the original to the Foreign Office, keeping a copy in his own handwriting, 'for it was too revolting to let anyone else copy it. It was this copy which gave some

---

19 The review was broadcast on Friday 13 Nov. 1936 at 7.55 p.m.
20 See also reviews by Edward Sheehy in *Ireland To-day*, vol. 1 no. 7 (Dec. 1936), pp. 80–1, and by P. E. Magennis (O. Carm.) in *The Catholic Bulletin* (Dec. 1936), pp. 1006–10.

British intelligence officer the basis for the forgery.' Gone are his scrupulous doubts of 1933 as to whether the copy had been sent to the FO or the original; absent is any indication that the Defence stemmed from his own recollections of 1912 and the parallel recollections of Bulmer Hobson. Ben S. Allen in the Californian Agriculture Department, the remotest of the witnesses, becomes the champion of the Normand Defence, which is thus liberated from any dependence on Casement's Irish friends and Maloney's managers.

An early contributor to the making of *The Forged Casement Diaries*, and one of its reviewers, O'Hegarty later published a series of 'Bibliographies of 1916 and the Irish Revolution' which also appeared in *The Dublin Magazine*. The seventeenth of these makes it clear that he and Casement had corresponded and, *en passant* or otherwise, discussed Casement's writing. Under Addenda, O'Hegarty cites tedious notes of his own 'which would point to a belief, at the time I wrote the notes, that [two items] were printed at the times stated, though I am not aware of any survival of them . . .'. Pointing to a belief held in the past scarcely amounts to a lively faith, and O'Hegarty the bibliographer is a cannier Casementite than the reviewer. Finally he refers to Parmiter's 1936 biography for brief details of Casement's official reports on the Congo and Putumayo, and declines to provide any collations for these. In all, O'Hegarty's bibliographical interest in Casement is clearly derived from a far earlier date than its publication. No recent discoveries or enquiries are mentioned, and there is conspicuously no reference to Maloney or forgery. This may distance the bibliographer from the theorist. Certainly, when O'Hegarty published his *History of Ireland Under the Union* (1952) he paid scant attention to Casement and none to any controversy about the diaries. In contrast, he praised Hobson as the 'sanest counsel' available to Eoin MacNeill in 1916, for which reason hard-liners had kidnapped him.[21]

THE GHOST OF HENRY WILSON

After the flurry of reviews and the greater excitement of Yeats's poems, the managers were entitled to feel that they had accomplished as much as they could have expected. 'With the Irish pretending now that they never did

21 P. S. O'Hegarty, 'Bibliographies of 1916 and the Irish Revolution: no. XVII Roger Casement', *The Dublin Magazine*, vol. 24 no. 2 (Apr.–June 1949), pp. 31–4; *History of Ireland Under the Union* (London: Methuen, 1952), p. 701.

believe the story, they could not well find fault with the proof.'[22] However, as in many Irish controversial matters, the fatal tendency to underestimate an enemy led to a strange epilogue. Near the end of May 1937, McCartan informed Hobson that 'the whispering campaign against Casement' had resumed. Publication of Maloney's book had not been greeted with unanimous acceptance of the Forgery Theory, nor even with a proper degree of silent disgruntlement. Joseph Bigger, professor of bacteriology at Trinity College, Dublin, had been in touch with the novelist Francis Hackett (1883–1962) and the eccentric landlord, Shane Leslie (Sir John Randolph Leslie, 1885–1971, 3rd bart.). In a statement designed for 'private consumption' only, Bigger made it plain that his family knew perfectly well that 'Casement was a homo'.[23] Hackett, who had been a journalist in America before turning to fiction, was living in County Wicklow in the mid-1930s. In his younger days, he had been friendly with the poet Thomas MacDonagh (1858–1916), executed for his part in the Easter Rising. In the same younger days, he had served on the first editorial board of the liberal American magazine, *The New Republic* (founded 1914). Coming from the other side of the contested field, Leslie was no less complicated. A cousin of Winston Churchill's who had converted to Catholicism and Irish nationalism while at Cambridge, in 1916 he had interceded vainly to saved the lives of the condemned rebel leaders. An enthusiast for ghosts throughout his life (and perhaps longer), Leslie too was a confidant with influence.

Joseph Warwick Bigger (1891–1951) was linked to Casement in very different ways. His uncle, Francis Joseph Bigger (1863–1926), had been an active cultural nationalist in Ulster, a book collector, and (with Casement) organiser of the Glens of Antrim *Feis* or festival. His devotion to youth activities led to rumours in Belfast about his sexual orientation, and some attention from the police. Maloney told Hackett that when he had been visiting Belfast many years earlier he had been aware of Frank Bigger's proclivities. 'I never knew him, and never had any interest in what he was doing: yet that did not spare my shocked ears from hearing that the Greeks had a name for Francis Joseph Bigger's habits, and that he wanted none to show him how to scout for

---

22 W. J. Maloney to B. Hobson, undated (NLI, MS 17,604 (1)).

23 NLI, MS 17604 (9). See Oliver St J. Gogarty to Patrick McCartan, [16 Apr. 1937], in which it is claimed that a 'so-called Casement diary' was burnt in 1922 'as a gesture of generosity'. The text of this letter, as published by Unterecker (*Yeats and Patrick McCartan*, p. 398), is so marred by diplomatic omissions as to be near unintelligible, but the import is that Casement material had been destroyed by the Bigger family in the presence of witnesses.

boys.' Having made this unnecessary declaration, the author of *The Forged Casement Diaries* poured scorn on the nephew's claim that Casement also was homosexual:

> The only proof a story like this usually needs is a nudge or a wink. To ask for further proof is scarcely decent. Accused of Sodomy one is presumed guilty unless innocence can be established: and innocence is never associated with such a charge.
>
> The 'proof' offered to you is the good faith of your informant, Joseph W Bigger. You 'think Bigger is telling the truth . . . He seemed a straightforward chap.' But he offered absolutely no evidence beyond his unsupported word. On the unsupported word of Spring Rice, Plunkett Sir Harris [?], Shane Leslie, John Quinn and other bigger liars this story has rested since it was first put out.[24]

While some truth can undoubtedly be found in the view that innocence was difficult to establish when sexual deviancy was alleged, Maloney's frame of mind is shockingly crude. John Quinn, on whom he relied in his published book, is now listed with even bigger liars. A few sentences later Bigger is described as an 'informer' and, with that emotive term released into the correspondence, Maloney appears to lose his grip even on his own book. Dealing with Bigger's apparent suggestion that references to Casement's brother, Tom, and his debts authenticated a diary destroyed twenty or so years earlier, Maloney writes, 'In my book, which the informer doubtless read, I specify with dates Tom's neediness.' But there are no references to Tom Casement's debts in *The Forged Casement Diaries*.

This confusion should not obscure an implied admission. For if the professor was rightly termed an 'informer', then he was presumed to be speaking the truth. And Bigger's intrusion into the well-laid plans of the Forgery Theorists excited more than the putative author. McCartan wrote from the United States to Hobson insisting that a response was necessary. 'Maloney was inclined to ignore it but I persuaded him to answer it as Hackett & others would assume that Maloney knew all about Roger. And he does know more than these people who whisper so confidentially & authoritatively but he has never found any evidence from those who knew Roger intimately

---

24   Copy of Maloney to Francis Hackett, 25 Apr. 1937 (NLI, MS 17,602). The doubtful reference is probably to Sir Horace Plunkett (1845–1932), founder of the co-operative movement who sat in the Irish Senate with Yeats in the 1920s. Sir John Harris, the anti-slaver, may also be mixed up in Maloney's phrasing.

of the charges leveled against him.' The note of hesitancy is again audible. How hard had Maloney (or Mr O'Keefe) looked for evidence of homosexuality, if at all? What might motivate such a search? What would knowing 'all about Roger' amount to?

Not pausing for an answer, McCartan moved beyond speculation:

> It seems there is but one way to stop this – it is a rotten way but still – I shall pass the word to the I.R.A. to give Bigger or any other Irishman found preaching this yarn one warning. . . . If [Shane] Leslie or any other Irishman help [*sic*] to substantiate the charges against Casement Maloney will have a lot more to say. Others who will say nothing may act. Some of the men involved in shooting [Sir Henry] Wilson on his own doorstep are yet alive & they will get all the facts from me.[25]

Of course, there were no charges against Casement, largely because he was dead and additionally because those who did not share the Theorists' view maintained a public silence. Maloney and Co. were in danger of protesting too much. In Colorado Oscar Wilde had found the only rational form of art criticism on a bar-room notice – 'Please Do Not Shoot the Pianist, He is Doing his Best.' In the eyes of at least one retired gunman, Bigger was now falling below Wild West standards. On a sheet of paper touchingly preserved by Hobson, McCartan ordered him to 'burn what I write on this page & show the rest to Leslie. It will help to shut him up for he is "yellow" as they say here. Show him also Maloney's reply to Hackett. Billy [i.e. Maloney] has enough on Leslie to make him run for cover. I hope to get Sean Russell or some of the boys to visit Bigger & give him some "friendly advice". He had no right to stick his nose in here.'[26] Whether the basis for a possible blackmailing of Shane Leslie lay in his youthful association with Frank Bigger is unclear but (in Theory at least) possible. Here the crude cynicism of the managers is plainly manifest. 'Accused of Sodomy one is presumed guilty unless innocence can be established' had been their mentor's dictum in defence of Casement, yet the same logic could be used to assassinate a dissenter from the Theory.

Then in a postscript McCartan advised Hobson, 'If you can [,] advise any Irishman who may be asked to keep off that Committee of Investigation. Let

25 P. McCartan to B. Hobson, 27 Apr. 1937 (NLI, MS 17,604 (3)). After Wilson's murder, two free-lance IRA men (Reginald Dunne and Joseph O'Sullivan) were tried and executed for the crime. Both had previously served in the British Army, O'Sullivan having lost a leg at the Battle of Ypres.
26 P. McCartan to B. Hobson, undated (NLI, MS 17,604 (3)).

it be a purely English Committee. I hope Shaw wont let himself be dragged in. Yeats took the wise course.'[27] That last remark suggests that the real motivation behind the ballads was the poet's desire to be excluded from any committee inquiring into the diaries. Equally certain was the disinclination of those who shouted Forgery to approve or assist a committee. Quite why McCartan, who was in America, became so excited by a Trinity professor's family recollections remains unclear. It is unclear on what grounds Maloney might have blackmailed Shane Leslie, but that was certainly McCartan's intention. *The Forged Casement Diaries* resembled a public opinion *putsch*, inflicted on Irish 'general readers' who would believe the worst of the British authorities without asking too many questions.

Civil War breeds congenital contempt. The progressive coarsening of sensibility which is traceable in these debates from the Tailteann Games onwards reaches its nadir in the threat of reprisals against a private correspondent. Nor can the gunplay be written off as hyperbole. Whoever the surviving unnamed killers of Sir Henry Wilson were, Sean Russell (1893–1940) was well known in the republican family, despite an inability to look anyone in the eye. A veteran of the 1916 Rising, he clung to the purist, 'physical force' version of the creed, in distinction to the leftward inclinations of those who seceded to found a short-lived Republican Congress (1934–5). While the charismatic but impractical Sean MacBride brought a limited renewal during his spell as Chief of Staff (1936–7), the IRA of these years was slipping into internal fractiousness and quasi-fascism. Russell was the embodiment of this tendency, and it is fitting that he should die on board a Nazi U-boat, in a venture more futile still than that of Casement in 1916.

The book-production framework provided for *The Forged Casement Diaries* by Hobson, McCartan and O'Hegarty could not have existed had it not been for the adjustments within republicanism which had taken place in the 1920s and early 1930s. Joe McGrath had been the bully boy overseeing Oriel House, the Free State's brutal interrogation centre. He had proposed an Irish Secret Service which (he insisted) should be organised along Scotland Yard lines.[28] His IRB links with Hobson and McCartan were not those of purist opposition to the compromise Treaty. On the contrary, each of these men in different ways had sought to accommodate himself to power while privately nodding to another

---

27   *Ibid.*

28   Other schemes were adopted instead. See Eunan O'Halpin, *Defending Ireland: The Irish State and its Enemies Since 1922* (Oxford: Oxford University Press, 1999), p. 53.

authority, visionary or vicious. Among their official opponents, the emergence of Fianna Fáil as a 'slightly constitutional' party contributed to the decline in die-hard republican morale. Settling scores, covering one's tracks, changing course – these were themes of the times in Ireland after the Civil War. Casement was a useful lightning-conductor in this psycho-political force-field, idealised and ambiguous, a hero of 1916 who had tried to prevent the Rising, an imperial servant and anti-slaver, a Protestant secretly baptised a Catholic in childhood, a gentleman-republican, half-forgotten. Preserved in Wilhelmine amber, he could even serve as a mascot for co-operation with the Nazis.

In America, Devoy's death in September 1928 led to publication of his *Recollections of an Irish Rebel* (1929). In a special sense, it contributed as much to the atmosphere in which Casement might be reassessed as the deaths of Quinn, Conan Doyle and F. E. Smith. Devoy had never wholly trusted Casement – and he quickly lost faith in Maloney – in the sense that he never believed Sir Roger's abilities were of the same mettle as his dreams. For this reason, he had wished Casement to stay in Germany rather than intervene in the Irish rebellion. Events had not conformed to Devoy's wishes. After 1928, a dead Devoy made the resurrection of Casement easier. Meanwhile, de Valera's government was playing cat-and-mouse with the IRA. Russell, who would become Chief of Staff in 1938, secretly met de Valera in 1935 to offer co-operation with the Fianna Fáil government: he was rebuffed, and the following year – the year of *The Forged Casement Diaries* – Russell provocatively described Ireland as still 'a nation subject to a foreign king'.[29] McCartan's threat to Professor Bigger was not simply of personal violence, but of punishment inflicted by an organisation in renewed confrontation with the government and the state itself.

As for the blackmailing of Shane Leslie, the rest was silence until 1 March 1937 when his review of Maloney's work appeared in *The Irish Times*. It was a masterpiece of evasion. 'Seldom has any post-war book called for a clearer or more impartial reading', Leslie began, and concluded 'It is only clear that a very serious confusion needs to be elucidated.'[30] Between these extremes of clarification, he referred to Maloney as 'the compiler' of the book and generally adopted a tone of grand caution. No elucidation followed until the Giles Document Laboratory report.

---

29 See Robert Fisk, *In Time of War* (Dublin: Gill & Macmillan, [2000]), pp. 81, 87.

30 In contrast, by 21 Apr. 1937 Hackett had given Maloney evidence to undermine the Forgery Theory (see NLI, MS 17, 604 (3)).

SIX

THE BUFF DIARY

STILL MISSING AFTER ALL THESE YEARS

—

Amidst the activities of successive protagonists of the Forgery Theory – Maloney, Mackey, McHugh, Ó Maille, Mitchell and others – it is difficult to trace any coherent pattern of response from the other side, the British authorities. As Home Secretary in 1959, R. A. Butler (1902–82) found it necessary to break the silence by admitting that the Black Diaries did exist – they had just been published from bad copy in Paris – and by releasing them into a semi-public domain of consultation. Though the documents progressively have been easier of access, no parallel growth in official eloquence has taken place. In February 2002 as publication of the Forensic Report approached, it seemed that the Foreign Office was wholly unaware that another diary, quite distinct from those collectively known as the Black Diaries, had been described in some detail during the 1936 controversy.[1]

Dr Maloney's basic approach to the problem posed by British use of diaries which they associated with Casement was to seek out discrepancies between various accounts of what had been covertly displayed. By this means, he was able to suggest – with characteristic sarcasm – that certain features came and went as the material was shown to this person or that. Some saw typescript, others saw manuscript, others again only saw photographs. Apart from highlighting the duplicity of the British, this procedure had, for the Forgery Theorist, the added psychological advantage of suggesting impermanence in the object itself. If type disappeared to be replaced on another occasion by holograph, or transcript by photograph, then (the inner logic argued) the diary would never finally materialise. It was a temporary thing, like the Saxon yoke upon the neck of Gaels.

Public evasion by successive Home Secretaries appeared to confirm these hopes. Challenges to the British authorities, like that of Maud Gonne, were predicated more on a confidence that nothing would emerge, less on the

1   In a conversation of 6 Feb. 2002, Dr Gill Bennett, official historian at the Foreign Office, undertook to search for any record of what I now baptise as The Buff Diary.

outcome of any forensic tests. Little attention was paid to the attitude of prime ministers – Stanley Baldwin and Ramsay MacDonald – whose response to family inquiries might be summarised in the phrase, Better Not to Know. Yet Maloney was in a particular regard imitating the behaviour of his enemies (his former wartime leaders). He assembled testimony with the intention of damaging a reputation. That his target was an entire government-cum-administrative system, and not an individual, did not alter the character of his enterprise. So what if the Maloney Papers, or associated archives, were to throw up discrepancies, gaps, irreconcilable documents?

Dispersed as well as assembled, these are not easily put to the test, for they are to found under the headings of Casement, Curry, McCartan, McGarrity, not forgetting Maloney itself etc. However, a comparison of three NLI files (MSS 5,588, 13,542 and 17,601) reveals some important interconnections. Somebody – almost certainly Maloney himself, or Hobson acting in his local capacity – designed a file (MS 5,588) of photostat documents for incorporation into the NLI archive, presumably to obviate the need to unearth the originals for each successive inquirer. Arranged alphabetically by author, the copy contents include statements and/or letters by Ben S. Allen, H. S. Dickey, Michael F. Doyle, Eamonn Duggan, O. St J. Gogarty and others. It is a relatively small file, bound in buckram to withstand sustained use. What is designed is, of course, more than a file – it constitutes in itself an argument from which reluctance, reservation, and personal factors have been expunged.

A SOLITARY AMERICAN WITNESS

One advantage which Maloney enjoyed lay in the winnowing of witnesses by death. For the most part these had accepted (with whatever personal or particular reservations) that the material they had been shown was genuine. The obverse side of this advantage was the difficulty of finding any survivor who held the material to have been fabricated. Though Maloney could not have predicted the outcome, Alfred Noyes eventually took up this position and, as a convert to the cause, helped to keep the Forgery Theory alive for a new generation. Back in the early 1930s, the search for any sympathetic surviving witness looked pretty hopeless. As luck would have it, the answer was a fellow American, even an erstwhile associate of Maloney's. But the resultant evidence in NLI suggests that some persuasion had been necessary.

Within these several files, the contribution of Maloney's only independent American witness is problematic. Indeed, his independence may be challenged without damaging his fundamental honesty. A native Californian, Benjamin Shannon Allen had been born in Grass Valley in 1882, the same year as Maloney. As he described himself 'just Irish enough to defend [his] action' in a particular dispute, it is possible that his second forename signals Irish associations. This in itself hardly jeopardises his independence relative to Maloney's theory, but it may prove to be an augury of other difficulties. In his youth Allen had studied (1903–7) at Stanford, a private university in California, where he edited the *Stanford Daily* as an undergraduate. In December 1909, he married Victoria French, a student at Mills, a women's college associated with Stanford.

By the first winter of the Great War, the Allens (with some offspring) were living in London. Ben S. Allen was chosen by Herbert Hoover (1874–1964) to present the first report of a Commission for Relief in Belgium to the King of the Belgians (the odious Leopold's successor). This involved him travelling within a few kilometres of the battle front (accompanied by his wife) where they spent two days under shellfire. The great conflict of that period in the war was the Battle of Mons. The episode marked the first stage in a long relationship between Allen and the future President, and between the Allens and the Hoover Institute at Stanford.[2]

For ten years, Allen had been on the staff of Associated Press 'under the matchless leadership of Melville E. Stone'. This period included much of the Great War, during which he represented the AP in London. At some point, Allen met Roger Casement for a lengthy formal interview, subsequently met him again, and grew to admire him tremendously. Though Allen gives no dates for the interview, the implication is that it took place in London (just possibly Ireland), but not in the United States. However, Allen's political allegiances themselves deserve notice: when his country joined the Allied cause, he joined Hoover's staff. The Republican president was later defeated by F. D. Roosevelt in 1932.

Maloney had reached New York by mid-1911 and entered upon a medical career unmarked by any concern with Irish affairs. It was, however, promptly associated with the Jesuit Order, which he seems to have held in high regard. The one published account we have of these years was written by an Ulsterman of Protestant background (Foster Kennedy) who leaves no

2   Ben S. Allen, 'A Mills Husband Looks at Reunions', *Mills Quarterly* (Aug. 1959), pp. 4–5.

impression of Maloney having an interest in nationalism. On the contrary, the public evidence records Maloney's prompt decision in August 1914 to join up and assist Britain in the war effort. Casement, for his part, arrived in America in July 1914, determined to assist in a liaison between Devoy's Clan na Gael and the German Empire. Although there is no evidence that Maloney ever met Casement at any time, Maloney knew Allen in the aftermath of the Great War, and Allen had interviewed Casement somewhere. These incomplete sides of a possible triangle do not strongly resemble a framework in which to posit a pre-war friendship amongst all three.

The evidence associating Allen with Maloney in the period immediately after the Great War comes from Allen's own typewriter. In one of two letters preserved in NLI, Allen referred to his association with the Scottish doctor in preparing 'the McCartan proclamation'. This can be dated roughly to the summer of 1919, when Patrick McCartan appeared in America as putative envoy of a newly established Irish Republic and sought recognition of it from the United States. When Allen in his December 1932 letter to Maloney additionally referred to 'our work in [sic] the later celebrated Shearer document', he stated that this had been carried at out at his (Allen's) home in Washington. This may refer either to *The Re-Conquest of America*, published in 1919, and/or to subsequent debates about its authorship in which W. B. Shearer had foolishly claimed a part.[3] But as Allen by his own account had moved to the west coast *circa* 1922 to be proprietor and editor of the *Sacramento Union*, it seems most probable that he refers here to activities he and Maloney pursued *circa* 1919–20. As someone who had served Hoover during the Great War, Allen would not have relished any publicity of his mildly subversive activities while his former boss was successively Secretary for Commerce (1921–9) and then President (1929–33).

Do these ephemeral publications and squabbles matter? Well, their common denominator is nationalism. When de Valera went to Sacramento in 1919, Allen editorialised with some hostility, a fact which in itself suggests his cussed independence of mind. Recalling this for Maloney, Allen admitted that he was 'quite a rabid nationalist' in those days. What the Irish leader on

3   William Baldwin Shearer (born 1874) was a fanatic on the naval aspects of Anglo-American relations, and the author of several books, including *The Cloak of Benedict Arnold* (1928). The debates, before a senate committee and in newspaper columns, occurred in late 1929 and early 1930. See, for example, the *New York Times* of 14 Oct. 1929 (p. 190), 15 Oct. 1929 (p. 9), and 17 Oct. 1929 (p. 24).

tour had offended was American self-respect, and Allen in response typified a particular strand of American nationalist/isolationist opinion – we keep out of the world's affairs, and nobody chides us on our own doorstep. A political climate of isolationism was conducive to the Casement project upon which Maloney was already embarked in 1932, because it discouraged moral comparisons of democracy and militarism and – after Hitler's election – contrasts of civil liberty and Nazism. In the 1930s, Allen seemed a useful ally for Maloney to acquire, an American 'nationalist' (in some limited sense) and a journalist who had actually seen both Casement and the alleged diary.

The recruitment of Ben S. Allen to the cause raises an issue which haunts several corners of the larger archive – financial indebtedness. In July 1932, Maloney complained that Allen had not answered letters despatched by registered post, 'He owes me much money.'[4] Yet Allen had evidently prospered, having become not just an editor but a newspaper proprietor. Replying eventually to the doctor on 29 October 1932, he began by admitting 'I am under very deep obligations to you, the material obligation, of course, I hope you know, I would be glad to meet any time that I was able to do so.' Perhaps Maloney had assisted him in acquiring ownership of the *Sacramento Union*. If so, why was Allen now a salaried state official? Had he surrendered ownership of the paper as well as the editor's desk? These questions may be unanswerable, but they arise from Allen's evident reluctance to confront his correspondent's single-minded purpose. In his letter, Allen dealt with non-Casemental topics of little consequence and, returning to Maloney's particular interest in 1916, he concluded 'I profoundly regret that I did not keep a diary myself at the time, because I find that my memory tends to become a bit treacherous.' He even went so far as to name a man on the editorial board of *The New Republic* who might prove more useful.[5]

Yet the New York doctor, having resumed contact with an indebted former associate, was not content with amiable but evasive responses. Palpably curtailing discussion of Casement, Allen had concluded

> This letter is written for the purpose of acknowledging your communication and in direct reply to the request which you made. Later I will supplement it with news

---

4   W. J. Maloney to Bulmer Hobson, 12 July 1932 (NLI, MS 17,604 (1)).

5   NLI, MS 17,601 (1). Whether Maloney took up the lead to *The New Republic* or not, the journalist in question (Bruce Bliven) does not feature in Maloney's published work.

about the family, particularly about the young man who, as a baby, enjoyed your much appreciated counsel.

With affectionate regards from the Allen family and hoping to hear from you again soon . . . [6]

There the matter did not rest. By means of some further letter or message – now untraceable – Maloney smartly brought Allen to a quasi-formal declaration about Casement rather than dilate on family matters: this is the second of the two letters preserved in NLI. Among the inducements had been a copy of Maloney's 'fascinating manuscript', the full-scale biography shortly laid aside to make room for the Forgery Theory. Thus Allen's second letter describes how he had been repeatedly shown what purported to be Casement's diary – the torn sheets of not quite legal size – some sixteen years earlier. This occurred in London while Allen was with Associated Press, the perpetrator was Reginald 'Blinker' Hall, (1870–1943), head of naval intelligence. It seems likely that Allen was the American to whom Mrs Dryhurst had alluded in July 1916.

Though *The Forged Casement Diaries* repeatedly quotes this (second) written testimony of Allen's, it fails to provide a date.[7] Maloney records the weekly incident with Captain Hall as if Allen had written his account some time between 1916 and – at the latest – 1921. Indeed, he promotes Hall to the rank of Admiral (which did not occur until 1926) as if to emphasise the colossal heights of his blackguardism. Nor is it anywhere admitted in print that Maloney had encountered considerable difficulty in locating the former journalist who, by 1932, was working for the State of California's agriculture department. Maloney's attempt at a direct tracing passed through 'several old addresses'. The successful and more indirect trail, however, can be reconstructed: the principal scouts were Jesuits, augmented by the services of the *Sacramento Union*.[8] Nobody provided Maloney with a home address for Allen,

6 Ben S. Allen to W. Maloney, 29 Oct. 1932 (NLI, MS 17,601 (1)).

7 See W. J. Maloney, *The Forged Casement Diaries* (Dublin: Talbot Press, 1936), p. 21, for an extensive quotation (with ellipses) from what is referred to as Allen's 'statement about the "Casement diary", now in the National Library of Ireland'. In the absence of a statement, we find Maloney constructing a passage by citing Allen's second letter in this order: paragraphs 12, 4, 13, 14, 5, 6, 15, 16. Elsewhere (p. 97) Maloney related how 'Mr Ben S. Allen of the Associated Press, in the letter [*sic*] which we have quoted, told how further American scope was officially sought for this story and was denied by him.'

8 W. J. Lonergan, SJ to W. Maloney, 2 Nov. 1932; Charles J. Lilley to Maloney, 2 Nov. 1932 (NLI, MS 17,601 (1)).

who conducted his subsequent correspondence from the San Francisco agriculture office.[9]

For his part, Maloney appears to have used the St Hubert Hotel on New York's West 57th Street as his dead letterbox. Both men manoeuvred with caution. Allen suggested that Maloney 'might do an injustice in not giving credit to some of the other American newspaper correspondents' who had been in London in 1916. Later in the same letter he named his proposed alternative collaborator for Maloney. In his second letter, which stressed the value of friendship, he submitted that 'since you must look to sympathizers with the Irish cause for support of your biography, my connection with the diary might alienate some of it'. But Maloney proceeded in *The Forged Casement Diaries* to quote other passages from this correspondence. Repeating his confusion of details in Alfred Noyes's journalism, and the unfortunate Casement-as-amanuensis-of-Normand theory, he declares that 'the testimony of Allen . . . leaves no room for doubt that a Casement atrocity diary did exist in 1916', omitting to qualify this with the doctrinal insistence on its being a forged diary.[10]

After 1932, he seems to have taken no further interest in Allen, at least as far as his accumulating archive in NLI is concerned. Though Allen comes across as an intelligent man, even-handed, spirited and honest, his relationship with Maloney remains problematic. Why was he not publicly invoked – even paraded – at the time of publication, a living witness to the diary/forgery? Why did McCartan not write him up in the two-part article which featured in the *Irish Press* (Dublin) at the time of serialisation? Had Allen been alienated by the manner in which his contribution to the cause was handled?

Allen's proposed substitute – the man at *The New Republic* – is a striking example of the dog who does not bark in the night. His absence from Maloney's team of witnesses is eloquent if obscure. Like Allen, Bruce Ormsby Bliven (1889–1977) had worked as a journalist in wartime London and had – Allen indicates – similar experiences with Casement's private papers. They had earlier been together at Stanford in 1907, and shared that formative education. The standard of *The New Republic* flew higher than California's Agriculture Department, and Maloney (one would have thought) should have welcomed

9   We know from Lilley that Allen was living in Palo Alto at the time. Maloney's New York address is given as 420 Park Avenue in Father Lonergan's letter, and 422 [*sic*] Park Avenue in Charles Lilley's.
10   Maloney, *Forged Casement Diaries*, p. 175.

testimony from that quarter, guaranteeing American publicity to a degree
never achieved by *The Forged Casement Diaries*. For whatever reason, no Bliven
evidence was forthcoming. He was, of course, decidedly liberal in outlook,
acting as New York correspondent for the *Manchester Guardian* from 1927 to
1977, unlikely to approve the McGarrity line on Irish relations with Germany.
And there remains an oddity about Bliven's appearance in the second of
letters despatched to Maloney above Allen's name – the misspelling of Bliven
as Blivens. We shall return to the letter and its oddities in due course.

In December 1932, Maloney could boast that he had 'traced another
American correspondent who was shown "the diary ["] found on Casement at
his capture – found by Scotland Yard. He was shown it about 1923. It con-
sistedly solely of episodes in Germany.'[11] If this breakthrough resulted from
Allen's suggestion of Bliven as an alternative source. Maloney does not admit
the fact. Nor is it likely. Allen implied that Bliven had seen material in 1916
and, in any case, there is little or no evidence that Casement had been in
possession of a diary when he landed in Kerry. It may be that the circulation
in 1923 should be attributed to Peter Singleton-Gates, the Fleet Street
journalist who obtained typescript copies of some material (probably from
Basil Thomson). We may be confident that this diary of 'episodes in Germany'
was sexually compromising, for no other kind of diary would be worth hawking
to journalists seven years after Casement's death.

On the central issue of Casement *per se*, Allen remained constant. In 1959,
his lifelong interest in woodland development was rewarded with presidency
of the Forest History Foundation. In 1960, when Maloney was several years
dead, the Californian travelled to London where he inspected the Black Diaries
in the Public Record Office on 2 August. He then proceeded to Dublin, which
the Great Theorist had successfully avoided. There, in the Gresham Hotel,
he swore an affidavit before a commissioner for oaths. A photostat copy was
duly lodged in NLI. By this date he was nearing his seventy-eighth birthday,
unable to remember more of 1916 than he had done in 1932.

Two features of his sworn evidence are noteworthy. Beyond declaring that
the diary he had been shown in 1916 'contained no definite locations, dates or
names', Allen provided no description whatsoever of its contents. He made no
use of terms like 'disgust', 'horror', 'perversions', 'ravings', which occurred in
his correspondence with Maloney. Perhaps this formalism derived from the
nature of affidavits as such. Perhaps it reflected altered attitudes towards

11   W. J. Maloney to Bulmer Hobson, 7 Dec. 1932 (NLI, MS 17, 604 (1)).

human behaviour on the part of a man who had by then lived forty years in California. Second, however, he specified the size of the document more particularly than in 1932 – 'It was of considerable thickness, and the pages were approximately foolscap size.' Nothing which is now in the PRO remotely resembles such a document. For that reason Allen remains the most valuable witness for the Forgery Theory, *despite* the absence of any statement from him in 1960 that he believed what he saw to be forgeries.

It seems reasonable to conclude that a prime mover in this last act was Herbert O. Mackey who, utilising the NLI archives as a platform for his own Zolaesque campaign, facilitated Allen's recital of the buff coloured pages, the torn composition book etc. This account of the materials circulated in 1916 was all the more valuable now that the British had opened the Black Diaries to limited inspection. Mackey had duly examined these, and Allen's testimony was required in legally sworn form. Alternatively, Roger McHugh may have been Allen's local contact in Dublin, in which case the American's silence on the issue of forgery is all the more eloquent as McHugh was at the time writing up his lengthy exposé for the Belfast magazine, *Threshold*. In this article and a follow-up letter to the editor, McHugh fails to note that Allen alleged no forgery in the Kew materials, merely noted their non-inclusion of what he had been shown in 1916.[12]

The notion that the Maloney Papers continued to serve the Forgery Theory does not carry with it any imputation of bad faith on Mackey's part. His voluminous writings about Casement (and his more valuable editions of Casement's own writings) testify to a conscience which is innocent if uneducable. *J'accuse* is little more than a vigorous statement of faith reiterated after a visit to London; obscene interpolations are reported in the PRO documents but never specified, the evidence of their interpolated status resting upon the obscene character. It is possible, however, to conduct a more acute examination of the Maloney phenomenon in Dublin, with Ben S. Allen as the chosen point of focus.

12 Affidavit by Ben S. Allen, sworn in Dublin, Gresham Hotel, 19 Aug. 1960 before J. Noel Tanham, commissioner for oaths. Two typed pages, Photostat copy (NLI, MS 13,542). Professor Roger McHugh refers to Allen's affidavit, but erroneously declares that Allen had written up his account of a manuscript diary in 1916. This grossly exaggerates Allen's authority on the subject, and flies in the face of testimony in NLI.

MISSING PAGES

MS 5,588 opens with Allen's second letter (2 December 1932) in photostat negative form, but does not however reproduce his first (29 October 1932). The originals of both letters are preserved in MS 17,601 (1). In the latter, we find an additional photostat negative copy of the second letter. But before turning to the copies, let us note that the four-page typed original lacks its third page. Several explanations come to mind.

Though NLI never makes available more than one file at a time, in the past the missing leaf may have been simply misfiled by a reader into an adjacent folder: if this is the case, page three may yet turn up. From a different perspective, it is possible to argue – but unlikely as a fact – that it was missing at the time of the letter's accession to NLI. No annotation records its absence. It is just conceivable that the actual page had been earlier absorbed by Maloney and his managers into the mass of paper required for the printer. There again, perhaps it was later deliberately removed by a curious reader at some time in the last sixty or so years: before the introduction of camera surveillance, such depredations were possible in NLI as elsewhere. It would be utter baloney to argue that Allen himself might have culled the files, when he visited Dublin in 1960. But why should anyone else remove page three of Ben S. Allen's second letter? After all, there are two complete photostat copies remaining, one of them in a bound volume resistant to vandalism.

It is of course technically possible that the two copies do not truly represent the unique original: the original against which these copies can be checked is incomplete. The disappearance of a page makes any such authentication ultimately impossible. Indeed, as Numbered Page Two concludes a paragraph and Numbered Page Four opens with a new one, it is even possible that there never had been a Numbered Page Three; instead, Allen might have wrongly numbered the final (signed) leaf as four.[13] Read straight through as a three-page document, it makes sense, and reveals no gaps or repetitions.

13 I am inclined to think that Allen did his own typing in this correspondence, which had no connection with the Board of Agriculture and involved matters of some delicacy. The first letter (but not the second) bears an office reference at the end, 'Ben S. Allen: b',which may mask Allen's own work as typist. Furthermore, though the typing and layout are neat, they are far from perfect. One punctuation mark is repeated and another elsewhere entirely omitted (these examples from the first letter). A gap between two words is omitted (this is in the second letter). In the second, Allen writes that he is 'sitting in the apartment of my wife in Mills Hall at Mills College where she is Chairman of Residents'. All in all, the letters declare him typist as well as author. He was clearly unwilling to delegate even the physical despatch of his communications with Maloney.

To test this entirely hypothetical suggestion, one needs to analyse the material contained in Copy Page Three, amounting to eight paragraphs. For the sake of clarity, reference will be made to these through a system of numbers covering the entire letter:

PARA 11 – of three lines. Explains the motivation behind the final paragraph (No. 10, of fifteen lines) on page 2, and contains no new material;

PARA 12 – of ten lines, commencing 'Now for a brief summary of my recollections of the way the diary was presented to me.' This paragraph repeats material from paragraphs Nos 2 and 3 of page 1, with more circumstantial detail. This paragraph is quoted in Maloney's book.

PARA 13 – of nine lines. Records Allen's conversations with Captain Hall, and his request to confront Casement.

PARA 14 – of four lines. Describes Hall's weekly display of the diary, and (once) of 'some typewritten excerpts'. Again repetition from Page One.

PARA 15 – of four lines (one sentence). Largely repetition.

PARA 16 – of seven lines. Deals with the post-execution period, refers to Bruce Blivens [*sic*] to whom a manuscript diary had been offered after the war. This paragraph repeats material in Allen's first letter where the surname was rightly given as Bliven [*sic*].

PARA 17 – a single line (one sentence). 'Then I heard no more until your welcome letter.' This sentiment, while admirably polite, is at odds with Allen's previous neglect of Maloney's registered letters several months earlier.

PARA 18 – of four lines. Refers to Maloney's manuscript biography, an error in it relating to Allen himself, and an undertaking to correct 'such unimportant details'. A holograph postscript on Numbered Page Four reads 'Please note insert on page 3 chapter 6 of Mss'.

One – tendentious – analysis of these successive paragraphs would suggest that the brevity of some and the repetition in others were efforts exactly to fill out an entire page which was to be inserted, *either* between Numbered Page Two and Wrongly Numbered Page Four, *or* instead of an original page three which has disappeared. The only objective of such a manoeuvre would be forgery. That this suspect page only exists in photostat may bolster the tendentious analysis, because acquisition of a sheet exactly to match the other sheets of paper (official Californian state stationery) would pose an additional problem in Dublin, neatly sidestepped by recourse exclusively to photostat copies.

Against the tendentious analysis, it should be noted that a characteristic feature of the typing is a dropped 'a', usually occurring when 'a' is the second letter in a word – see appendix 1. That the second letter cites (on Copy Page Three) material already covered in the first letter may suggest that the second was intended both as a personal communication and as a quasi-formal, reasonably full 'statement' concerning Casement and the diary, written in the knowledge that it would be used by Maloney in some fashion. This is borne out by the contrasting references to the AP boss who, in the first letter was scarcely flattered: 'Whatever else one may ever say against the Associated Press under the regime of Melville Stone . . .'. By the second, he has become 'matchless'.

Let us therefore take the charitable view, that Original Page Three did exist but was removed by the managers because it particularly was to be quoted in *The Forged Casement Diaries*. Apart from mitigating the accusation (levelled at Maloney) of foul play, this view is supported by a consideration of what Allen had written on Numbered Page Two. Much of this could not be admitted into Maloney's book or, perhaps, even be admitted to Maloney's managers. Allen referred affably enough to Captain Reginald Hall – 'He too was my friend' – and spoke approvingly of Douglas Brownrigg, a wartime British naval censor. Like Frank MacDermot TD, Allen could appreciate the larger moral arena created by the Great War, in which scruples about the use of private papers might have to be sacrificed for a greater good. This larger perspective was of no interest to Maloney, except as an arsenal for sarcasm. Allen also made some indiscreet revelations of Maloney's involvement with the McCartan proclamation and likewise with the naval business which later involved Shearer. All that had been good sport at the time. But any admission of undercover activities could now damage the impression of righteous indignation which Maloney projected as the saviour of Casement. Better, therefore, to isolate Page Three for selective quotation.

Having noted that references to Maloney's post-war propagandistic work occur in Allen's testimony, one is obliged also to recall how forgery – albeit satiric forgery in print only – played a large part in that work. *The Re-Conquest of America* was the most substantial of his publications, with Sir William Wiseman as its target. It was true that McCartan, in *With de Valera in America*, celebrated Maloney's contributions to the Irish nationalist cause, but the Casement project was to be conducted at a higher level in which British propaganda would fall under scrutiny. To this end, propaganda itself was abjured, for no moral victory could be achieved by 'setting a thief to catch a thief'. Though McCartan's book had appeared while Maloney was seeking out Allen and while Hoover was serving out his last days in the White House, the Forgery Theorist had little to gain if Allen (once Hoover's aide) repeated the same stories. Apart from anything else, these would discredit Allen as a witness, revealing him as an American journalist who had aided and abetted fugitive publication on behalf of an alien interest. Indeed, they might even suggest that Allen had somehow been under Maloney's influence in 1919–20, just as McCartan had been.

We are left, however, with an *embarras de richesses* – two photostat, negative (that is, white on black) copies of Missing Page Three. If, however, each copy reflects the other exactly then we could infer an unproblematic page three or, to put it another way, the argument in favour of accepting these copies as true is greatly increased. The establishment of this conclusion would go a long way towards mitigating the suspicions aroused elswhere in the Allen–Maloney relationship. A close examination of the two copies (in MS 5,588 and MS 17,601) quickly established that it is precisely their third pages which constitute a paradoxical area of identity-and-difference between them. Textually, they are identical *ad literatem*. That is to say, each reflects the other on an alphabetical letter-to-letter basis, even to the point of possessing the same crunch of punctuation marks at a juncture where a period is oddly (but legitimately) followed by a comma and the latter followed by a capital initial *without* the spacing proper to the context. From such evidence, we can deduce that these copies are indeed copies of the same original (which may not, of course, be automatically assumed to possess authorial status).

Despite this identity in the text and type, there are differences of scale between the two copies. By taking a series of measurements (*a*) between the several pages of Allen's letter preserved in MS 17,601 (1) and the copy preserved alongside, one can establish that the copy was reproduced in a process which involved virtually zero magnification. However, by applying the same comparisons between (*b*) Allen's letter in MS 17,601 and the copy preserved in MS 5,588, one finds a magnification ratio of *circa* 1: 1.1346 to 1: 1.2777 *for the third page only* of MS 5,588. This hardbound MS 5,588, as we have established, was put together as the display case *summum* of the core evidence for forgery, the file especially constructed for readers at NLI. Why does it prefer a copy over an available original? Why does it prefer a copy made on two separate occasions, employing two different reproductive technologies?

The tendentious approach might argue that the Copied Page Three of MS 5,588 was a trial-piece, a stage in the construction of a plausible substitute for the (now missing) original page three. As such it should never have been allowed to survive, and its preservation effectively rules out the tendentious approach. An alternative answer might be sought by returning to the larger plethora of 'Papers' in NLI which loosely constitute the archive relating to the Forgery Theory. MS 17,601 (1) is part of the Joseph McGarrity Papers, and Maloney's personal liaison with the Philadelphian philo-nazi is touchingly inscribed on the obverse of the second page of Allen's letter of 29 October 1932. There one reads the following holograph notes:

Married   1 Indian had a boy
              2 Then married a German & had 2 children 1 died – girl lived
                went back to Germany
              3 Jailed for dope importing in N.Y.
              4 Strike breaker in San Francisco

McGarrity's report on Alder Christenson[14]

This annotation indicates Maloney's casual way with paperwork, and we might speculate whether or not an original page three of Allen's second letter was withdrawn because it had been used for notes he did not wish to preserve in NLI. Of course, the annotation also records McGarrity's methods of dealing with Christensen's allegations against Casement – that is, (1) to demonstrate the Norwegian's married status and (by implication) eliminate the homosexual liaison between the two men, and (2) to blacken Christensen by digging up his criminal record. The oddest feature of the Maloney Papers at large is the extent of the incriminating detail which is preserved.

14 Eivind Alder Christensen [recte, born *c.* 1890] was the Norwegian manservant whom Casement acquired in the United States and who accompanied him to Germany, via Norway. In Oslo, Christensen betrayed his master to the British authorities and hinted strongly at a homosexual relationship which he enjoyed with Casement.

At the end of an enquiry into the incomplete nature of an original document lodged in NLI to support the Forgery Theory, we have not demonstrated that the letter in question was itself forged, either in part or in its entirety. However, a large number of discrete difficulties emerge. These are worth listing.

1 The extreme paucity of American evidence which amounted to a statement from Michael F. Doyle (one of Casement's lawyers in 1916), and just two letters from Ben S. Allen.

2 Allen's admission of a debt owed to Maloney.

3 Allen's admission of collaboration with Maloney in propaganda work *circa* 1919.

4 Allen's political/professional involvement with Herbert Hoover.

5 Allen's insistence on the relative good conduct of Reginald Hall and Douglas Brownrigg and, hence, his declining to cast Casement as victim in absolute terms.

6 Allen's description of his memory as 'treacherous', and his admission that he had no diary for 1916.

7 Allen's attempt to curtail his account of his dealings with Hall and to conclude his first letter with an expressed wish to stay in touch with Maloney but to discuss other topics.

8 The questionable repetitions in the second letter, especially with reference to a page the original of which is missing.

9 The misspelling of Bliven's name in copies of this missing page, despite Allen's familiarity with Bliven over many years, and his correct spelling of the name elsewhere in the correspondence.

10 Maloney's strong preference for quotation from this page, together with his re-ordering of quotations from what he describes as Allen's 'statement'.

Given a willingness to blackmail Shane Leslie, and the threats to Professor J. W. Bigger's life, it would be naïve to ignore these anomalies, likewise the analysis of typing summarised in appendix I below. Was Allen the victim of extortion? It is clear that Maloney was no CMG in shining armour, even if John Devoy's charge of undercover work on England's behalf remains unproven. That charge was based on a mixture of historical research and personal prejudice. 'Maloney's family has been sending members into the British Army in every generation since Waterloo', Devoy told McCartan, adding his own objections to the neurologist's 'furtive eyes' and 'thin velvety voice'. 'I am morally certain that he is a British agent.'[15]

Perhaps the Forgery Theorists would like to have the documents purporting to be Ben S. Allen's evidence submitted to forensic examination.

15 J. Devoy to P. McCartan, in the Cohalan Papers, American Irish Historical Society (New York), quoted (without a date specified) in Terry Golway, *Irish Rebel: John Devoy and America's Fight for Ireland's Freedom*, 2nd edn (New York: St Martin's Griffin, 1999), pp. 262–3.

SEVEN

CAPT. DICKEY OF US INTELLIGENCE

ARRIVES LATE ON THE SCENE

We are alright at last, we have no friends in America.

JOSEPH MCGRATH (1921)

Introducing what he variously calls Casement's 'Amazon Journal' and 'Putumayo Journal', Angus Mitchell declared Herbert Spencer Dickey 'the most important and convincing witness' to his hero's conduct in 1911.[1] If Gwynn's biography of Roger Casement is a source which Maloney misused, and Allen's testimony leaves at least one page to be desired, the recollections of Dr Dickey apparently endorse the Forgery Theory. Herbert Spencer Dickey (1876–1948) was an American who spent a good deal of time in South America, where he briefly met Casement and assisted him in opposing the brutality of rubber company bosses in the Putumayo region. It is important to note Dickey's various allegiances.[2] He sometimes worked directly for commercial companies actively exploiting the natural resources of South America, while also interesting himself in humanitarian work: during the Great War, he had served as an intelligence officer in the American army. His rather casual publications have an air of amateur anthropology about them, as if Bronisław Malinowski had never lived. Dickey's commentary on Casement emerges in a piecemeal fashion, none of it contemporary with the Irish hero's life or death. One biographer has suggested that the American doctor's view constitutes 'an imaginative sexual embroidering of a hazy recollection'.[3]

1   Angus Mitchell (ed.), *The Amazon Journal of Roger Casement* (Dublin: Lilliput; London: Anaconda, 1997), p. 35 n 32. In his diaries, Casement mentions a Dickey family of north Antrim, including Ned Dickey who also knew Frank Bigger. No possible connection has been investigated.
2   Casement's Putumayo report gravely affected not only the business interests of rubber companies but also their shareholders. In 1912 Wm Henderson Mair (of Pollockshields, Glasgow) took an action against Rio Grande Rubber Estates Ltd, alleging fraudulent descriptions in a prospectus: he lost in the Scottish courts, but won on appeal to the House of Lords a year later. I have not attempted to establish the degree of kinship (if any) between W. H. and G. H. Mair.
3   B. L. Reid, *The Lives of Roger Casement* (New Haven: Yale University Press, 1976), p. 480 n.

Recent Forgery Theory, while invoking Dickey, has refrained from quoting Casement's own opinion of him. For despite the doctor's casual suggestion that, having parted in South America, the two had little or no connection, Dickey not only entered into correspondence but despatched instalments of a book-in-progress during the first six or so months of 1912. Casement was encouraged to assume 'carte blanche to cut or add on or amend anything' in Dickey's not well-written narrative. There is some evidence that the former consul noted possible improvements, even though the document nowhere makes it clear that he was one of those whose South American adventures were being related. In August 1912, Casement in Belfast sent an official memorandum to Sir Edward Grey casting doubt on Dickey's suitability as a travelling companion with later investigators into the rubber industry. As if to substantiate these doubts, Dickey in February 1913 wrote to Casement promoting the claims of one administrator and lauding the improvements the man had allegedly introduced.[4]

Dickey's immediate's plans for publication were – he suggested to Casement – eclipsed by the publication of the latter's official report.[5] Nevertheless, he cultivated this ambition for more than fifteen years. With the aid of a co-author, Dickey published his *Misadventures of a Tropical Medico* (New York: Dodd Mead, 1929) virtually under Maloney's nose and from within the profession Maloney still pursued. Yet the book nowhere features in Maloney's argument. The presence of a co-author is of some interest, given that Dickey will be understood later single-handedly to undertake a biography of Casement, a task for which he had little training. Hawthorne Daniel (born 1890), however, was a professional and prolific writer, mainly of adventure stories. The year before his collaboration with Dickey, he published *Seal of the White Buddha; Being the Tale of a New England Girl in the Year 1847, Sailing Aboard her Uncle's Clipper to Distant China, and of the Mystery, Adventure and Great Good Fortune which Befell Her* (1928). Daniel's ideological position might be

4   See Rhodes House (Oxford) MSS Brit. Emp. S 22 (Anti-Slavery Society file G344a) for Dickey's three letters of Feb.–July 1912 and a typed copy of Casement's memorandum of 24 Aug. 1912. N.B., from the latter, 'The despatch of Senor Carlos Rey de Castro, the Peruvian Consul Generate at Manaos, to the Putomayo who, as I opine, is now there, accompanied by Senor Arana himself and Dr Dickey is a very disquieting circumstance. The journey of these men along with Mr Mitchel and Mr Fuller cannot facilitate the enquiry of the latter gentleman into the actual condition of the Indians.'

5   Dickey to Casement, TSL dated 1 Feb. 1913 from La Chorrera (Rhodes House, Anti-Slavery Society file G344c). Having visited some previously deplorable sections of the rogue company's operation, Dickey now found that the Indians 'apparently want for nothing'.

judged from later work, including *Uncle Sam's Navy: The Ships and Men of the American Fleet* (1940, with official navy illustrations).

Almost twenty years had elapsed since Dickey had met Casement. He had no exposure to the diaries in any of their transient forms, and thus was not a witness in the sense that Ben S. Allen and Eamonn Duggan were witnesses. Indeed, his links with Casement were considerably less than those of another American, Walter Hardenberg (1886–1942), who had done much more to bring the Putumayo atrocities to public notice. Maloney made no apparent effort to contact Hardenberg in the 1930s, though the engineer had (like Casement) been accused of blackmail by a Putumayon boss in 1910.[6] Neglect of Hardenberg can be explained in several ways – he never met Casement, there is no evidence he ever was shown diary material in 1916, at which date he may have been persuaded to stay silent when he could have testified to the prisoner's success as a humanitarian. But it also throws the later reliance on Dickey, as an American witness, into a strange relief.

To judge from his 1929 book, Dickey was blithely ignorant of what had happened to Casement's reputation in 1916. The two men had spent some weeks together during 1911, when Dickey was well placed professionally and personally to observe any sexual activity in his fellow traveller.[7] Maloney declares that Casement never returned to Putumayo after 1910 (correct), nor (by incorrect implication) to South America, from which it naturally would follow that he never met Dickey.[8] This gaffe may be assigned to ignorance, though other explanations present themselves. The fact that Dickey reported no sexual activity in his associate might have been seized by Maloney as evidence that there had been none, but the Forgery Theorist wisely forbore from that illogical manoeuvre. For the *Misadventures* had other observations which could not safely be introduced into *The Forged Casement Diaries*.

A large part of Maloney's book was devoted to a scathing attack on the allegation of madness repeatedly advanced by the British authorities against Casement. Though the New York doctor does not concede the point, the same diagnosis was discussed amongst Casement's supporters in 1916 and

6   See W. E. Hardenburg's anonymous article in the magazine *Truth* (London, 1909) and his *The Putumayo: The Devil's Paradise* (London: Fisher Unwin, 1912).

7   Letitia Fairfield, who had known Casement, held that the extent of Dickey's association with him had been greatly exaggerated. See her letter to the editor of *Threshold* (Belfast), vol. 4 no. 2 (autumn–winter 1960), pp. [91]–2.

8   W. J. Maloney, *The Forged Casement Diaries* (Dublin: Talbot Press, 1936), p. 180.

amongst later commentators. Even figures as different in their outlook as Patrick McCartan and Denis Gwynn concurred in regarding the German diary as the work of someone close to, if not already afflicted by, mental illness. In 1932, Gwynn observed that 'Casement's own diary of his activities in Germany reveals the extent to which his mind had become unbalanced by the horrors of his experience in the Putumayo'.[9] Maloney, we have some reason to believe, had assisted in getting that document into print.

Maloney's specialism was said to be neurology, yet his argument entirely lacks technical detail and professional interest. Dickey, a mere general practitioner in tropical regions, had things to say about Casement's mental condition not at odds with the views of McCartan (privately in 1924) and Gwynn (publicly, eight years later). His first stab at a retrospective and informal diagnosis is hardly conclusive. 'That he [Casement] was slightly unbalanced I fully believe, but I am certain that he was as sincere and as honest as any man who ever breathed.' Within less than ten pages, however, a shift in emphasis is evident. 'He wasn't exactly mad, but he was extremely eccentric, and who can draw the line between the two?' Dickey had good reason to acknowledge Casement's honesty and courage in defence of native rights, but the drift of his reminiscences is damaging. The final comment on proportions of decency and eccentricity in the Foreign Office's man turns, ironically enough, on the unauthorised release of a report the doctor had sent to him in London. Having emphasised that its release would endanger his life, Dickey was astounded to read his own material in the *Daily Mail* while he was still in South America. 'It may be, of course, that he [Casement] had not received my message concerning it – either that or he had definitely gone mad.'[10]

Maloney's neglect of Dickey's book may have sprung from an unwillingness to deal with these cumulative doubts about Casement's sanity, lightly expressed though they were. He was presumably unaware of May Casement's mental deficiency, and had no reason to anticipate Tom Casement's suicide (in March 1939). In 1931, he had attempted to interview his hero's far from heroic brother, 'which was not very productive'.[11] The previous year, another brother, Charles, had died in Australia: back in 1916, the shock of Roger's trial and execution had disturbed the balance of Charlie Casement's mind for

---

9 Denis Gwynn, *The Life of John Redmond* (London: Harrap, 1932), p. 482.
10 H. S. Dickey, *Misadventures of a Tropical Medico* (New York: Dodd Mead, 1929), pp. 156, 163, 197.
11 It is not clear where Maloney met Tom Casement, who had been living in South Africa.

months, if not longer.[12] As a family sub-set, they did not exemplify mental robustness. In a late, strangely touching letter to his Congo comrade, E. D. Morel, Roger Casement had confessed 'I am dreadfully bothered too – over Irish things in part – but much more over family failings which always come home to roost.'[13]

Anything which trumped Ireland in Casement's card-game was serious beyond description, and family failings must come under that heading. These cannot simply be reduced to Tom's perennial indebtedness, to which Roger usually responded with generous aplomb. Maloney's contempt for a diagnosis of his hero's madness in 1936 sprang from deep-seated feelings of his own, and led him also to treat Conan Doyle in a grossly off-hand manner. As for Dickey's observations, Maloney may simply not have known of *The Misadventures*' existence – hardly reassuring in an academic crusader. Dickey published a second account of his career, *My Jungle Book*, in 1932 which had absolutely nothing to say about Casement. Its appearance two years after Gwynn's biography will ultimately help in dating Dickey's revised opinion of Casement.

Despite his marginality in the context of Irish propaganda and British perfidy, Herbert Spencer Dickey, whose 1929 comments on Casement's sanity were best ignored in 1936, unexpectedly emerged as a willing ally of the Forgery Theorists – perhaps too willing. According to Angus Mitchell, in the late 1930s Dickey entered into correspondence with Maloney and began his own work on a Casement biography. It is plain they were also in cahoots. *The Incorrigible Irishman* and/or *Casement the Liberator* were possible titles. B. L. Reid, in the most thorough of the recent biographies, attributes Dickey's sudden return of interest in Casement to Denis Gwynn. On 4 May 1936 – when the Maloney project was in full swing – Dickey wrote to Gwynn volunteering an explanation of the diaries' blackness out of his own experience. But Gwynn's 1936 biography contained no account of the diaries' controversy, and the earlier edition of 1930/1931 (which contained very little on the topic) appeared in its American form while Dickey was bent on tracking the Orinoco River to its source.[14]

---

12 See NLI, MS 13,075, quoted in part in Reid, *Lives of Roger Casement*, p. 450 n.

13 Casement to Morel, 26 June 1912 (LSE, Morel Archive). Money constituted part, but not all, of the recurring Casement family problem.

14 For details and dates of his expeditions, see Dickey's *My Jungle Book* (Boston: Little Brown, 1932), esp. pp. 283 (1930), 272, 286 (both 1931), 298 (1932). It is likely that Gwynn's discretion on the issue of the diaries and Casement's sexuality was prompted in 1936 by his desire to find a post in the National University of Ireland.

There is some reason to see Maloney and Co. as the principal agents directing Dickey's interest rather than Gwynn.[15]

Otherwise it is impossible to explain why Dickey's letter to Gwynn is preserved in NLI – there are no Gwynn Papers. The explorer-doctor had indeed written (from Ecuador) to the historian on 4 May 1936, enclosing two typed pages from what he described as 'the rough draft of a book' about his South American experiences. These abruptly reported a conversation of some twenty-five years earlier in which

> Casement said that he'd always been of the opinion, until he went to the Congo, that sexual perversions were found only among civilized persons. That he'd been amazed to find among the Congo natives the 'most horrible examples of perversion.' He said also that Sir Aryhur [*sic*] Conan Doyle, his friend, had been much interested in his findings and that he had asked him to learn what he could about the existence of such things among the primitive folk of South America. Casement continued that he'd not had time while in the Putumayo to delve into the matter, and that I, as a physician, perhaps had come across some cases which might be of interest to Doyle. I replied that of course I had, that I could give him dozens of cases. He asked me to wait until he got his note-book. Then we sat down together and I reeled off to him some of the most terrible examples of human depravity of which it has been my misfortune to learn. Casement took notes of these.

A number of points deserve emphasis here. First, we are told that Casement already had an interest in, and collected findings about, sexual perversions in Africa. Second, the name of Arthur Conan Doyle only arose after the topic had been discussed by Casement and Dickey and there is no reference to any letter arriving from Conan Doyle. Third, the conversation between Casement and Dickey took place after the Putumayo inquiry, during which Casement allegedly had no time to study Normand, whose behaviour was central to the inquiry and whose diary he had appropriated (according to the Maloney Managers). Fourth, Casement actively sought information from Dickey, went to the trouble of fetching his notebook and then took notes. Fifth, the notebook is not described as to the colour of its binding or its paper. Sixth, there is no reference in these two pages to any 'Normand Defence'.

15 It may be strange that Gwynn, writing to Hobson late in 1936 to regret the imminent publication of *The Forged Casement Diaries*, did not think it fit to mention the striking new testimony he had apparently received from Dickey a few months earlier.

Dickey's two-page excerpt continues directly:

I must jump ahead now many years. Casement had been hanged for treason and
buried. I in 1920 was at the Bath Club in London where I met a Capt. Peter Wright
of the British Intelligence service. This gentleman afterwards was sued for slander
by the Gladstone family, but that was a long time later. Now, Capt. Wright
astonished me by saying that Casement himself was homo sexual and that Scotland
Yard had in its possession a note book of his displaying 'the depths of oriental
decadence.' I paid little attention to this stuff at the time, except to say that
Casement, with whom I'd been associated for many weeks was the last man in the
world I'd suspect of anything queer, and that was that.

And then, not very long after, I came upon a copy of Denis Gwynn's *The Life
and Death of Roger Casement*. I learned then that there had been a deliberate attempt
to prove Casement homosexual, in order to offset the effect of a petition . . .

I hold no brief for Casement, so far as his treason is concerned, and I certainly
have no reason, as you will find if you finish this book, to go out of my way to aid his
memory. But, there are some things that one doesn't wish, for even an enemy, and
if my slight contribution will lift what I am sure is undeserved obloquy from the
name of one who, after all was doing what he thought was right, according to his
lights, I'll feel much better.[16]

In this passage, Dickey clearly suggests that his first intimations of immorality
in Casement came as late as 1920 – the date has been added in the typescript,
creating syntactic awkwardness, but (it seems) chronological precision – and
that his source was a British intelligence officer.[17] (As a US intelligence officer
during the Great War, he can hardly have wholly missed the *cause célèbre* of
1916.) That the setting for his initiation into the mystery was a Pall Mall club

16 NLI, MS 13,078 (8). Dickey will remain an enigma until the de Valera papers, recently
transferred from the Franciscan Library in Killiney to University College Dublin, are fully
accessible. The preservation of his letter to Gwynn among the Casement archives in NLI raises
the issue as to whether Gwynn ever received it.

17 Wright had been a translator with the Supreme War Council, and published *At the Supreme
War Council* (London: Nash, 1921) and *Portraits and Criticisms* (London: Nash & Grayson, 1925).
Though he discusses Birkenhead and Reading (both of whom were involved in the prosecution
of Casement) there is no reference to the trial. Dickey's recollection of time's ebb and flow is
unreliable here as elsewhere. Viscount Gladstone's description of Wright as 'a liar and a coward'
tempers one's acceptance of him as a reliable informant. See Charles Mallet, *Herbert Gladstone: A
Memoir* (London: Hutchinson, 1932), pp. 299–301.

gives one some clue to his own privileged social and economic status, quite different from Casement's. Indeed, it was in such pleasure grounds of the British upper class that the rumours of a perverted diary had been originally circulated.

Why none of this was mentioned in 1929 when Dickey was writing up (one version of) his conversation with Casement about South American perversion remains unexplained. There are other problems. From 1920 to the reading of Gwynn's book in (or after) 1930 cannot easily be accommodated with a casual 'not very long after', for at least ten years elapsed. To send Gwynn this account of progressive enlightenment about the blackguarding campaign seems obtuse, for no one was better placed than Gwynn to measure the gap between 1920 and his own book. Finally, Dickey's undisguised animosity towards Casement is not wholly explicable in terms of Great War politics and the Irishman's Germanism. Why then should Dickey 'feel much better' if Casement is cleared of a sexual immorality imputed twenty years earlier? The observation about 'Casement himself' being homosexual could be read as pointing to Dickey or Wright (or both) also being homosexual. Had Dickey been, in some treacherous fashion and at whatever distance, involved in the imputing?

The communication with Gwynn was essentially private, though there may have been an intention to lead Gwynn into some more extensive reiteration or revision of his views. In May 1938, Dickey swore a twelve-page affidavit much of it simply culled from *Misadventures of a Tropical Medico*. In one significantly new passage, Dickey described how in September 1911, Casement had received a letter from Arthur Conan Doyle inquiring about sexual practices in South America. As a consequence, 'For at least the next half hour, perhaps even three quarters, I recited instance upon instance of sexual perversion among the Indians. As I dictated Sir Roger copied word for word into his notebook' – bound in black with yellowish pages. Casement 'filled several pages'.[18]

This is a much more dramatic account of the two men's discussion of sexual perversions in South America, wholly without any distracting reference to Africa. Conan Doyle's role is now crucial, for his letter prompts and hence justifies the evidence spoken and recorded. The notebook has acquired a very specific appearance, which is likely to render the account convincing. Unfortunately no one has ever discovered this notebook among either Casement's or Doyle's papers, nor does Casement's diary (though it frequently

18 NLI, MS 17,601 (3), pp. 7–9. Homosexuality was a conventional mode of existence in certain areas of remote Peru (to go no further) and Dickey's use of the term 'perversions' is questionable; for a fairly recent account, see Tobias Schneebaum, *Keep the River on Your Right* (London: Cape, 1970).

mentions Dickey) record an extraordinary conversation. Between *Misadventures of a Tropical Medico* (which nowhere mentions this striking incident) and the first writing up of the incident, there had died the one man who might have confirmed it – Doyle.[19] Forty-five minutes of dictation might have resulted in two or three thousand words ('several pages') of sexual description but could hardly have constituted the dossier of depravity which was alleged to encumber Casement's private records.

By November 1938, the intrepid explorer was in touch with Joe McGarrity seeking funds for his book. In curiously slack terms for a doctor, he reported that Maloney was now 'a very sick man . . . he has developed some infection of the throat, and he looks worse than I have ever seen him'. Within less than a month, however, Dickey was under Maloney's medical supervision, and taking a rest cure of five to six weeks.[20] Who was seeking advice from whom? A related mystery surrounds the whereabouts today of Maloney's extensive pre-1936 writings on Casement. Strikingly absent even in carbon copy form in the NLI, they may have been absorbed without trace into Dickey's care. For a non-professional writer in his late sixties, the undertaking of a Casement biography was no light burden – as Dickey knew nothing of Irish affairs, apart from excessive drinking. We may wonder if the undertaking is not related to the demise (or transfer) of Maloney's longer project. Ghost or no ghost, Dickey's biography was never published, though work-in-progress was evidently reported to Eamon de Valera. This fate may explain its non-publication, for at no point can one discover de Valera actively advancing detailed inquiries into his dead comrade's life.

As with Ben S. Allen, personal finances complicate the matter. Between May and November, McGarrity paid $1,500 to Dickey who had also borrowed $100 from Maloney. This income was additional to whatever Dickey's employer – never named – paid him by way of salary. Cheerfully reporting the Graystone Press's scathing opinion of his efforts – too much Inca history – Dickey persisted with his task as biographer. It was a lucrative undertaking for one who had once expressed hostility towards Casement whose life he now wrote to order. Maloney was kept in the dark about McGarrity's financial

---

19 A considerable portion of Conan Doyle's papers are still (2002) inaccessible, owing to a legal dispute as to ownership. However, as Doyle did not advance this defence in 1916 it is reasonable to conclude that he did not have the basis for so doing.

20 H. S. Dickey to J. McGarrity, 30 Nov. and 25 Dec. 1938 (NLI, MS 17,443), the latter written from The Lotos Club, New York.

involvement, and the Philadelphian took philosophically the endless post-ponement of Dickey's final delivery of a typescript.[21] (A cousin dies, an old friend falls ill, a trip to Florida cannot be avoided.) In 1937 de Valera's declared opinion was that 'Roger Casement's reputation is safe in the affections of the Irish people'.[22] And so it has remained.

21   Dickey to McGarrity, 30 Nov. 1938 (NLI, MS 17,443).

22   Mitchell (ed.), *Amazon Journal*, pp. 35, 21. Mitchell cites de Valera MS 1,334 (as numbered while these papers were preserved in the Franciscan Library, Killiney, Co. Dublin), but gives no indication as to whether the evidence is a letter from Dickey or some independent source. No biography has been traced in the de Valera Papers which are currently being recatalogued in UCD. I am grateful to Dr Seamus Helferty of the UCD Archives Department for his assistance on this point.

EIGHT

AN ORIENTALIST FANTASIA

ABOUT OTHER NORMANDS BEHIND THE DEFENCE

Let the Volsces
Plough Rome and harrow Italy; I'll never
Be such a gosling to obey instinct, but stand
As if a man were author of himself
And knew no other kin.

SHAKESPEARE, *Coriolanus* V, iii 32–6

—

FICTION AS REALISM

It is a long way from the concerns of de Valera in 1937 to the world of Gustave Flaubert, the master of French realist fiction, and it is difficult to see how any helpful encounter with Roger Casement could be expected *en route*. Nevertheless, in methodological terms it may be useful to look to literary as well as political history, for the Casement problem is centred upon relations between the imagination and the world. Furthermore, the author of *Madame Bovary* (1857) and the framer of Ireland's new Constitution were alike concerned with provincial realities, seeking to understand the possibilities for moral action amid circumscribing inanities. The story of Emma Bovary's indiscretions and extravagances is accompanied by a running commentary – or running sore – personified in the grotesquely blind beggar who dogs her carriage. When he removed his hat, 'he revealed where his eyelids should have been a pair of gaping holes all stained with blood. The flesh was shredded into red ribbons, discharging matter which had congealed in green scabs down to his nose.'[1] This is a virulent reality deceitful Emma – 'the best wife in Normandy' – cannot face, and instead she accumulates useless objects in any attempt to turn latter-day Yonville (=Yawnville?) into a bourgeois Babylon.

---

1   Gustave Flaubert, *Madame Bovary*, trans. Alan Russell (Harmondsworth: Penguin, 1983), p. 278.

This recourse to sentimental orientalism is directly related to Emma's inability to confront the horrors around her. Or rather, it provides her with an unreality which, for the time being, keeps death, disease and her own delusions at bay. In Thomas Mann's *Death in Venice* – written in the year Casement's Putumayo report was published – a similar juxtaposition of self-delusion and general decay is examined. This time the sexual register is homosexual, or at least homo-erotic, as Gustav Aschenbach fantasises about the boy Tadzio in a city enduring a cholera epidemic which, for commercial reasons, it will not publicise. As with Emma, Gustav is moved towards death against a general condition of human suffering, but the individual in each case resorts to extremes of fantasising which compound his and her crisis. Listening recently to the exposition of Ignes Sodré on these themes, I was struck by the parallel with the non-fictional Casement exposed to monstrous human suffering and concomitant human violence.[2] Just as the characters in Flaubert's and Mann's fiction eroticise objects, images and incidents in a self-defeating escalation so Casement is driven to lavish desire upon those whom he sees brutalised. And while Emma sought to build Babylon from the resources of Rouen's shops, so Gustav visioned a sexual utopia at odds with the real city to which he moved – 'he saw it, saw a landscape, a tropical swampland under a cloud-swollen sky, moist and lush and monstrous, a kind of primeval wilderness of islands, morasses and muddy alluvial channels; far and wide around him he saw hairy palm-trunks thrusting upwards from rank jungles of fern . . .'.[3]

But Casement actually saw that landscape. And endured, however damaged, however unable to recognise the symbolic nature of his predicament.

EFFECTS WITHOUT CAUSES

A primary intention in writing this book has been to explore the structure and rationale of Maloney's Forgery Theory – and to attempt that, irrespective of the results which forensic examination of the Black Diaries would produce in

2   Mrs Sodré spoke at a symposium in the London Institute of Psycho-Analysis on 23 Feb. 2002. Her title, drawn from Milton's *Paradise Lost*, was 'Imparadis's in hell' which uncannily echoed Walter Hardenberg's *The Devil's Paradise* (1912), proofs of which Casement took to the Putumayo as evidence of atrocity.

3   Thomas Mann, *Death in Venice and Other Stories*, trans. David Luke (London: Secker, 1990), p. 199.

2002. There has always also been a tacit assumption that a broader interpretative framework must ultimately be called into existence if the complex
cultural phenomenon conveniently labelled 'Casement' is to be understood.[4]
A further part of such a framework can be derived from the study of other
Europeans who spent extended periods of time in tropical climates and
conditions of very great stress – anthropologists, explorers, missionaries etc. In
similar fashion, forensic examination has a larger scientific context. Many
disciplines may be drawn upon to interpret its findings, and these cannot
regarded as transparent or final beyond the very specific terms upon which
Audrey Giles conducted her examination of the Black Diaries, part of the
White Diary, a large file of Casement correspondence for 1903, 1910 and
1911 – but not of course the Buff Diary. Like the Buff Diary, the concepts
by which we consciously or unconsciously try to make sense of the world do
not submit to spectroscopy.

Nor is the confusion which surrounds, and informs, *The Forged Casement
Diaries* wholly susceptible to textual analysis, because some of it arises from –
quite plainly – blankness, silence, the absence of words, the total absence of
the author as image. In this regard, Maloney's project is only an extreme
example, for any topic of historical inquiry will at some point present limits
and boundaries to the most determined investigator. But the limitations
imposed by one mode of historical inquiry do not invalidate all others; on the
contrary, they constitute a challenge to our preconceptions. An exhaustive
trawling through documents may ultimately be justified in a quite different
context. The absences, or near-absences, can be rendered articulate if the concepts upon which the inquiry is based are themselves subjected to scrutiny.

Among the detailed allegations contained in Roger Casement's official
report on the South American rubber trade, one name had recurred with
disturbing frequency. The most accessible text of the report is, ironically, to
be found in the piratical *Black Diaries* (Paris, 1959) where (in substance) it
appears interleaved with the pages of Casement's 'degenerate' record of his
own activities in 1910.[5] Prior to this exposé of the diaries' authenticity, the

---

4   Although Teresa Brennan makes no reference to Casement, or indeed to any possible specific
focus of enquiry, her *History After Lacan* (London: Routledge, 1993) is rich in methodological and
conceptual insight. See Chapter 11 below for a more detailed response.
5   See Peter Singleton-Gates and Maurice Girodias (eds), *The Black Diaries: An Account of Roger
Casement's Life and Times with a Collection of his Diaries and Public Writings* (Paris: Olympia, 1959),
pp. 220–308 (versos only); references to Normand occur on pp. 236–8, 254–8, 260, 274, 282, 294.

more ingenious explanation of the unnatural writings linked to the prisoner in 1916 was to attribute them ultimately to Armando Normand. The name had not emerged immediately as part of a refutation by Casement's friends, as they strove to save him from the gallows. It did however feature prominently in Maloney's argument, published to miss the twentieth anniversary of Casement's execution.

Though the Normand Defence is no longer openly maintained by the vindicators of Casement's virtue, it deserves attention as a historical phenomenon in itself. In strictly conceptual terms, the action attributed to Casement is categorically similar to that of the apprentice artist working within the Victorian academy context – he is a copyist. A recurrent anxiety in both the general practice of art and the specific act of transcribing the sadist's words fixes on unconscious identification between subject and object as an unthinkable motif, because it amounts to an annihilation of the self. This may sound suddenly philosophical in the midst of ordinary historical plodding, but it is wholly in keeping with concerns raised by participants in the 1936 controversy.

As Alfred Noyes suggested, the idea that Casement might have copied another man's diary was flattering neither to his gentlemanly honour nor to his astuteness as a would-be accuser: an un-Irish stratagem. Nevertheless, Bulmer Hobson and P. S. O'Hegarty committed themselves to the Defence, and had little difficulty in persuading Maloney to adopt it. It even shimmers through the instability of Dr Dickey's several accounts of Casement's interest in sexual deviancy though – it might be noted – as one who had actually trodden a few of the same jungle paths as Normand and indeed worked for the same employer, the Tropical Medico never named the name.

At the time of the Putumayo report, Armando Normand's liability for atrocities was acknowledged by the authorities in Bolivia and Peru and reported in *The Times*. 'The Bolivian Minister informs Reuter's Agency that he has received a telegram from the President of the Bolivian Republic stating that Normand [*sic*], who figures so prominently in Sir Roger Casement's report on the Putumayo, has been captured by the Bolivian police and handed over to the Peruvian authorities.' The following day, the same paper pursued the story: 'The man Armando [*sic*] Normand mentioned in Sir Roger Casement's report on Putumayo is now in custody at Lima, and will be sent to Iquitos to be tried.' The two-stage release of the prisoner's full name mimics a construction of his role as one of many perpetrators of the violence detailed in the report. The presence of so many names, and now the highlighting of this obscure name, stands in contrast to the concentrated attention given to King Leopold in Casement's earlier account of 'red rubber' atrocities in the Congo. As if to emphasise the consistency of Casement's humanitarian work, the next news paragraph in *The Times* announced that 'On the Foreign Office Vote, which will be taken in the House of Commons today, Sir Edward Grey's chief topic will be the affairs of the Congo.'[6] There, however, the question of bringing Normand to justice disappeared from view.

While Casement's biographers have been content to assign this disappearance to corruption in the police and legal systems of South America, other issues remain equally undisturbed. In 1912, nobody in the Foreign Office was concerned with the possible causes of Normand's extremely violent behaviour. If British subjects had been killed, maimed or otherwise injured, then it was enough that the law should move against the alleged offender, without reference to motivation or cause. Indeed a Board of Trade memorandum noted with some embarrassment that 'Sir Roger Casement was only enabled to conduct his investigations because of the suggestion that certain coloured British subjects were being ill-treated in Peruvian territory, the fact being rather that these coloured British subjects, who were employees of the Company assisted in the illtreatment of the natives.'[7] Yet it was clear that the culprits were by no means all of them black – Andreas O'Donnell, who (to Casement's disquiet) was of Irish origin, was even arrested but managed to elude justice by a timely writ of *habeas corpus* in the Barbadan courts.

No universal sense of human rights underpinned the official inquiries, though something very close to that concept certainly informed Casement's report. The encompassing sense of outrage which Casement voiced, implying a shared and equal humanity, had not always been his hallmark. Writing to Lord Terence Blackwood in March 1908 shortly after his first arrival in South America, the new consul had spoken of 'hideous cross breeds . . . a very large admixture of native blood . . . the resultant human compost is the nastiest form of black-pudding you have ever sat down to'.[8] Happily, these

6   *The Times*, 28 May 1913, p. 7 col. f; 29 May 1913, p. 8 col. d.

7   See BT 58/44/cos/3637 for the memo dated 2 Oct. 1912.

8   Quoted in Roger Sawyer, *Casement the Flawed Hero* (London: Routledge, 1984), p. 70. Jeffrey Dudgeon, in his yet-to-be-published gay biography cited Casement's altering views on the future Home Secretary, Herbert Samuel (1870–1963), who, in 1905, was 'a kindred spirit' but by 1914 had become 'an Asiatic half caste or half-bred Jew'. If such utterances were found to be more than incidental instances of spleen, then Casement's sympathy for race-pure people in the jungle becomes a kind of racism in itself, of a kind which ultimately resulted in South African apartheid.

The German authorities produced postcards depicting (certain suitable) aspects of life in their prisoner-of-war camps for use by the prisoners in communicating with home. A picture of the Catholic Chapel at Limburg (which Casement visited) shows little distinctive imagery while one of Giessen (which he did not visit) displays a wealth of Gaelic lettering, indicative of some Irish nationalist feeling. The altar may have been thus decorated by prisoners after the 1916 insurrection.

(B. Britland Papers (IWM, Department of Documents))

As a painter and worker in black and white, Harry Kernoff
(1900–74) was a distinctive figure on the Irish artistic scene
throughout the middle decades of the twentieth century. Born
in London of continental Jewish background, he was decidedly
a 'man of the left', designer of a masthead for *The Irish Workers'
Voice* in the early 1930s. His woodcut of Casement is one of a
series devoted to Irish political figures, and its suggestion of a
tropical forest backdrop does not conceal a Mephistophelean
dimension to the central image.

Dr Maloney Edinburgh

Supplied by Kevin Haley of Queensland, Australia, this is the only verifiable visual image of W. J. Maloney so far traced. (A press photograph of the Dolphin Hotel dinner – see pp. 66–7 – may feature him as an unnamed foreground figure, though there is no other evidence of his presence on that occasion.) Patrick McCartan certainly had access to an earlier photograph of Maloney, which he did not like, in March 1936, his source being a Seamus O'Doherty of Claude Road, Drumcondra, Dublin.

The statue of Seán Russell (1893–1940) is located in Fairview Park, Dublin. Inscriptions on the plinth include a list of republicans who died in action (or were executed by Irish governments) closely resembling that in Austin Clarke's poem, 'The Last Republicans'. ('Last' in this context usually comes to mean 'latest' rather than 'final'.)

This confident photograph of Herbert Spencer Dickey (1876–1948) is one of many to be found in his *Misadventures of a Tropical Medico* (1929) in which he comes close to declaring Roger Casement insane in 1911.

By permission of the British Library (BL, 10482.bb.17).

A late image of Benjamin Shannon Allen, taken from an alumni magazine (*Mills Quarterly*, Aug. 1959). The following year, he travelled from California to inspect the newly released Black Diaries in London. While noting the absence of what he had been shown in 1916 – the Buff Diary – he declined to declare the material forged.

The London-based painter, Ernest Normand (1856–1923), painted *Bondage* in 1895, by which time Casement had already visited the Belgian Free State, met Joseph Conrad, and begun to acquire the detailed familiarity with conditions there which later informed his 1903 report.

(Royal Institution of Cornwall)

Bia. Monrovia.   _15_

Keri Kamara.   1

m ~~chains~~ Timang boy
Came himself a year ago
from Bonda looking for
~~souri.~~ M. Bathro
Chain for Bon.
Djara ~ Monrovia

2 Atimi Accraman   } not
Came himself.   } in chains
3 Sonde Came himself   }
Signature..... Accraman

No.   Date
From   To
Place   Place
Despatch   h.   m.   M Receipt   h.   m.   M

Casement's notes on conditions of labour in the Congo Free State
frequently recorded the use of chains. This page additionally
illustrates his practice of revisiting and annotating his own diaries.

(PRO, HO 161/1)

This entry in the 1910 diary records an episode in Casement's sexual relationship with Joseph Millar Gordon (known as Millar). The evidence of re-inscription, the use of various writing instruments, the attempted return to moments of emotional pleasure, are all evident here. Note in particular the large X with which he retrospectively identified occasions of sexual activity, perhaps to assist him in quick consultation of his diary.

(PRO, HO 161/3)

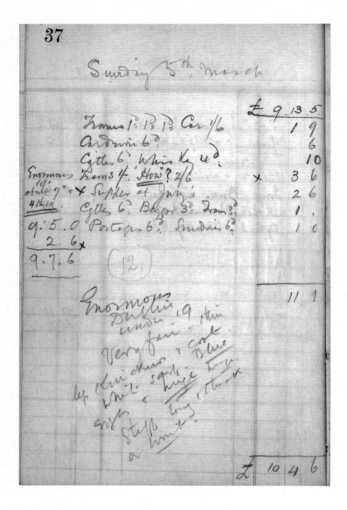

The last item in the Black Diaries series is a ledger, containing
annotated expenses for the year 1911. On line 4 of the text,
'"How"?' is Casement's code-name for a youth whom he had
previously done sexual business with. The layout of this page,
with diagonal writing in the lower portion, illustrates some of
the easier problems confronting a would-be editor of the diaries.
The number 12, lightly inscribed and enclosed in a circle,
appears to be a tally of sexual encounters; its position and
texture suggest a retrospective calculation.

(PRO, HO 161/5)

cannibalistic metaphors did not endure. Defending native peoples three years later, Casement aligned himself with a quasi-aboriginal purity threatened by intrusive breeding as well as aggressive exploitation. The psychology of his final alignment with the victims of processes at once exterminating and procreative deserves close attention on some other occasion.

If the labourers mutilated and killed by Normand earned Casement's sympathy by their unsullied wild passivity, they earned official significance in London only if they (or at least some of them) were British subjects. The alleged multiple murderer was sought irrespective of whether greed or insanity might feature in a subsequent explanation of his conduct. The Peruvian Amazon Company was, of course, registered in London: legal purism conveniently dissolved this uncomfortable fact by emphasising the exceptional character of Normand's behaviour. Greed was to be regarded as a personal vice, never as a systematic feature of industrialisation, wild farming, or Capitalism itself. The possibility that Normand was mad – which Casement seemed to discount – only served to underscore the untypical character of his behaviour and so further exonerate the system.

At the time Casement recognised that national definition was bound up with the manoeuvres of capital. In his White Diary, he exclaimed, 'And where is the Law and Authority of Peru in this region that this British Company has asserted to be in supreme existence here?'[9] Insofar as the systematic brutality of the Peruvian Amazon Company in 1910–11 took place in a world market which was rapidly changing – from the harvesting of wild rubber to the development of cultivated plantations – then the conduct identified in Normand could additionally be understood as a temporary phenomenon, and marginalised even further. In such a context, personal greed acquired the same 'wildness' which characterised the resources upon which it fed. These resources were not simply rubber trees in the forest, they included the indigenous peoples required to gather the crop. In such an argument, Normand becomes a vehicle for a covert libelling of entire peoples as themselves murderous, violent, cruel, and so undeserving of any general protection. A good deal of capital could be made from the stigmatisation of Normand, especially if he remained wholly

---

9   NLI, MS 1622 f. 22. Norman Thomson argued that the registration of Arana's company in London was not just a financial stroke, but intended to force the recognition of certain international frontiers in a manner favourable to Peru. Thomson, it should be noted, published on behalf of the Colombian government. See his *Colombia and Peru in the Putumayo Territory* (London: Thomson, [1914]).

out of view, a near-absence, simultaneously a personification and a non-person. The White Diary – which was not lost amid British official pronouncements – endangered this sequestration of Normand from view.

The suspicion of insanity raises different issues. Quite distinct from lucrative amoralism, fundamental psychological derangement is audible in Richard Collier's descriptions of Normand as 'insane' and 'crazed'.[10] Although Collier was a populariser, writing late in the day, he knew members of the Hardenburg family and perhaps may be relied upon for this detail. It had been Walter Hardenburg's unpublished accounts of the Putumayo atrocities which served as Casement's rough guide when he went out in 1910 on the Foreign Office's behalf. But the American had repeatedly named the villain as Norman [sic]; his editor retained this spelling in Hardenburg's text and simultaneously reprinted parts of Casement's report which gave the name as Normand.[11] In the pages of *The Devil's Paradise*, a degree of nominal instability afflicts a central actor in the vile proceedings. It is as if agreement as to his identity were negotiable, that is, avoidable. It is tragically ironic that Casement should have insisted on what appears to be the more precise or full version of the name, for no sooner had the consul completed his investigation than he divested himself of his imperial role and commenced on a course of political reorientation which quickly led *him* to be regarded as mentally unstable. In 1913, he was an Irish cultural nationalist in defiance of his family origins and professional training; by 1915 he was residing in Berlin in wartime alliance with Britain's enemies. A year later, he was executed in London for treason and his character blackened by a whispering campaign alleging unnatural sexual practices on a grand scale.

It is not Normand alone, but his accuser, who is 'crazy'. To add to the irony of this duplication, Casement found himself regarded as insane (or nearly so) by some of his own friends and supporters. Their concern focused on experiences and behaviour pre-dating the conversion to militant nationalism,

10   Richard Collier, *The River that God Forgot* (London: Collins, 1968), pp. 157, 141.

11   The distinction between a Normand spelling and a Norman spelling is maintained in a recent collection of documents focused on the Putumayo, though once again it is through republication of material by Casement that the longer form of the name is introduced. See Augusto Gómez et al. (eds), *Caucherias y Conflicto Colombo–Peruana: Testimonios 1904–1934*. Bógota: Disloque, 1995. The collection includes a short piece by H. S. Dickey (first published 1921) in which neither Casement nor Normand is mentioned. At the time of original publication, Dickey was described as a Major in the Military Intelligence Division of the US Reserve Corps.

and relied on descriptions of Casement's own mental condition after he had been exposed to the evidence of sadistic brutality in the Company's management of labour. The context in which the discussion of his sanity occurred was defined by his trial, and thus, by his political activity; his friends' efforts were devoted to saving him from the scaffold. But the evidence to which they looked was drawn from the period immediately after Casement's saturation in the Putumayo inquiry. The kinds of violence alleged of Normand might arise from an extreme mental disorder in the perpetrator, but might also give rise to very different kinds of disorder in those confronted with the evidence.

The convergence of two such contrasting men in the notoriously difficult term 'mad' could be traced in various ways. For his political change of heart, Casement paid with his life after a trial before judge and jury. For his many acts of homicide, torture and extortion, Normand appears to have suffered nothing more than a few days' (protective?) detention. Though convicted of treason, Casement died as a consequence of his sexual as well as political offensiveness. His homosexuality – never mentioned in court – was used to alienate potential admirers of his humanitarianism and unblemished public character. Normand, in contrast, had been shown by Casement to have been an extremely violent heterosexual, who commandeered women for sexual gratification and mutilated the genitals of male prisoners – to say no more.

In a narrative where irony has already been hyperactive, one can only marvel at the turn of events which occurred in the 1930s. When Casement's 'unnatural' diary or diaries were alluded to, they had been explained by some of his defenders in 1916 as transcripts which he had made in seeking evidence against those whose brutal conduct he was recording for the Foreign Office. This had been Nannie Dryhurst's role, assisted by Sidney Olivier. Twenty years later in 1936, this unlikely proposition had crystallised into a dogma, a semi-divine mystery. Normand's perverted diary existed; but only in Casement's handwriting and thus it had been used by the British authorities to destroy his chances of a reprieve. In some deluded and spectral region, Casement and Normand were now identical. Maloney's role was to rescue his hero from a conundrum partly of Maloney's own making.

A NAME IN SHORT SUPPLY

It is striking that none of Casement's biographers, vindicators or other commentators have looked beyond the brute facts of murder, mutilation, rapacity, starvation, terror and torture in the Putumayo. As far as Casement is their focus, his efforts to put an end to violent exploitation are of greater significance than the anaysis of an entire economy or the prosecution of one or more murderers. This priority of the desired result over systematic or individual culpability leads to paradox. Undocumented by any court of law, Normand becomes 'the personification of evil', a phrase which oddly discounts any complex sense of personality. While Hardenburg's book title – *The Devil's Paradise* – was well chosen to attract public attention in 1912, at another level it removed Normand from rational discourse and forensic inquiry. It was as if Normand had invented himself in the one part of the globe which he ruled absolutely.

To the best of my knowledge, Casement never claimed that Normand was subject to British law by being himself British. On the contrary, he referred loosely to him as a Peruvian or Bolivian on at least one occasion. There is, however, an element of ambiguity in another remark that 'even Peruvian white men said to me [i.e. Casement] that Normand had done things that none of the others had done'.[12] Does this assign Normand to the category of Peruvian white men or, in contrast, mark him off from that group? Some of the loudest declarations of his British origins were uttered by his boss, Julio Cesar Arana, at the London inquiry.[13] Uncertainty as to his nationality may have assisted Normand in eluding justice when the Bolivians handed him over to the Brazilians, as reported by Reuter's correspondent. Yet Casement's comments on Normand, whom he met on several extended occasions and with whom he spoke at some length, imply that the latter was a European rather than a South American (though the distinction cannot be regarded as an absolute one). They evidently spoke in English, and the promptness with which Casement noted Normand's appearance suggests that there were no barriers of exotic

12 Quoted in Geoffrey Parmiter, *Roger Casement* (London: Barker, 1936), p. 75.
13 The Peruvian Amazon Company was registered in 26 Sept. 1907: the directors were Abel Alarco, Julio Cesar Arana, Baron de Sousa-Deiro, J. Russell Gubbins, Sir John Lister Kaye, T. F. Medina, and Henry M. Read. Lizardo Arana was a director by Sept. 1910. The Company's first secretary was A. Vernon Smith, succeeded by J. Golding, with offices in Salisbury House, EC.

physiognomy to be crossed before describing 'a little being, slim, thin, and quite short – say 5' 7" – and with a face truly the most repulsive I have ever seen... perfectly devillish in its cruelty and evil'.[14] By naming him repeatedly in his report to Sir Edward Grey, Casement gave the impression that Normand could be made subject to British justice, declaring that 'if anyone on the Putumayo deserves punishment this man should be made an example of'. As we know, not enough happened to advance this possibility. But did Casement know more about Normand than he committed to his reports? Even the White Diary, which will be more revealing about Normand than the 1936 Forgery Theory ever conceded, managed to record the fact of one particular conversation between the two men but to omit its substance. In November 1910, Casement was profoundly disturbed by the prospect of travelling down the Putumayo on the same steamer with Normand, and begged a Company official to send the repulsive little being on a different boat. These are not the reactions of a powerful diplomat in command of his feelings.[15]

It is therefore advisable to look closely at the near-absence, conceding that the national and parental origins of Armando Normand are as yet unknown. This can be attempted through two routes – first (in this chapter) by means of external research, second (in chapter 11) by an analysis of Casement's own 'white' diary. So – to the facts. If Richard Collier is right in assessing the villain to have been 22 years of age at the time of Casement's investigations (or in 1913 when Julio Cesar Arana gave evidence in London), then Normand would have been born towards the end of the 1880s – say between 1885 and 1890. Casement, however, alleged that Normand had been brutally active since 1904, which might push a date of birth back to 1880. He is variously said to have been educated at an English public school and/or given a commercial education in the East End of London.[16] Beyond this, nothing but vague claims as to his Bolivian nationality are recorded, and these may reflect his local affiliation rather than his country of birth.

---

14 Roger Casement, diary entry for 17 Oct. 1910; see NLI, MS 13,085/6 (the White Diary); quoted by B. L. Reid, *The Lives of Roger Casement* (New Haven: Yale University Press, 1976), p. 113.

15 Parmiter, *Roger Casement*, pp. 75, 82. The Peruvian Amazon Company's near monopoly in the region is reflected in its ownership of fifteen river-steamers and the Iquitos tramway system.

16 See 'The Crimes of Armando Normand', the fifth chapter of G. Sidney Paternoster, *The Lords of the Devil's Paradise* (London: Stanley Paul, 1913), pp. 92–116.

Quite apart from variations of spelling, there is no guarantee that the name used in South America was in any sense an inherited one.[17] It is not unfamiliar in South America – witness the eminence of Enrique Normand in Peruvian legal circles at the beginning of the twenty-first century, whose company specialises in (wait for it) natural resources. Naturally, France has also known many bearers of the name, amongst whom one might note Charles Pierre Normand (1765–1840), whose *La Troie d'Homère* was republished in Paris at late as 1895, and also the novelist Suzanne Normand (born 1902) whose non-literary publications include a book on Yugoslavia under Marshal Tito (1954). Another exotic was Charles William Blyth Normand (born 1889) who published a book on *The Climate and Weather of Iraq* (1919) in Baghdad. The American comedienne, Mabel Normand (1892–1930), was of French-Canadian descent: none of her siblings can be identified in Casement's villain. Today Roger Normand is policy director of the Center for Economic and Social Rights, based in New York and critical of US policy towards Iraq.

Given this diversity, the only practical place to begin a search for the villain's origins would be among English Normands. Immediately any such narrowing of focus is introduced, bearers of the name become relatively few in number. The practical imperative serves a higher abstract purpose, allowing reflection on the metropolitan culture supported by enslavement – the pneumatic bliss of Eliot's *The Waste Land* was rubber-based. It would be misleading to assume that a search for Normand is merely academic positivism fuelled by a desire to fill in gaps and multiply facts. To know in some reflexive way who Normand was, where he came from and why, to re-place him (for a moment) in a social and cultural world which he had abandoned for butchery in the Putumayo, would be to advance our understanding of Roger Casement, just as an acknowledge-ment of the consul's racial distaste for half-breeds is part of the larger picture.

But where to begin? *The Times* offers a few – remarkably few – leads from which one can build up more complex histories:

1   Amand Normand, a teacher of languages in Brighton, was listed for a bankruptcy hearing on 18 March 1863 at the County Court in that town – see issue of 4 March 1863. He died in 1880, aged 54, and hence must have been born *c.* 1826. No will has been traced.

17 Local newspapers seem to have consistently given the name as Norman, which may reflect pronunciation; Normand's certificate as a bookkeeper, displayed in his living room at Matanzas, provided Casement with the longer spelling.

2 The obituary for the somewhat-known painter Ernest Normand (1856–1923) appeared on 27 March 1923, p. 15. He died of heart failure, aged 66.[18]

3 Ernest Normand's wife was also a painter (a better one), named Henrietta Emma Rae (1856–1928, daughter of Thomas Burbey Rae and his wife Anne Eliza Louisa, *née* Graves). Her obituary appeared on 28 March 1928, p. 11.[19]

4 Mr Arthur Normand, of Trelyon, St Ives, Cornwall, died on 2 September 1934. He left an estate of just under £20,000, gifting money to the Royal National Lifeboat Association, and the Royal College of Music.[20]

HOLLAND PARK

Of these, the most promising subject of inquiry is the painter whose work displayed an interest in the sexually exotic and in female bondage – themes deriving in part at least from the Flaubert of *Salâmmbo* (1862). The younger son of George Barten Normand (died 1901) and his wife Mary Ann (formerly Craggs), Ernest Normand was born on 10 July 1856. He left England in 1869 to study in Germany at a government school in Gotha and, for a further two years in Augsburg where he concentrated on commercial law. As G. B. Normand's will of 1890 refers to land owned at Fritzlar (in Hesse), a family project may be detected behind the thirteen-year-old's dispatch to Germany. Back home by 1876, he entered his father's City firm but pursued artistic interests at weekends and in the evening. Arthur Fish's description of the family business exceeds the facts. Normand & Reddan had premises near the junction of Old Compton Street and Greek Street, from which the

18 Normand's date of birth has generally been given as 1857, but the registration is unambiguous – 10 July 1856 at No. 7 Hereford Road, in the sub-district of St John Paddington, London. This lies in the registration district known as Kensington, which contained localities of humbler status than the name Kensington suggests. In 1870 a Maria Normand died at the age of eighty.

19 Like her husband's, Henrietta Rae's age has been consistently underestimated: she was born on 30 Dec. 1856 and not in 1859 as stated by Arthur Fish: the place of birth was No. 1 Grove Villas, The Grove, Hammersmith.

20 See issue of 26 Oct. 1934, p. 16. The death in 1872 of Frances Cooper Normand in Truro at the age of fifty-five suggests a Cornish family of this name.

firm traded as 'manufacturers of india rubber balloons and christmas tree deco-rations'.[21] As for the budding artist, the influence of John Pettie (1839–1893) was important in directing Ernest Normand out of Soho into a career as painter. By the early 1880s, he was living in Fitzroy Square, and in 1881 he and Henrietta Rae announced their engagement. In the catalogue for an exhibition of December 1883, Henrietta Rae is listed with an address at 5 Fitzroy Square, where Normand had a taken a studio for them both in 1881.[22]

Ernest Normand married Henrietta Radcliffe Rae on 26 May 1884 in the parish church, Croydon. Though the second forename had changed since the registration of her birth, there is no reason to doubt that she was the same daughter of Thomas Burbey Rae, a civil servant and a minor figure on the outer edges of W. M. Thackeray's literary circle, the friend of minor writers such as Mark Lemon and Dion Boucicault, and secretary of the Whittington Club. This gilt-by-association is fondly recorded by Fish, in the one book devoted to the daughter, while the plainer details of public records indicate that T. B. Rae was clerk to a board of guardians, later a resident in Stock Orchard Crescent, a nondescript North London address. After an initial sojourn in Wright's Lane, Kensington, the young couple moved to Holland Park Road (1886 onwards). In an elaborate studio block beside the home of Valentine C. Princep (1838–1904), other occupants included the painters Herbert Schmalz (1856–1935), Wm Robert Symonds (1851–1934), and [Sir] William Blake Richmond (1842–1921). In this ménage, mild sexual irregularity and ordinary bad taste went hand in hand.

Normand's favourite theme of bondage is already evident in his student work. 'A Palace Yet a Prison' (1884), painted in the year of his marriage, brought in the impressive sum of 300 guineas. The following year he exhibited 'The Bitter Draught of Slavery' also at the Royal Academy, in which a naked white girl clings to the knees of a Negro who in turn points out her attractions to a vaguely Arabic potentate. The Normands suffered a good deal

21   The firm occupied Nos 51, 52 and 54 Old Compton Street, and also No. 41 Greek Street. According to the commercial directories for 1873–4, it also had premises in Birmingham and Sheffield. William Taylor Reddan is listed as the warehouseman, with G. B. Normand presumably conducting the more public side of the business. None of the Board of Trade documentation relating to the Peruvian Amazon (Rubber) Company suggests that any of the Normands were shareholders or directors: see PRO: BY 31/18220/95023 and BT 58/44cos/3637.

22   *Institute of Painters in Oil Colours: A Catalogue of the 1st Exhibition* (Piccadilly: The Graphic, [1883]), p. 53. Rae exhibited 'Shadows of Memory' in this large show, which did not feature any of Normand's work.

of technical criticism even while they achieved popular success, at least that is the explanation subsequently offered for their departure overseas. In 1890, both Ernest and Henrietta studied in Paris under Benjamin Constant and Jules Lefebvre, then Ernest (perhaps alone) paid an extended visit to Morocco in 1891. His uncharacteristic 'An der Schwelle des Lebens' (as the German trade reproduction is named) shows a chronically depressed young man – so much for the Threshold of Life! Normand's continuing preoccupations can be gauged from 'An Alien' (1894), showing a captive white woman standing nude before two (again Arab-looking) men and an impassive slave girl. A picture of 1895, 'Bondage' featuring an entire harem, confirms his regular collocation of sex and slavery. By 1897, his regular 'flying visits' to the orient were the subject of affable comment.[23] Little of his work rose above the level of cluttered pornography.

It was, however, a distinctly racialised, if soft, pornography. The figures invariably conformed to one of a few stereotypes – Arab, Negro or 'White'. In this, they conformed to the imperialism of the day, or at least represented the Near East sphere of British and French imperial activity – India and the Far East lay beyond Normand's brush. If the human landscape was composed of distinct and compartmentalised racial types, the drama in his paintings bespoke a different arrangement. Not separation by race, but congress between the sexes, was implied, with the white female playing the subordinate, if not always submissive role. Yet beyond coitus, division was reinstated; for this was a purely male, purely pleasurable sexuality, without the possibility of generation, of half-breeds. One way to read Normand's art is of course to convert it into a photographic negative, in which one would discern the dominant male White beckoning the black slave girl to his thigh. Yet the *non*-development of this theme anywhere in Normand's art indicates the importance for him of some equation with the submissive role.

In addition to the demi-gods of Rowsley House, Sir Frederick Leighton, Sir John Millais, and G. F. Watts provided an elevated circle for Normand and his wife to move in. Henrietta Rae had also reached public success through 'prentice work in the British Museum's galleries, and her ascent in the art world had been achieved through hard work. Her great success came in 1894,

23 Details drawn from the cuttings preserved in the Witt Library, Courtauld Institute, London, and from Frank Ritter, 'The Art of Ernest Normand', *Art Journal* (1901), pp. 137–41. 'Bondage' is in the Royal Cornwall Museum. See also A. T. C. Platt, *People of the Period* (London, 1897), vol. 2, p. 217. The 'orient' in question may not have been more distant than North Africa.

when 'Psyche Before the Throne of Venus' was deemed one of the wonders of that year's Royal Academy show.[24] Rae's thematic range was more conventionally classical than her husband's, though they were both celebrated painters of the nude. Her 'Loot' (1903) maintained the conjoined imagery of vigorous female nudity and scattered classical relics, in an ambiguous picture which finally assigns the figure neither to the category of loot nor that of looter.

In contrast to her husband's galloping orientalism, Rae also took on conventional portrait commissions. In that idiom, she enjoyed a large practice in Northern Ireland, and regularly visited Belfast where she maintained a studio in the Scottish Provident Buildings. Her subjects there included the Marquess of Dufferin (died 1902), as well as lesser worthies. Though the very model of high liberal diplomacy, Dufferin had been severely embarrassed by the crash of the London and Globe Finance Company at the end of his life.[25] In 1903, Rae's husband exhibited 'The Story Teller', a comparatively well-clad picture of 1896, at the Royal Hibernian Academy. But this seems to have been his Irish debut and swan song; from a date closely associated with Rae's contact with Dufferin (1899), the Normands' fortunes were diverging. She spent more and more time in Belfast, and abandoned the sobriquet 'Mrs Ernest Normand' which had been part of her identity-kit. His productivity declined, while she maintained her new line of business in Ulster portraiture. The impact of modernism virtually obliterated the kind of painting in which the Normands traded, though one might note the exhibition of her 'Echo' in Buenos Aires during 1910. The only readily traced connection between Holland Park and the more astringent artists with whom Yeats and his Irish circle associated involves the daughter of Richmond's favourite model who ran off with Edward Gordon Craig.[26] Princep's adopted daughter, Julia, was the second wife of Leslie Stephen, and the mother of Virgina Woolf.

It is difficult to reconcile Casement's fluid emotional nature with the new aesthetic shortly to emerge from Yeats's collaboration with Craig on one side

24 See Frank Ritter's article on her work in *Art Journal* (1901), pp. 303–7.

25 Frederick Temple Hamilton-Temple Blackwood (1826–1902 1st marquess of Dufferin and Ava) was a major figure in the diplomatic corps, holding ambassadorships successively in St Petersburg, Constantinople, Rome and Paris, as well as serving as Governor General of India. Rae's other Ulster subjects included Sir Daniel Dixon (1844–1907), Henry Musgrave (1829–1922) and Lady Winifred Renshaw and son (1903).

26 See Caroline Dakers, *The Holland Park Circle: Artists and Victorian Society* (New Haven and London: Yale University Press, 1999), p. 217. For Craig's association with Casement's friend, Nannie Dryhurst, see chapter 2 above.

and Ezra Pound on the other – and with Joyce sitting apart. Leaving aside moralistic considerations, Joseph Conrad may have acted on this basis when, in 1916, he signally failed to support the man he had met in the Congo more than twenty years earlier. Certainly Casement was alert to innovations in cultural exchange within the United Kingdom. As he moved closer to Irish nationalism, his literary commitments were expressed partly through enthusiasm for a language, Gaelic, of which he knew little. In keeping with this, his ideal was the local féis, with a concomitant faith in the art of little places, retreats from modernity. Though lacking the scholarship of Douglas Hyde (1860–1949), he too was convinced of the need to de-anglicise Ireland. London was corruption itself, and only a complete break could assuage the insurgent spirit.

In contrast, one notes everywhere in the career of the Normands sustained and useful links with the world of commerce. Both had emerged from the struggling mid-Victorian middle class. Ernest began in trade and never quite painted himself out of its corner. His father had evidently thrived in rubber, moving from Soho offices to a residence in Norwood large enough to accommodate the younger Normands' studio in its grounds. In many ways, the career of Normand senior fits a pattern well described by Arthur Conan Doyle in his Sherlock Holmes stories, that of the London businessman turned suburbanite in retirement. In both its generations, the Normand family demonstrates the economic logic of orientalism, from the manufacture of balloons out of cheap imported rubber, to luxurious (and expensive) depictions of colonial sexuality as an anti-dialectic of oneness and separation. Ideally, if not actually, Armando Normand fits in here, becomes a near-presence.

Henrietta Rae's parents knew better when to die, or at least disappear from view, for she had been a free and enterprising spirit by 1883 when she lived in Fitzroy Square, perhaps co-habiting with her future husband. Successful Victorian painting was big business, and the once-off price paid for a canvas was systematically augmented by the sales of reproduction rights. In Germany, the Berlin Photographic Co. had bought the copyright on her 'Ariadne' as early as 1885, while Hildesheimer & Co. marketed colour prints of other paintings. At home, Messrs H. Graves & Co. held rights to her work. These arrangements provided important souces of income for artists who could never quite afford to step off the treadmill of production. The only monograph devoted to either of them – Fish's book on Rae – was published by a company with proprietorial interests in her work.

Contrary to the impression given in their obituaries, the Normands did have children – a son born on 20 May 1885 at Rowsley House, and a daughter (Florence) born on 21 June 1892 at the same Holland Park Road address. At registration, the first-born was confusingly given his mother's family name (Rae) as his fore- or christian-name, when his father registered the birth.[27] Florence's birth, unusually at the time, was registered by the mother. Other kinds of confusion are, however, minimised among the Normands. Attempts to trace the Armando of Putumayo infamy are assisted by the infrequency of the surname in British records of birth, marriage, and death. Between June 1837 (when publicly accessible registration began) and 1892 (the year Ernest and Henrietta's second child was born) only fourteen infants (apart from theirs) are listed.[28] Frankly, the villain does not feature, at least not under his own forename.

However, the involvement of George Barten Normand in the manufacture of goods from imported rubber, and the enthusiasm of his son for the depiction of female slaves is sufficiently curious to justify further consideration of the latter and his wife. It was between the births of Baby Rae and Florence that the parents left London for the Parisian Latin Quarter, and later to settle at Grez on the road to Nemours (July 1890 onwards). To facilitate this attempted reinvigoration of the parents' artistic genius, the boy was sent somewhere in the English countryside with a nurse. Though the only extensive account of Henrietta Rae's life and work provides no detail implicating the Normands, it is clear that life at Grez was hectic, 'suggestive of a Bohemianism that was somewhat appalling even [*sic*] to Mrs Normand and her husband'. The inn they stayed at 'reeked of an indefinable combination of cheap *caporal* and absinthe' and their sudden return to London was prompted by a sexual scandal involving 'a pale drowned corpse in an outhouse'.

27 Later, the boy acquired a second forename – Princep – in honour of the Indian-born painter. When Rae Princep Normand acted as executor of his uncle's will in 1934, he was described as a 'coal contractor'.

28 For the record these are: George Warren Normand (born in the Strand district of London, 1841); Georgina Maria Normand (the Strand, 1847); Janet Frances Normand (Stepney, 1850); William Frederick Normand (Greenwich, 1850); Arthur Normand (the Strand, 1851); Martha and Mary Normand (twins, St Giles, 1852); Ernest Normand (Kensington, 1856); Louisa Normand (the Strand, 1867); Elise Josephine P. M. Normand (Marylebone, 1890); George Normand (Chorlton, 1890); and William Charles Alfred Normand (St George's, Hanover Square, 1891).

Back in Holland Park Road by June 1892, after their daughter's birth the Ernest Normands moved to Norwood at the suggestion of his father.[29] G. B. Normand built a studio for the couple in the garden of 'Aucklands' (his own home); he owned several houses in the area including 'Tronmaca' where his daughter lived with her husband, W. A. Surridge. In time, Ernest could refer proudly to a Normand Mausoleum in Brookwood Cemetery, but this investment in the future may not have been made during his father's lifetime.

In 1896, the Normands toured Italy and its galleries, though their regular place of annual retreat was Scarborough. The Queen's jubilee in 1897 saw Henrietta Rae installed as president of the Women's Art section of the Victoria Exhibition, a position which presupposes respectability. Her sponsors included [Sir] Charles Holroyd (1861–1917), later the Tate Gallery's first keeper. For some months, the owner of the Doré Gallery provided free space for the couple to display and sell their works, even to the point of claiming the gallery's commission fees. In 1902, Rae fell victim to an unnamed near-fatal illness, from which she was rescued by Henry MacNaughton Jones (1844–1918), her Irish physician best remembered for *Manual of Diseases of Women* (1884).

LONDON, CASEMENT AND THE NORMANDS?

Having arranged these fragments of artistic biography and critical prejudice, one should assess their relevance to the study of Roger Casement in death. Indeed, the question was framed earlier in the chapter – did Casement know more about Armando Normand than he ever committed to his official report or to his private diaries? First, it must be conceded that nothing has been established to link the sadist of Putumayo to Ernest Normand, except their common connection with the rubber trade and to enslavement – informal but hyperactive in Armando's case, formal but only by representation in Ernest's. Normand's wife does provide a more banal link to the diplomatic service on whose behalf Casement investigated Armando Normand's crimes: she twice painted the Marquess of Dufferin whose son and heir – we should now add – was the Foreign Office clerk to whom Casement reported prior to and during his appointment as British consul at Para in 1907–8.[30] The Dufferins were

---

29   Arthur Fish, *Henrietta Rae* (London: Cassell, 1905).

30   Lord Terence Blackwood (1866–1918), 2nd Marquess of Dufferin and Ava from 1902.

Ulster grandees of the grandest kind, and their home at Clandeboye, County Down, was not likely to have attracted the new generation of nationally inclined intellectuals and activists with whom Casement associated on his visits to Ulster. Henrietta Rae's choice of portrait-subjects – her clients – were invariably of the Unionist stripe, mainly businessmen. Yet Belfast was a small place where the cultural nationalists gathering round Casement's friend, Frank Bigger, were well acquainted with such activists as were to be found on the other side. And Casement did acquire paintings in Belfast (probably through the Rodman Gallery), though these were of the local landscape variety.

As our examination of the White Diary will demonstrate, polar opposites constitute a field force, however, at least in the eye of the historian who acknowledges both material and symbolic powers. A more familiar image is to be found in the opening pages of Erskine Childers's novel, *The Riddle of the Sands* (1903), with out-of-season London described in terms of empty streets and clubs temporarily closed. Absence implies an elsewhere and, for Childers, German shipping lanes not the grouse-moors of Scotland demanded attention. The author's social position neatly mediates between that of Casement and his superior, the younger Dufferin. Like Casement, Childers had been effectively orphaned and brought up by relatives, with a subsequently intense attachment to symbolic places – Antrim for Casement, Wicklow for Childers. It is strange that the Barton home in which the author of *The Riddle of the Sands* grew up should lie close to the home of Julius Casement into which young Roger was not invited. Like Dufferin, Childers held the faux-humble position of Clerk (in the House of Commons rather than the Foreign Office) and did so partly by virtue of his family's earlier service to the imperial government. Of the three, two became traitors, the one executed by the government he abandoned, the other by the rebel government he assisted into being.

Childers's London is the metropolis in which Casement never had a permanent home. Instead of title deeds or leases, he was attached through transient and (in some respects) illicit associations – with anarchists, hired typists, landladies, pressmen, rentboys. Viewed historically it is an unexceptional urban landscape, for the Victorian gentleman had long practised the art of living in two worlds – that of the home and the brothel, with his business interests or office commitments acting as a mediating alibi. More recently, a more risky re-enactment of the age-old subterfuges had been exemplified in the trials and punishments of Oscar Wilde. Against this background, the art of the Normands takes on a new light.

The architecture of some latter-day Babylon or suburban kasbah can be read as Carlton Terrace or King Charles Street, with the human figures now fused as a compound image of the imperial theme itself – master and slave; male and female, force, money and gratification. Ernest Normand had begun to exhibit during the heyday of Rider Haggard, and his work followed the sexualisation of empire into a period of diminished confidence, where the Great White Painter is colour-coded into his art as the imminently to be ravished slave girl and as the alien potentate *in negativo* who gestures with a brush-like hand. The *disjecta membra* of Mrs Normand's 'Loot' match the photographs of amputation which the colonial investigator took in the Congo and (later) of the flogged buttocks of children in the Putumayo. Where do Casement's photographs fit into the picture; were they part of his evidence against Leopold II and Armando Normand, or were they (also) trophies in themselves? Consider, for example, this white entry under 18 October 1910 – 'Bustamante hid from us, or tried to. He was taken upstairs with a hankerchief on his bare buttocks. I spoke to several of the men and boys, but all seemed half dazed and wholly frightened, and when I got some of them to stand for their photos they looked as if under sentence of death.'[31]

Death was all pervasive under the sway of Normand and his peers, gross in the manner of its infliction and in the subsequent casual neglect of its victims, dogs often playing the part of undertaker. Casement had faced brutality in the Congo, yet his moral constitution was not that of the hardened traveller. Profoundly moved by the sufferings of native Indians, he also picked up the idiom of their persecutors – of Normand he wrote 'This wretch is only fit for the flogging triangle and then the gallows'.[32] The emotional impact of sustained exposure to the evidences of recent extreme violence, borne often in the company of those responsible, was all the greater on a man who – while regarded as the Foreign Office's strong arm – did not fully measure up socially or professionally in the eyes of the FO itself. Appearing as the knight errant, Casement exactly lacked armour plating. If the 1903 'black diary' is taken as authentic, he had long ago developed a sexual life in which this lack sought to

---

31 Angus Mitchell (ed.), *The Amazon Journal of Roger Casement* (Dublin: Lilliput; London: Anaconda, 1997), p. 265. Roger Sawyer (ed.), *Roger Casement's Diaries: 1910, the Black and the White* (London: Pimlico, 1997), p. 191. César Bustamante was Normand's deputy at one of the rubber-gathering stations; see *ibid.*, p. 98, n. 138.

32 Mitchell (ed), *Amazon Journal*, p. 280; Sawyer (ed.), *Roger Casement's Diaries*, p. 201. This is one of the occasions where Casement explicitly compares Normand and Leopold II.

negotiate with forbidden realities. Photography was not a feature of his hidden life in Dublin, London or Paris, nor indeed of his non-hidden life. But it emerges in prolific and ambiguous form in the tropics.

Some illumination of Casement's predicament can be derived from the private writings of Bronisław Malinowski (1884–1942). In his early days, the Polish anthropologist kept what was posthumously published as *A Diary in the Strict Sense of the Term*. Compiled between 1914 and 1918 – mainly in New Guinea – it plainly records his ill temper, sexual anguish, aggressive feelings towards the natives, and his use of photography, together with much valuable reflection on the problems of the participant-observer. Longing for his Australian fiancée led to visions, and the diarist found he could not 'say that *her real self, as brought home by her letters* is infinitely closer to me than her *Double*. *There is always a process of adaptation.*'[33] Malinowski, then aged thirty-four, was able to deal with the body through the mind, and vice-versa. He also read his fellow Pole's novel of anarchist violence, *The Secret Agent* – 'poor, unnecessary, drawn out'.[34] Clearly, he was familiar with Casement's Congo Report of 1903, for he confides violently to his diary for June 1918, 'I understand all the German and Belgian colonial atrocities'. [35] In due course, Malinowski married Miss Elsie Masson of Melbourne and became a pillar of the social sciences. He had never lived among sadistic torturers and mass murderers. Casement in contrast died on the scaffold above complaints of homosexual excess. The two men shared a commitment to fieldwork, one transforming it into an academic methodology. But the other found his terrain to be littered with objects, images, *disjecta membra*, and damaged human figures which did not succumb to intellectual reflection. Did a further alteration in the emotional significance of such photographs as those of Bustamante and sundry young boys take place between the Congo inquiry and the Putumayo Report, an alteration prompted by the shock of recognition which Norman + d's name inscribed in Casement's diaries, and which led to a heightened eroticisation of objects? Or was Casement well fashioned sexually long before he stepped into Conrad's darkness?

These are questions which Drs Freud and Jung were more competent to address than Drs Maloney and McCartan.[36] Closer to Casement than any of

33 Bronisław Malinowski, *A Diary in the Strict Sense of the Term* (London: Routledge, 1967), p. 178.
34 *Ibid.*, p. 199.
35 *Ibid.*, p. 279.
36 Cf. the work of Ronald Britton and Ignes Sodré.

the four was William Hope Hodgson (1877–1918) whose fiction darkly explored the effects of psychic flaying and consequent exposure of the human soul to hellish images. If there is any validity in the proposed diagnosis of a breakdown suffered by Casement after his prolonged association with the sadism of Normand and the others whom Nevinson wished to hunt down like animals, then the attractions of Irish nationalist politics for the damaged consul will have to be reassessed. The desire for independence from London needs to be examined as an instance of desire as well as a route towards independence.

NINE

MORE ABOUT MALONEY
THAN HE WANTED YOU TO KNOW

Raze out the written troubles of the brain.
SHAKESPEARE, *Macbeth* V, iii

—

The world of the Normands is remote from Irish America. It is difficult to imagine any connection between the lurid confections of Ernest and Henrietta and the monkish chastity of John Devoy – except perhaps to offer the jungle encounter of Casement and Armando Norman + d as an allegory of some conceptual breaks-down or aporias which divide cultural theory from scholarly practice. One further way to summarise these difficulties would be to lay out the photographs Casement took in the Putumayo and to question their place in a spectrum of images ranging from bourgeois orientalist decoration at one end to functionalist legal data at the other.

No photograph of the Great Forgery Theorist has yet been discovered. In this regard, he remains in stark contrast to his hero. Unlike Casement, however, he also eludes biographical summary. Time and again, a line of inquiry turns backwards into the dark. Dr Maloney is more cipher than author, an ambivalent presence at best, and more often an intimidating absence. Nevertheless, some effort at recording the known facts is required, if only to lay bare these grounds for suspicion.

A MODEL STUDENT

Born in Edinburgh on 16 October 1882, the eldest son of Bernard Joseph Maloney (*c.* 1847/8–1923) and his wife, Isabella (*née* MacNees, married 1879), the future theorist came from a family which probably had been Irish a generation or two earlier. The Maloneys may have come to Scotland from County Louth, in north Leinster. Bernard Maloney was a curio and art dealer, and a worshipper in the Sacred Heart congregation.[1] Six children were born to the couple before 1891, William having two elder sisters, and at least three (perhaps four) younger siblings. One other possible brother (born 1885?) may have died in infancy. An 'army' household, in John Devoy's view.

A pupil first at Edinburgh's Catholic School, and later for four years at George Herriot's (very distinguished) school, William Joseph may have acquired part of his secondary education in France though no confirmation of this has been established. From these details, we can assume that his background was financially secure, even comfortable. The Maloneys were emerging from the shadows of ancient prejudice in a nervous bourgeois security. They could boast kinship with Mr F. Henry, a Justice of the Peace in Glasgow who sat on the Catholic Schools Board. Birth registration and educational records consistently give Maloney's Christian names as William Joseph, and no more. 'Marie Alois' may have been picked up in France.

As an undergraduate in the University of Edinburgh's medical school, Maloney was joint Ettles Scholar of his year (1905), having previously won the Wightman Prize (1904) for clinical work.[2] For his MB and ChB finals, he was awarded first class honours. While he was completing his undergraduate course, the Congo controversy visited Edinburgh in the form of a 'monster meeting' held on 15 February 1904.[3] At least two pamphlets were published in the city, rubbishing Congo Reform to the unknown authors' own satisfaction.[4] Catholic spirits in the Scottish capital were buoyant, and the prizewinner was regarded as a model for emulation. A eulogy published in the *Catholic Herald* in the summer of 1905 credited him with the James Scott Scholarship in Midwifery and a Research Scholarship in Pharmacology.[5] Simultaneously, the

1 The communist, C. Desmond Greaves, one of the very few historians who even mention Maloney, describes the latter as the son of an Edinburgh watchmaker; see his *Liam Mellowes and the Irish Revolution* (London: Lawrence & Wishart, 1971), p. 130 n.

2 Information provided by Jean Archibald of the Library, University of Edinburgh, 16 Aug. 2001.

3 See Charles Sarolea, *A propos du rapport Casement sur l'administration du Congo* (Bruxelles, 1904), p. 3. The author was in the audience. Sarolea signed off another pamphlet 'University of Edinburgh, August 1906' – see *The French Revolution and the Russian Revolution: A Historical Parallel and a Forecast* (Edinburgh: Oliver & Boyd), 1906.

4 Anon., *A Complete Congo Controversy Illustrating the Controversial Methods of Mr Morel*, and Anon., *Dr Guinness Self-Refuted: Inconsistency of the Congo Balolo Missionaries*. Both published in Edinburgh through Oliver & Boyd, 1905, both 24 pp. A series title, Congo Pamphlets, appears on the cover of each, suggesting that the topic remained a hot one in the year of Maloney's graduation.

5 *Catholic Herald*, location untraced. I am grateful to Kevin Haley for supplying a cutting either from a regional version of the *Herald* or a similar paper quoting from the *Herald*.

Herald in 1905 was campaigning for the Belgian King Leopold. In these articles Casement scarcely featured, while anonymous wrath was concentrated on E. D. Morel (1873–1925), the Reverend John Harris and the Reverend Grattan Guinness (1835–1910). This neglect of Leopold's principal British critic might prompt reconsideration of the extent to which Casement was recognised as hero of the hour.[6]

Ignoring the disputes to which he would later contribute, Maloney was entered on the Medical Register on 1 September 1905, and proceeded MD in 1907. (His highly commended graduating thesis on infantile diarrhoea ran to two vols.) Interest in this latter condition tends to confirm his claim that, in 1906 he 'became an interne at the Hospital for Sick Children in Great Ormond Street, London'. Later brief reminiscences allude to the influence there of 'Dr. Frederick John Poynton, being comely and gallant . . . armed with hypodermic syringe and vaccine, going forth to slay the dragon of rheumatism.'[7] Maloney is said to have pursued further medical studies in Europe (Paris and Munich) yet, according to *Nisbet's Medical Directory* of 1908, his address was the Royal Infirmary, Bradford, and he was described as 'late H.P.' (house physician) at the Royal Maternity Hospital in his native city. The author of a doctoral dissertation on the history of medicine in Bradford has been unable to confirm his presence.[8]

Two early publications reflect Maloney's continental interests, albeit as translator or facilitator of other people's work.[9] Contrary to claims sometimes

---

6   See for example *Catholic Herald* for 1, 8, 15 and 29 Sept. 1905. For Leopold's manipulation of Catholic opinion in the United States, see Adam Hochschild, *King Leopold's Ghost* (London: Macmillan, 1999), p. 244.

7   W. J. Maloney, 'Foreword' to Leopold Lichtwitz, *Pathology and Therapy of Rheumatic Fever* (London: Heinemann, 1944), p. ix. F. J. Poynton (1869–1943) was a leading paediatrician with a special interest in rheumatic fever.

8   See C. Alvin, 'Medical Treatment and Care in Nineteenth Century Bradford: An Examination of Voluntary, Statutory and Private Medical Provision in a Nineteenth Century Urban Industrial Community', PhD thesis, University of Bradford, 1998.

9   Pierre Budin, *The Nursling: The Feeding and Hygiene of Premature and Full-term Infants . . .* Authorised translation by William J. Maloney (London: Caxton, 1907). As this item dates from the year of Maloney's MD qualification, and as he had referred to Budin in his graduating thesis, *The Nursling* can be classified with his degree work, rather than as postgraduate research. The second publication indicates a marked change of interest: see *[Emil] Kraepelin's Reckoning Test as used in the Crichton Royal Institution, Dumfries* (Key . . . by William J. Maloney). (Edinburgh: 2 pt. John F. MacKenzie; London: Simpkin, Marshall & Co., [1911].

made, he was never a Fellow of the Royal College of Surgeons (Edinburgh).[10] The *Medical Register*'s listing him in 1910 at the Kasr-el Ainy Hospital (founded 1828) in Cairo remains a mystery to which Maloney makes only passing reference as late as 1944. This obliquely autobiographical fragment must be read in the context of the World War during which it was written, and the related radical modification of Maloney's public attitudes:

> After a year in Paris, I escaped for a while from rain and cold by going to Egypt. . . Among those who then came to winter at Shepheard's was Professor Daniel J Cunningham, our Edinburgh anatomist. . . . As [he] was lonely and in pain, I was privileged to wait on him until he went home to die. When he felt able, we drove together. On one of these outings, our archaeological friend, Elliot Smith, showed us rheumatic bones of ancient Egyptians . . .[11]

Shepheard's Hotel was a venerable Cairo base for well-to-do globetrotters on the orientalist Grand Tour. Destroyed by fire in the year Maloney died, a century earlier Anthony Trollope had thought it more English than the English themselves. Crossing its exotic terrace to collect his charge, the young Edinburgh Catholic doctor asserted his place in the order of things. As Cunningham – who had strong Irish interests – died in June 1909, we can set a *terminus ad quem* to his attendant's Egyptian excursion. In his 1907 thesis, Maloney referred to 'nine months . . . spent in France as M'Cosh Scholar'. According to the 1944 'foreword', he attended the Saltpétrière in 1908 and other hospitals in 1908. He also alluded to time spent at Munich where he examined rheumatic joints shown to him by 'kindly old Professor Roentgen'. All of this implies a reliable private allowance and a peripatetic approach to postgraduate experience.

Maloney's early publications establish his linguistic abilities, as a translator from French and German. His one real professional distinction – election to the Royal Society of Edinburgh – was initiated on 4 December 1911, with

---

10 Information provided by Simon Johnston (Library, Royal College of Surgeons, Edinburgh), 12 July 2001. The sister institutions in London and Dublin also deny knowledge of Maloney.

11 Maloney, 'Foreword', pp. vii–xiv, esp. pp. ix–x. The Australian anatomist and anthropologist, Grafton Elliot Smith (1871–1937), studied anatomy in London before taking a chair in the new government medical school in Cairo (1900–9); he subsequently contributed a preface to W. H. R. Rivers, *Conflict and Dream* (1932), a work which directly took up the experience of war victims and the psychoanalytical use of dreams.

fellowship conferred for the year following onwards. His four proposers were Sir William Turner (1832–1916), who had become Principal of Edinburgh University in 1903 (the first Englishman to hold the office), Sir Thomas Richard Fraser (1841–1920, professor of materia medica for forty years); Sir Alexander Russell Simpson (1835–1916, sometime lecturer in midwifery, and a prolific writer in gynaecology) and Sir John Halliday Croom (1847–1923, also a writer on gynaecological and obstetric medicine).

Apart from the knighthoods, these men have little in common with Roger Casement; they are pillars of an establishment Maloney was keen to enter. Simpson came from a strong evangelical background in which a medical forebear had also distinguished himself. According to *Who's Who* the younger Simpson 'takes an interest in evangelistic work in Edinburgh, and especially in the mission movement among students'.[12] In the year of Maloney's graduation, Sir Alexander was going into retirement, and delivered a farewell address in which he outlined his *Religio Obstetrici* (1905). Dedicated Bible-Protestantism, maintained in the professional and educational arena, confronted the growing confidence of Scottish Catholicism evidenced in the *Herald*'s celebration of Maloney's success in his finals. Such signs as can be identified indicate that the young doctor heeded the Establishment rather than the faith of his fathers. By the time of his election as FRSE, Maloney had already left Edinburgh to pursue his career overseas. Yet compared to the Astronomer Royal for Scotland, Ralph Allen Sampson (1864–1939) who was elected FRSE the same day, Maloney was as yet a nobody.

SETTING UP IN NEW YORK

However long or short his continental studies, Dr Maloney moved to the United States in 1911. The presence of a cousin, William Power Maloney, among New York's prosperous attorneys may offer an explanation. He served on the staff of Fordham University (New York) in 1911–12 as Professor of Neurology, and this constitutes his best claim to an academic career.[13] In April

12 In 1887, Simpson published *Christ and the Beginnings of Christianity by a Physician of the First Century* (Edinburgh: Murray), and in 1890 wrote in the *Edinburgh Medical Journal* on the opportunities open to medical students. He died on 6 Apr. 1916, a few days before Easter and the events which would so profoundly affect his protégé.

13 In June 1923, Maloney was awarded an Honorary Doctorate in Laws. Fordham being a Jesuit institution with strong Irish associations at the time, it is reasonable to conclude that the award

1911, he was offered a post by the specialist, Joseph Collins (1866–1950), at the newly established Neurological Institute, though by January he was advising a 'retreat from it' – advice which his Ulster-born colleague, Foster Kennedy (1884–1952) did not heed. Despite these contradictory impulses, Maloney was listed as Physician-in-Chief at the Neurological Hospital on Blackwell's Island, in the East River. (Now called Roosevelt Island, Blackwell's had a prison, an infirmary, a smallpox hospital etc.) By 1913, Nisbet has him at a New York address and describes him as the author of *Pressure Sense in Eye, Face and Tongue* (1911). This monograph has proved elusive. However, the journal, *Brain*, carried an article entitled 'The Sense of Pressure in the Face, Eye, and Tongue' which is attributed to Foster Kennedy whom Maloney had probably first met in Edinburgh.[14]

There were additional avenues of advance in America. In 1913 came marriage to Margaret Sarah, only daughter of Charles Follen McKim (1847–1909), a distinguished New York architect whose social position earned President Taft's attendance at his funeral.[15] The McKims were related to the Garrisons, an American press dynasty. The Reverend James Miller McKim (1810–74), a noted anti-slaver and abolitionist, had been one of those to whom the moldering body of John Brown was consigned after his execution in 1859. In the next decade, McKim had been a founder of *The Nation*, the New York magazine through which Maloney would conduct some of his more balletic ideological gyrations.

In October 1874, McKim married Miss Annie Bigelow at Newport, Rhode Island, and their only child was born there on 13 August 1875. The marriage was not a happy one, with the husband travelling a great deal, and the wife insisting on separation in 1878. For twenty years father and daughter never met. In 1897–8, Margaret McKim suffered a serious breakdown, and was

---

13 *cont.* reflected his propagandistic achievements. On the other hand, one might read the LLD as a means of politely jettisoning Maloney *honoris causa*. I am grateful to Patricia Kane of the university's archive department for information on Maloney.

14 A reviewer of this article referred (perhaps pointedly) to the 'author' [i.e. singular], see *Review of Neurology and Psychiatry*, vol. 9 no 11 (Nov. 1911). See also the privately printed tribute volume, *The Making of a Neurologist: The Letters of Foster Kennedy* ([n.p.:]1981). To judge from the two fleeting references, by 1911 Maloney was known to Isabel McCann, Kennedy's fiancée, who was still living in Belfast. Kennedy served in the RAMC and his letters provide much detail. However, he nowhere mentions Maloney after 1912.

15 He is best remembered for the design of Boston Public Library, the Agricultural Building at the 1893 Chicago World Fair, the New York State Building, and the Pennsylvania Railway Station.

taken to Europe by her grandmother. The eventual reuniting of father and daughter took place on 2 January 1899, that is, after her return to America: the *mise en scène* at Jamaica Plain strongly suggests that she was staying at a clinic. In merging his life with hers again, McKim averred that what she needed was 'diversion, cheerful surroundings' – and the care of Dr Hitchcock at Narragansett Pier.[16] No parental home was planned for her. By this point, C. F. McKim was top of his profession, mixing with leading artists, financiers and politicians of the day. In 1903 and 1904, he spent extended periods in Europe (including Germany, France, and Scotland) and was presented at court in London. His daughter, fondly addressed in dutiful letters, led a lonely struggle into adulthood. How she met the Edinburgh doctor has not yet been established, though one cannot rule out a patient/physician relationship.

McKim died on 14 September 1909 aged sixty-two. When a biography of the late architect was prepared by a Library of Congress staff member, Maloney corresponded with the author, assimilating himself quickly as the bereaved daughter's partner in all things, social as well as marital.[17] Not enough is known of Maloney's background to confirm a judgment that he was – in Roy Foster's classifications – a 'Mick on the make', though the dual attachment to Jesuits and Unitarian McKims deserves notice. The patronage of Scotland's medical knights no doubt counted for much, but their protégé's American circle was never that of consultant specialists in diseases of the rich.

In 1913, William Alanson White (1870–1937) and Smith Ely Jelliffe (1866–1945) included a contribution by Maloney in their two-volume collection of essays, *The Modern Treatment of Nervous and Mental Diseases*. Both editors were not only practising neurologists of great distinction but historians of their science who continued to publish prolifically until their deaths. There is, however, no further sign after 1913 of an association with the newcomer in New York. Publication is by no means the best measure of clinical ability, nor is historical research necessarily a higher calling than curing one's patients. Yet it is notable that the Scottish prize-man, who would write much outside medicine, did not hold a place in this American league.

16 Charles Moore, *The Life and Times of Charles Follen McKim* (Boston, New York: Houghton Mifflin, 1929), p. 166.
17 See papers in the New York Public Library.

THE ONSET OF WAR

The Great War obtruded on Maloney's career as it did upon so many promising lives. Still a British subject, in August 1914 he returned home to enlist, and served in the Royal Army Medical Corps, while attached to the 4th Worcestershires. Though he is said to have been awarded the Mons Star, his unit did not serve in that disastrous campaign (August–September 1914). In any case, this decoration should be recognised for what it was, a gong issued in bulk to rally survivors of Britain's early reversal in the War. Far from being a personal achievement, the 1914 Medal (its official name) was given to every soldier – officer, NCO, or private – who saw active service in France or Belgium between 5 August and 22 November 1914. Campaign medals such as these were minted by the ton. As for the claim that he was twice mentioned in despatches, his absence from Lord French's list does nothing to confirm it.[18]

In the official regimental history, the earliest sign of Maloney is among the officers who embarked on 22 March 1915 from Avonmouth for the eastern Mediterranean. He is listed also among eleven officers who survived the action of 12 May (the 2nd Battle of Krithia) in the Dardanelles campaign. 'We spent a pleasant hour together free from shells, which was very nice although it was raining' (Battalion Diary). Even the mechanical cheerfulness of military narrative fails to conceal the horrors which followed. 'By dawn of June 7th both sides had ceased to attack . . . The Medical officer, Captain W. J. Maloney was severely wounded while trending a wounded man outside the front trenches. Apart from his skill as a surgeon, his bravery and kindliness made him the most popular man of the Battalion and his loss was regretted by all.'[19]

The rudimentary details provided by army records of promotion are consistent with the view that Maloney's first sight of action came in 1915, not at Mons. Contrary to the impression given in annual directories of the American medical profession, he never held a regular or permanent RAMC commission.[20]

18 *The Despatches of Lord French* (London: Chapman & Hall, 1917). These covered the western front up to 31 July 1916, well after the conclusion of Maloney's military career.

19 H. F. Stacke, *The Worcestershire Regiment in the Great War* (Kidderminster, 1929), pp. 78, 85, 87. See also W. G. Macpherson and J. J. Mitchell, *History of the Great War Based on Official Documents: Medical Services; General History* (London: HMSO, 1924), vol. 4. Appendix 4 establishes that only one RAMC officer was awarded the MC in the Gallipoli campaign; Maloney is nowhere mentioned.

20 Consequently he does not feature in the 'Roll of Officers' given in Robert Drew (ed.), *Commissioned Officers in the Medical Services of the British Army 1660–1960* (London: Wellcome Historical Medical Library, 1968), vol. 2.

He had enlisted as a temporary lieutenant in September 1914, and advanced
to the rank of temporary captain exactly one year later. That promotion falls
later than the reference to Captain Maloney at Krithia in June, but wartime
paperwork may not have kept pace with developments in the field.

Shane Leslie (whom Maloney had been briefed to blackmail in 1937) has
left the only personal account we have of the Scotsman's wartime experiences.
Unfortunately, he refers to 'Dr W. S. [*sic*] Maloney, a fellow Irishman [*sic*] who
had been wounded at the Dardanelles.' As the two men had crossed the
Atlantic together in 1915 or 1916, it is likely that Leslie got the following from
the doctor himself – 'He was an unrecorded hero who on an occasion when all
the officers in the regiment to which he was attached had been disabled and
the line broken, dropped his medical gear and took over. He led a counter
charge restoring the line of the regiment.'[21] As an *unrecorded* hero, this version
of Maloney cannot have been the recipient of the Military Cross to which the
New York doctor much later laid claim. Indeed, the extensive papers of Sir
Ian Hamilton (1853–1947) in King's College, London, do not substantiate any
of Maloney's claims.[22]

The official date of his being 'invalided with honour' was 4 August 1916,
the day after Casement's execution. Thus ten months between Krithia and dis-
charge remain unaccounted for, presumably spent in hospitalisation, recovery,
etc. Writing in 1937, McCartan records that the wounded Maloney had 'sent vain
cables of protest to London as the merciless shooting [i.e. the Dublin execu-
tions] continued'.[23] That would be May 1916. According to an autobiographical
interpolation in *The Forged Casement Diaries*, on 13 August 1916 Maloney

---

21   Shane Leslie, *Long Shadows* (London: Murray, 1966), p. 176. During the war, Leslie had
served in the ambulance corps.

22   Hamilton was in command of a joint Anglo-French army in the Dardanelles in whose dispatches one clearly discerns dissatisfaction with the War Office's attitude towards recommendations
of awards for gallantry. However, the archive includes lists of officers and men who were commended and *not* rewarded as well as those who were rewarded. Chaplain Ken Best met 'Dr Henry
and Dr Maloney' on 4 June. When Henry was wounded, Best carried him to the beach. Next day,
he 'c[a]me once more on Dr Maloney'. With the Worcesters on Sunday, he found stretcher-bearers
exhausted, though playing cards while men died. One officer was 'having to shoot friends down to
save panic'. There is no mention of Maloney after 5 June, and by Monday (the date given for his
injuries), the battle was more or less over. Best provides no verification of Shane Leslie. 'Hell
impossible? We have seen it.' (IWM, 81/17/2).

23   Patrick McCartan, 'The Man Who Exposed the Casement Forgeries', *Irish Press* (Dublin),
11 Jan. 1937.

returned home to the United States. As the ship docked, a reporter from the *New York Herald*, full of the Casement story, came to [him]. Photographic specimen pages of the diary . . . had been brought to the *Herald* office . . . [24]

Whereas the book dedicated to the redemption of Casement locates its author arriving in New York in a timetable synchronised with Casement's own death and denigration, Maloney's private correspondence has him snug at home in the American capital by 21 May, well before Casement had been tried. He admitted, however, that he had suffered 'psychic disturbance' arising in part at least from the inexplisability [*sic*] of the Irish situation.[25]

With this frank admission and public lie, the conundrum begins to exfoliate. In 1917, Maloney published a brief analysis of conscription and its likely deleterious effects on the prospect of victory: critical of the new measure, he looked forward to the victory of Britain and her allies, and recorded the death of his brother in the war against Germany. His main preoccupation seems to have been Canada. No protests about the execution of Connolly, MacDonagh and the others; even fewer Casemental heresies.[26] On 2 May 1917 in the *New York Evening Post*, Maloney billed himself as 'Captain in the Royal Army Medical Corps'; on the following 25 January, he wrote as an 'Ex-British Officer'.

24 W. J. Maloney, *The Forged Casement Diaries* (Dublin: Talbot Press, 1936), p. 25. In an endnote, Maloney adds that the following day, he protested to the *Herald*'s editor about any contemplated use of these photographs but his action was 'uncalled for'. This seems an extraordinary bout of activity in a man sent 'home' to New York by the British Army on the grounds of permanent disability.

25 See W. J. Maloney to S. Leslie, 21 May 1916, written from 40 East 62nd Street (Georgetown University, Lauinger Library, Shane Leslie Papers).

26 These pamphlets are complicated in their bibliography and I am grateful to Lucinda Thomson for examining copies in the NLI to confirm details. There is no reference to Casement's sexuality or to alleged diaries, though the *Irish Issue* refers to him in the context of British attempts to paint the Irish as pro-German. The anti-conscription item first appeared in the *New York Globe* on 11 Apr. 1917 and – according to a pencilled note on the NLI copy – it was based on an 'interview for which Maloney [was] threatened with indictment'.

THE RAMC AND CASEMENT'S TRIAL

The earliest publication devoted to Casement was written by L. G. Redmond Howard (born 1884), a prolific author and nephew of John Redmond whose biography he also wrote. Issued between the trial and the execution in 1916, the pamphlet account of Casement's character has, by the way, nothing to say on the question of diaries or sexual morality.[27] In discussing Casement's attempt to set up an Irish Brigade, the author quotes the evidence of one Irish prisoner of war at Limburg, the German camp at which Casement had picked up Mrs Dryhurst's anguished letter in April 1915.

Corporal John Robinson of Belfast testified to Casement's conduct as manifestly treasonable. Robinson was not only from Ulster, he was a member of the Royal Army Medical Corps, who had been wounded at the Battle of Mons, and captured by the victorious Germans. His availability at the mid-war trial in London resulted from a swap of prisoners, almost certainly engineered on the British side with the long-term intent of having witnesses to Casement's treasonable activities. The engineering may not have been without unconscious assistance from the other side. In March 1915, a group of Irish prisoners at Limburg had been released by the Imperial authorities at Casement's urging. The names he recorded in passing reference did not include Robinson, though he pointedly if pathetically observed that if more of the same were repatriated 'we shall have soon the Orangemen of the North on our side'.[28] Neither was Robinson on the list of remaining undesirables whom Casement sought to have removed from Limburg in the spring of 1915 as hostile to his projected Irish Brigade though – if we accept Redmond Howard's account – the RAMC man was still in Limburg till May.

Though hardly a star of the courtroom, Robinson played his role as the third of seven low-ranking army personnel (two of them RAMC men) to give evidence after the preliminaries about arrest etc. were completed. In this sense, Maloney's RAMC contributed to Casement's downfall. It would be helpful to establish whether Robinson or Private Michael Moore (the second RAMC

27   Louis G. Redmond Howard, *Sir Roger Casement: A Character Sketch without Prejudice* (Dublin: Hodges Figgis, 1916). The author wrote several other books on Irish affairs, including *John Redmond, the Man and the Demand* (1910), *The Last Speech of Robert Emmet: A Recitation in Verse* (1911), and *Ireland, the Peace Conference and the League of Nations* (1918).
28   Roger Casement to Richard Meyer, 15 Mar. 1915; see Reinhard R. Doerries, *Prelude to the Easter Rising: Sir Roger Casement in Imperial Germany* (London: Cass, 2000), p. 95.

witness) had perhaps – the possibility is not great – served with Maloney in the same or in adjacent field stations at Mons. That is, *if* Maloney had ever served at Mons as he claimed, before being shipped to the Dardanelles.[29]

Between his removal from the battlefield in June 1915 and his self-proclaimed arrival in New York over a year later, where had Maloney been treated? Emergency hospitals throughout the length and breadth of Britain treated severely damaged soldiers to *regenerate* them: Sinn Féin had no monopoly on religious rhetoric. As Pat Barker's novel of 1991 serves to remind us, the convalescent wards did not lightly admit failure in mid-war nor release useable military personnel into civilian life.[30] Hence the conditions upon which Maloney was permitted to leave Britain are of vital importance for any interpretation of his subsequent conduct. But these conditions remain obscure.

Maloney's particular relationship to the RAMC becomes even more opaque if the *New York Times* obituary is consulted. According to the anonymous author who claims that Maloney was twice mentioned in dispatches during 1915, he

> was sent to this country [i.e. the USA] as a British Army medical recruiting officer. He held that position until his indignation at the execution of Irishmen after the unsuccessful Irish rebellion of 1916 led him to quit the British service. Then he helped edit a paper called Ireland . . .[31]

In this version, the telegrams to London would have been dispatched from America, and one can only speculate as to the authority Maloney invoked in so reprimanding his superiors. His correspondence with Shane Leslie in May 1916

---

29 Redmond Howard, *Sir Roger Casement*, p. 43. Robinson's biography deserves note: Joined army in June 1906, at the outbreak of war was stationed in Dublin; sent to France on 19 Aug. 1914, attached to 13th Field Ambulance; taken prisoner by the Germans at Thulin, wounded in the head, knee and shoulder; taken to hospital at Recklinghausen, then to camp at Sennelager; on 23 Dec. transferred to Limburg. Stated in evidence that Casement had said the Irish Brigade would land in Ireland; stayed five months at Limburg, then transferred to Giessen; on 8 Oct. exchanged and returned to UK; in 1916 living at 45 Ross Street, Bristol. For the trial details see H. Montgomery Hyde (ed.), *Trial of Sir Roger Casement* (London: Hodge, 1960), pp. 25–9 and 33–4. Hyde held that 'the most promising of these witness from the defence point of view was John Robinson' (pp. lxxxii–lxxxiii).

30 Pat Barker, *Regeneration* (London: Penguin, 1992). The novel is set in Scotland, and opens with Siegfried Sassoon's July 1917 protest against the continuance of war.

31 *New York Times*, 5 Sept. 1952, p. 27.

strongly suggests that he was working closely with British Embassy staff though hardly in pursuit of official policy. Certainly, his political position was obscure. *Ireland* had been founded at the behest of John Redmond 'to uphold [him] in supporting the prosecution of the war'.[32] This puts Maloney quite remote from the attitudes of Casement and Pearse. Indeed, a newspaper cutting from late 1916 or early 1917 proclaims his intention of returning to active service in the British Army. However, in the Philadelphia *Irish Press* of 9 July 1921, he declared that he had been 'disgusted by the brutality of the English towards the Irish revolutionaries in 1916' and, moreover, he 'had resigned [his] commission on excuse of my wounds August 4, 1916'.[33] To say such things in 1921 does not in itself affect the past except, possibly, to conceal it.

THE CONSCIOUS IRISHMAN

Back in America, Maloney had begun a second career, despite being (somewhat) housebound by war injuries. The editor of his final, posthumous work judged that the invalided doctor made enough money in journalism to set himself up as a consultant neurologist.[34] A series of articles on *The Irish Issue* in a Catholic journal, *America*, in October–November 1918, led to its being banned from the US mails. The offending material was subsequently published by the author as a pamphlet. The same year saw the publication of a lengthy medical study.[35] Privately, Maloney deplored the failure (or real non-existence) of British democracy as evidenced in the treatment of Ireland, and condemned 'Junkerdom' at work behind the Asquith government. He approved of Woodrow Wilson, while recognising an impractical streak, and even suggested that Irishmen might be recruited to new American regiments specially raised. But pamphleteering continued to occupy his time. *Ireland's Plea for Freedom* appeared in 1919 from the America Press, New York. Maloney's

---

32 See *The Nation*, vol. 106 (21 Mar. 1918), p. 325.

33 Quoted in Patrick McCartan, *With de Valera in America* (Dublin: Fitzpatrick; New York: Brentano, 1932), p. 267.

34 F. N. L Poynter in his 'Editor's Note' prefacing Maloney, *George and John Armstrong of Castleton: Two Eighteenth-century Medical Pioneers* (Edinburgh, London: Livingstone, 1954). Up to this point I have drawn on Poynter – a major contributor to medical bibliography – for bibliographical data, also on American medical directories; but see chapter 4 above.

35 *Locomotor Ataxia-Tabes Dorsalis: An Introduction to the Study and Treatment of Nervous Diseases for Students and Practitioners* (New York, London: Appleton, 1918).

interest had been fired by the Sinn Féin election (autumn 1918) when post-war feelings produced a landslide endorsement of the party presenting itself as the heir to 1916. *The Recognised Irish Republic*, which he produced in 1920, took the story further. Several of these pamphlets are attributed to printers or publishers with an address at 164 East 37th Street.[36]

By far the most striking (if digressive) of these contributions to the paper war of Irish independence was *The Re-Conquest of America*.[37] To confirm Maloney's authorship of this pamphlet one has recourse to later proceedings of a Naval Affairs Committee of the United States Senate, though the East 37th Street address pretty well gives the game away.[38] The text provided an account of British propaganda in the States, a carbon copy of which had supposedly been sent to the publishers, with an anonymous note stating that it had been found near 500 Madison Avenue. This had been the New York headquarters of Sir William Wiseman, later Britain's principal adviser on American affairs at the Paris peace talks.[39] In form, the document purported to be an unsigned letter to Lloyd George, dated June 1919, outlining progress in a campaign to re-anglicise America. (The cost of rewriting textbooks to portray George III as a German monarch is estimated, together with other fatuous satirical details.) Issued when Woodrow Wilson was vainly seeking support for the Versailles treaty on Capitol Hill, this clumsy effort at counter-propaganda is the germ of all Maloney's forgery theories. Wilson was by now a villain, having ignored Ireland's claim to nationhood. Maloney now talked of making the President 'the metaphysical tragedy of the age'. To this end appeared *The Book of the Prophet Wudro, and the Fifth Book of the Kings of Eng; being the Hypocrypha Translated out of the Original* . . . published in 1920 under the Statesman Press imprint. Maloney's own 1919–20 exercises in satirical forgery preceded his allegations of British malpractice by seventeen years.

36 For an account of these publications, and the destruction of J. E. C. Donnelly's printing press at the East 37th Street address, see McCartan, *With de Valera in America*, pp. 129–30. McCartan's book had also been published in New York in 1932 by Brentano.

37 *The Re-conquest of America: Full Text of the Most Astounding Document Ever Discovered in the History of International Intrigue* ([New York]: Statesman Press, 1919), p. 29 [3].

38 I am grateful to Dr David Trithart of Potsdam, New York State, for assistance in this connection.

39 From 1915 Wiseman (1885–1962) had been both an unofficial and influential link between the Foreign Office and the White House, and the covert head of MI 1c (later MI6) in the United States. In the latter capacity, he directed operations not only against Irish but also Hindu separatist organisations. After American entry into the war, Wiseman continued to operate clandestinely. (I am grateful to Eunan O'Halpin for his assistance on this topic.)

Writing in the midst of a second World War, Lewis S. Gannett of the *New York Herald Tribune* recalled 'the day in 1920 when Dr William J. M. A. Maloney came into our editorial conference [at *The Nation*], his heart aflame with a fire that inspired us all'.[40] From it resulted an American committee of inquiry into conditions in Ireland. This is not the only tribute to the former British officer's charisma, though its warmth should be measured in the context of 1942 and a battle for survival in the chilly Atlantic sea-lanes (see chapter 10). *Entre les deux guerres*, Maloney was the crippled Minuteman of Irish America, who swayed editors but also launched anonymous broadsides. Kinsman by marriage to the great Garrisons, he peddled pamphlets from a suitcase.

IDENTITY AND INTEGRITY

In August 1916 or earlier, the British Army had deemed Maloney permanently incapacitated, and for the rest of his life he could only travel with difficulty. The nature of his incapacity raises two questions. Was he merely physically injured in the Battle of Krithia, or had he suffered psychic damage of the kind sometimes resulting in war neurosis and sometimes more commonly known as shell-shock?[41] This first question may not be wholly distinct from the second – to what extent did his condition preclude travel? In July 1917, he could boast of 'about fifteen visits to Canada' since his return to New York permanently incapacitated. Some time in September he made a tour of Canada with Oswald Garrison Villard (1872–1949), his newspaper-owning relative-by-marriage.[42] Later, he 'deluged' British Columbia with 'atrocity reports' of British behaviour during the Anglo-Irish War, reports which (in the words of one well-born Irish politician) 'had a peculiar effect, confusing the minds of the ignorant professional classes of that province'.[43]

40 Lewis S. Garnett, '"The Nation" and Ireland', *The Nation*, vol. 154 no. 5 part 2 (31 Jan. 1942), p. 125.

41 See Wendy Holden, *Shell Shock* (London: Channel 4 Books, 1998). The term was coined by Charles Myers (1873–1946), editor of *The British Journal of Psychology*, who also lived among primitive peoples in Borneo and Malaya. Among leading commentators on the authorities' treatment of shell-shocked soldiers was G. Elliot Smith, whom Maloney had known in Cairo; see Holden, *Shell Shock*, p. 44 for an excerpt from Elliot Smith's report in *The Lancet* of April 1916.

42 Maloney to Leslie (Leslie Papers), 8 July and 1 Oct. 1917.

43 Report to the Department of External Affairs (post July 1921) by Osmonde Grattan Esmonde; see Ronan Fanning *et al.* (eds), *Documents in Irish Foreign Policy*, vol. 1 1919–1922 (Dublin: Royal Irish Academy, 1998), p. 188.

The two issues can be focused on his relationship with Roger Casement. There is no evidence in NLI to suggest the two men ever met, and the well-nurtured account of Maloney's change of heart after the execution of 3 August 1916 implies (and perhaps requires) that they had no association in life. (The analogy of Saint Paul again serves to underpin this mythopoeic construction.) The correspondence with Leslie between May 1916 and April 1918 only mentions Casement once, and that to accommodate an anti-Semitic remark.[44] Nevertheless, Maloney later refers to Roger quite familiarly, as if to a dead friend. Perhaps this is a mode of speech he picked up from McCartan and McGarrity, who certainly had known Casement well, and use of the hero's Christian name served to integrate him – a former British officer – with these nationalist veterans. The Royal Army Medical Corps was remote from their world, remote even from the recruiting drive Casement conducted in German prisoner of war camps.

Only three accounts of his ever having visited Ireland emerge. In 1931, Maloney told Hobson that he had been to Ballymena, County Antrim (i.e. to Northern Ireland), looking for Casement family graves, but gave no indication of when this trip occurred. The only other admission of travel to Ireland relates to Belfast in his youth, when he had some contact with Frank Bigger's circle – enough to hear of Bigger's sexual reputation. Indeed, the question has to be asked – did Maloney ever set foot in the Irish Free State?[45]

Though he remained publicly silent on the point, he and an American priest, the Very Reverend Peter E. Magennis, met members of the Irish cabinet (including Richard Mulcahy and Eoin MacNeill) in Dublin on 24 August 1922 to discuss a possible truce in the Civil War; shortly afterwards, Maloney met the republican Mary MacSwiney near Cork, but nothing came of his endeavours.[46] This is the only dateable occasion on which he can be located in Ireland. There is one other, ambiguous reference, to an important textual incident apparently falling between the more external Belfast and Ballymena

44 'Untainted Jew Reading, who sentenced Casement, should incite a pogrom here [i.e. in New York], see Maloney to Leslie, 1 Oct 1917 (Leslie Papers), addressed from New York but evidently written in a garden near Newport, Rhode Island. In Dublin, the *Catholic Bulletin*'s endorsement of the dead Casement as a beloved recruit was paralleled by a three-part article on 'Ritual Murder Among the Jews' by the Revd Thomas H. Burbage (see issues from May to Aug. 1916).
45 For Ballymena see W. J. Maloney to B. Hobson, 8 Sept. 1931 (NLI, MS 17,604 (1)).
46 F. M. Carroll, *American Opinion and the Irish Question 1910–23* (Dublin: Gill & Macmillan, 1978), pp. 184, 285 n23. See under Magennis in the Biographical Register below. See also Maloney's memorandum in Box 20 of his papers as preserved in the New York Public Library.

ones. In *The Forged Casement Diaries*, Maloney records his own initiation into the labyrinth of copies and duplicates which characterise the problem. 'At the close of the Anglo-Irish war, Mr. G. Gavan Duffy, Casement's solicitor at the trial, and one of the Irish plenipotentiaries who signed the peace treaty, gave me a typewritten transcript of the daily record actually written by Casement while he was in Peru' – that is, the latter part of 1910.[47] However, as Gavan Duffy signed the Treaty in London, it seems likely that he met Maloney there, for we also know that the doctor's wife was under medical care in Wimpole Street six months later. Certainly nothing in this establishes that Maloney had been in Ireland at the time, though it raises further questions about his alleged physical inability to travel. Likewise there are questions to be answered about his presence in the outer circles of the Irish delegation. Later, the committee established to draft a Free State Constitution included one obscure member whom Desmond Greaves regards as Maloney's protégé in the absence of the great propagandist himself.[48] Maloney's political identity is bound up with the extent and nature of his war injuries.

Why should Gavan Duffy – renowned for his sagacity as a lawyer – have entrusted so valuable a document to a comparative stranger? How many typescripts did he possess, and where was the original manuscript from which these had been made? It is clear from Maloney's description of what he obtained that the original is the manuscript so-called White Diary, now in NLI.[49] In November 1923, Patrick McCartan had reported that 'The British Gov. has Casement's diaries & photographs of the Putumayo but won't give them up.'[50] Either this corpus included the 'Black Diaries' now available at the PRO (Kew), or the White Diary for 1910 (now in the NLI) – or both, or more than both. If the White Diary had been in the hands of the British authorities, it cannot be regarded as wholly above suspicion of forgery, at least in the eyes of one NLI official. And if its provenance included a spell in the hands of Dr Maloney, that suspicion is not mollified. For it is clear that the

---

47 Maloney, *Forged Casement Diaries*, p. 184. The typescript (NLI, MSS 1622–3) is a good carbon copy, with corrections in various forms, bound in two volumes. Some of the corrections deal with misspellings of proper names, others appear to be designed to bring the work ready for publication: the most significant are, perhaps, two tipped-in pages (vol. 1 ff. 2–3) replacing the originals.

48 Greaves, *Liam Mellowes*, p. 289. The committee member was C. J. France.

49 The manuscript is NLI, MS 13,087, and the typescript (bound in two volumes) is MSS 1622–3; see Angus Mitchell (ed.), *The Amazon Journal of Roger Casement* (Dublin: Lilliput, 1997), p. 29.

50 NLI, MS 17, 675 (4); see chapter 4 above.

history of the Black Diaries is duplicated in that of the White – first copies emerge, and then apparent originals.

Amidst these questions of scribal authority and priority, the issue of Maloney's British military honours might seem a matter of simple fact. But efforts to authenticate his Military Cross do not unearth a gazetting before 30 January 1920, that is, two years after he had declared himself a former British officer, now devoted to Irish independence. However, the army card index links his award to 5 May 1919, a date falling six months after hostilities had ceased on the Western Front but falling also into the period of renewed conflict in Ireland.[51]

With whom was Maloney fighting that late spring day of 'Nineteen Hundred and Nineteen' (Yeats's preferred near palindrome) to an extent which eclipsed the heroics of Krithia? And – come to think of it – what do we make of the reference to his 'loss' at Krithia? Whatever the event which earned him the MC, the slow-motion effect continued. Maloney was not finally decorated until 14 August 1928, when he was sent the medal by registered post. By then an old hand at Irish-American propaganda, he could scarcely betake himself to London or Aldershot for the ceremony. One wonders if the British authorities were aware of Maloney's activities, not only as publicist for Irish independence, but also as a friend to former German prisoners of war.[52] Eccentric ecumenism on this scale could hardly be welcomed on the parade

---

51   The similarity between Mair and Maloney, in their both gaining the MC after 'the guns fell silent' might argue to confirm the doctor as an intelligence officer (as Mair certainly was). However, MC awards were delayed in many instances. At least equally intriguing is the evidence of PRO, WO 339/54110, the career file of Captain W. Molony [*sic*] of Limerick, which has been mistaken by at least one Casementalist as the Scottish doctor's. A farmer from Rathmore near Croom, Molony (various spellings feature, including Maloney) joined the Royal Munster Fusiliers in Feb. 1916. His MC was won (evidently in France) before 18 Aug. 1917, when he was temporary 2nd lieutenant. In August 1918, his location was unknown to the military authorities in Cork. By December, he was serving with the 52nd Rifle Brigade at Colchester, though Irish military HQ at Parkgate conceded to the War Office (11 Dec. 1918) that 'there was great difficulty tracing the whereabouts of this Officer'. In January 1919, he was in a reserve battalion at Fort Stamford, Plymouth, and he seems to have taken 'harvest leave' at some point. Molony finally retired, with the rank of 1st lieutenant, on 13 Sept. 1920, and his claim to the rank of captain remains unexplained in the file. However, portions of the file were destroyed – deliberately it would seem – in 1932. Without impugning the Limerick man's integrity, one might wonder if the Scottish doctor occasionally used his near-namesake's identity at times, especially his bona-fide wartime MC. No comparable file for our Maloney has been located.

52   See papers in the New York Public Library.

ground. Did the well-connected medical man, denounced as England's 'cleverest and most subtle agent . . . among Irishmen', receive in his mail-box an award for these services while John Devoy was dying in poverty?

FROM JAMAICA TO THE EMBASSY IN WASHINGTON

Not only the winning of medals and the conferring of awards, Maloney's physical movements continue to tease the analyst. The Dublin executions took place in May, and Casement's in London was last of the lot (3 August). In *The Forged Casement Diaries*, Maloney recounted his arrival in New York on 13 August 1916, and his prompt efforts to rebut the allegations made post-humously against Casement in America. An *Irish Press* (Philadelphia) article, written fifteen years earlier, had opened with Maloney arriving in New York on 19 April 1917 'on board the *Zacaapa* from Jamaica in the West Indies where I had spent nine months trying to recover the use of a leg which had been paralysed by gunshot wounds on June 7, 1915'.[53] It is barely possible to accommodate both dates of arrival in New York, and an intervening nine – more like eight – months of convalescence in Jamaica.

About the ship's movements, there can be little doubt: she sailed from Kingston (Jamaica) on 2 April and docked in New York between 17 and 20 April.[54] What is doubtful is the motive behind Maloney's uncharacteristic precision in announcing his personal movements. While Lloyd's Register does not invalidate his claim to have arrived on a particular date and boat, this

---

53   The ship (recte, *Zacapa*) had been built in Belfast for the United Fruit Company Line, a politically and economically powerful force in Atlantic trade. The Company maintained a medical service, hospitals etc. in the Caribbean and Maloney may have been attached to one of those during his recuperation. For its continuing political significance, see two German publications: Wilhelm Bitter, *Die wirtschaftliche Eroberung Mittelsamerikas durch den Bananen-Trust: Organisations und imperialische Bedeutung der United Fuit Company* (Hamburg: Westerman, 1921); and Ewald Baatz, *Die Bananwirthschaft auserhalb den United Fruit Company* (Hamburg: Friedenischen, 1941). A more recent and popular account, Thomas P. McCann, *An American Company: The Tragedy of United Fruit* (New York: Crown, 1976), relates the company's intrusion into Honduran politics *circa* 1924, with the assistance of Guy 'Machine Gun' Molony [*sic*] and notes that 'in the mid 1930s, United Fruit entered into a barter contract with Nazi Germany' (p. 25). There is, however, no sign of Dr Maloney or any of his associates.

54   See (Lloyds) *Overseas Shipping Intelligence: Confidential Movements*, 26 Apr. 1917, p. 2 col. 10, and 3 May 1917, p. 3 col. 13.

diverts attention from the issue of what an army officer was doing in the Caribbean when his country needed him in or just behind the trenches. If Maloney left England no earlier than 4 August 1916 (by his own account) and reached New York on 13 August, he cannot have had much time for recruiting in America before he departed for Jamaica where he stayed (again by his own account) until 19 April 1917 (or till May in a different account). As for any post-Jamaican recruiting, two weeks before Maloney's return the United States had entered the war against Germany, and no British recruiting for American military doctors would have been in progress. Jamaica puts a name on the place where Maloney recuperated, but it simultaneously obscures what he was up to.

In the *Irish Press* (Philadephia) article, Maloney claimed to have been one of six delegates – representative Irish-Americans – chosen by Shane Leslie to wait on Arthur Balfour in Washington in the spring of 1917. Yet McCartan, who reprinted the article, declared that Maloney 'had never spoken at an Irish meeting and only once to my knowledge had he been seen on an Irish platform. He was not then a member of any Irish Society' – this at the time of the second Race Convention – in 1919. Again, it is possible to reconcile Shane Leslie's initial choice of Maloney as a representative Irish-American in 1917 (fresh from Jamaica) with McCartan's admission that Maloney had no public profile as a spokesman before 1919. But the exercise of accommodating and recon-ciling is difficult to sustain, for there are no less than three dates advanced as marking the doctor's arrival back in New York. Amid this smokescreen of detail, Maloney's immediate career after Easter 1916 shows little evidence of an attachment to the Irish republican cause.

Contradictory accounts of what Maloney was up to from the late summer of 1916 through to spring 1917 in turn complicate what little we know of his relations with the Embassy. In the *Irish Press* (Dublin) McCartan described how Maloney 'was received kindly by his bewildered friends on the staff there'. Refusing their hospitality, the doctor took himself on his crutches to a hotel whence Shane Leslie followed 'and sincerely voiced many fears of what the British might do to Maloney'.[55] He was advised to heed Brigadier-General Charles D. Norton, who was related by marriage to Mrs Maloney (*née* McKim). As an extension of these warnings, his patron O. G. Villard, owner of the *New York Evening Post* and *The Nation*, was threatened. On the positive side, the

---

55 While devoting a chapter to Casement and another to 'Irish America During the War', Leslie refers neither to Casement's sexuality and the diary controversy, nor to Maloney in *The Irish Issue in its American Aspect* (New York: Scribner, 1917).

newly 'conscious Irishman' (McCartan's phrase) was offered a British consulship at Newport, Rhode Island (vacation haunt of the McKims).[56]

Desmond Greaves, whose resourcefulness should be acknowledged, recorded that Maloney 'resigned his commission on the 9th August 1916 after a violent quarrel with fellow-officers in a club after he had condemned the hanging of Casement'.[57] This has the smack of authentic detail, were it not for Maloney's own declared timetable which puts him mid-Atlantic on the date stated. Of course Maloney made contradictory claims about his return to America, and Greaves concurs in the one which gives 1917 as the momentous moment. He adds that Maloney had been steered towards the Socialist Party by his friend, Norman Thomas, but introduced into the American-Irish movement by J. C. Walsh.[58] Nothing of socialism marks the Forgery Theory.

Casement had been a British consul who, in his last years, affected to call himself an Irish one, even though no Irish state existed. His would-be biographer caused as much confusion, with greater effort. In his autobiography, McCartan printed a statement made by a leading Irish American, Judge Cohalan, repudiating suggestions of pro-Germanism. The occasion was one on which Maloney showed his distracting charisma to the full. The statement described a meeting *circa* 6 May 1917 at the embassy with Shane Leslie, Maloney, and Lord Eustace Percy present.[59] Maloney's objections to Leslie's scheme ensured that 'the invitation was not repeated', though Maloney published his own demands upon Balfour in Villard's *Evening Post* of 2 May 1917. And despite these sudden manifestations of Irish patriotism, he was back the next day with Leslie and others, in Spring Rice's embassy from which the ambassador had circulated the Casement material ten months earlier.[60]

Any account of the Cohalan statement requires the same distinction between the proclaimed and actual author which was noted with regard to H. S. Dickey.

56 *Irish Press* (Dublin), 11 and 12 Jan. 1937.

57 Greaves, *Liam Mellowes*, p. 130 n.

58 *Ibid.*

59 Eustace Sutherland Campbell Percy (1887–1958) was the 7th son of a 7th duke (Northumberland). Educated at Oxford, he served in the diplomatic corps, in government (where he interested himself in education and industry), and was Minister without Portfolio in the early 1930s. In 1918, he married Stella Drummond, daughter of Major-Gen. Laurence Drummond: they had two daughters. An interest in Irish land and distress is evidenced in two official reports to which he contributed in 1923–4. He published extensively, and after the Second World War adopted a decidedly Christian outlook on world affairs.

60 McCartan, *With de Valera in America*, pp. 267–71, esp. p. 268.

Denying that certain documents originated with him, the Judge declared 'they attempted to destroy Parnell by use of the forged Piggott [*sic*] letters and . . . they waited until they hanged Casement before they began to print his forged alleged diary'. If, as both McCartan and (apparently) Maloney concede, this defence of Cohalan's was in fact written by 'Captain William J. Maloney', then it contains information of a kind available to no one else in May 1917 – that the British had actually *printed* parts of an alleged Casement diary.[61]

There is some understandable imprecision in these various recollections – if Maloney returned in May, how did he meet Leslie on 29 April? But McCartan's account of these events (in which he did not take part) is more oddly imprecise on the central issue of Cohalan's relations with the Germans. At the time, those named in the defence were instantly unavailable for comment:

> the veracity of the defence was, therefore, substantially uncontradicted. A few in our organization publicly emphasised the silence of the British Embassy as a proof of Judge Cohalan's innocence . . . The Government, fearing further accusation from him, then left him alone; and he kept silent.[62]

This is what Maloney – in a different context – called a nudge or a wink. We are to ask no further questions about the judge's pro-Germanism.

By these means, Maloney's 'Defence of Cohalan' won a famous propaganda victory among Irish Americans, pleasing no one better than John Devoy. It resurfaced in 1921, in no tribute to the judge but as part of an internal battle between factions. At the beginning of July 1921, Maloney took the extraordinary step of accusing a leading Catholic churchman of accusing him (Maloney) of being a British spy. This American row – see the *New York Times* of 2 July 1921 – arose as preliminary moves were being made in Ireland towards a settlement with the British. *The Nation* in 1942 was inclined to gloss over any involvement of Maloney's in these earlier fractious events, for wholesale Irish endorsement of the war against Germany was the urgent priority. Yet the suspicion of

---

61 *Ibid.*, pp. 18–19. Leslie's presence is readily explained as liaison officer between the Embassy and the Catholic hierarchy in America, which in turn derived from his editorship of the influential (English) Catholic journal, *The Dublin Review*. As far as one knows, prior to the Olympia Press edition of 1959, only Charles Curry of Munich had published (in 1922) a Casement diary, and he had been assisted by Maloney. Fragmentary printings in the Irish-American press can also be ascribed to Maloney or his associates, and these too date from well after 1917.
62 *Ibid.*, p. 20.

deliberate troublemaking is not entirely concealed.[63] Differences had arisen
as early as the Race Convention, at which the Doctor (or Captain) had obdu-
rately stuck to an amendment he was deputed to press at this his Irish-American
début. Devoy now 'vilified him, and shook his fist in Maloney's face', and the
two never met again. In February 1920, the patriarch circulated his diagnosis
of the political medicos. 'McCartan is constantly with Maloney in all sorts of
places – public dinners, etc., and the look of abject submission and adoration
in his face when with him shows the doctor is hypnotized by the expert on
nervous diseases.'[64] Shortly, Maloney fell out with the Judge, accused the
Right Rev. M. J. Gallagher, and thereafter aligned himself with Joe McGarrity.
McGarrity had appointed McCartan to edit the *Irish Press* (Philadelphia), and
from that point through to 1936, Maloney travelled with his fellow doctor.

63   Suzanne La Follette, 'America's Role in Irish independence', *The Nation*, vol. 154 no. 5 part 2
(31 Jan. 1942), p. 126.
64   McCartan, *With de Valera in America*, pp. 84, 150–1.

TEN

SECOND THOUGHTS AFTER PEARL HARBOUR

Well said, old mole! canst work i' the earth so fast.
SHAKESPEARE, *Hamlet* I, v

—

So much for the life of Maloney as far as it can be at present recreated for the years before 1930. It is possible that his bizarre shifts of perspective were occasioned by a conjunction of total disillusion with his country and a renewed, even strengthened faith in the religion of his childhood. Shane Leslie's ill-fated attempt to recruit him as an Embassy-aligned Irish American doubtless relied on some apprehension of Maloney's Catholic origins, just as Maloney's response took into account Leslie's conversion to Rome. Against this tapestry of altered allegiances, progress through George Heriot's to Edinburgh University and the British Army could look like apostasy.

These new gods had hats of brass and feet of clay. Military bungling in the Dardanelles could hardly be distinguished from the stupid executions in Dublin. Contradictory forces – of revulsion and devotion – could only be reconciled by invoking an aspect of his ancestry in which religion and nation were assumed to be in harmony. Maloney's Irishness emerges out of the complex traumas of 1915 in Gallipoli, of 1916 in Dublin, and 1919 in New York. If it is oddly diminished by his apparent avoidance of Ireland as a staging point on his journeys between America and Germany, America and Scotland, so does his Catholicism lack personal expressions of piety. He worked with Jesuits, he regarded Casement as a martyr: beyond that, one encounters little evidence of a religious sensibility. Yet, at least once he looked into the depths.

EXPERIMENTAL TRAUMA

Several explanations present themselves. Psychically damaged in the Great War, Maloney's affiliations were devices of survival, unconscious or deliberate. John Devoy's allegations – in effect that the New York doctor remained a British loyalist after Gallipoli – only appear extraordinary in a context from which Maloney's army service and military decorations have been excised. Viewed in the round, his record is not manifestly inconsistent with that of a low-grade agent provocateur. Indeed, if one were to apply the procedures of Maloney's own disciples among the Forgery Theorists, then the case against his being 'authentic' is undeniable, and no further tests are needed.

Before concluding that the Forgery Theorist was a fraud, we should look more closely at what can be established of that career cut off by the guns of August 1914. In collaboration with Dr Alwyn Knauer, Maloney had devised two new instruments for use on the physiological side of his profession; the prototypes for these were manufactured by a Detroit firm which employed a relative of Knauer's. Dr Knauer is described in the *Journal of Nervous and Mental Disease* as recently an assistant of Emil Kraepelin's at Fordham University, a datum which goes some way towards linking Maloney's immediate post-graduate concerns in Dumfries with his migration to New York. The founder of modern psychiatry and co-discoverer of Alzheimer's disease, Kraepelin was a contradictory figure, a conservative German who disliked Jews but also opposed the death penalty, corporal punishment, and alcoholic beverages. Maloney claimed to have studied in Munich, where Kraepelin worked alongside Alois Alzheimer (1864–1915); while no accessible accounts of the German professor mention the Scottish disciple, it seems reasonable to conclude that any contact between them occurred in Bavaria.[1]

At a Fordham International Extension Course in September 1912, Maloney presented a treatment of ataxia using techniques acquired by studying the

---

1   Smith Ely Jelliffe, 'Emil Kraepelin, the Man and His Work', *Archives of Neurology and Psychiatry*, vol. 00 (1932), pp. 761–75 includes a photograph of visitors with Kraepelin in 1906 (after Maloney's graduation), but there is no sign of the Scotsman in either text or illustration. Kraepelin visited the USA in 1923–4, but again there is no traceable link to Maloney. See also *Allgemeine Zeitschrift für Psychiatrie* (1926, dedicated to Kraepelin), and the later Benjamin Pasamanick (ed.), *Epidemiology of Mental Disorder* (Washington: American Association for the Advancement of Science, 1959) also dedicated to the memory of the German psychiatrist. None of these publications alludes to Maloney either for the pre- or post-war periods.

way blind people relate to bodily movement.[2] By March 1913, he was parti-
cipating in meetings of the New York Neurological Society. When Pearce
Bailey, president of the American Neurological Association, read a paper on
the topic of traumatic neurosis, Maloney was among the respondents, and he
cited evidence gathered by the Society for Psychical Research.[3] If he and
Knauer publicised their 'cephalograph' and 'pneumograph' through the
journal, with accompanying diagrams, their most striking contribution pointed
to other approaches to medicine and its relation to the mind. 'A Preliminary
Note on the Psychic Action of Mescaline [*sic*], With Special Reference to the
Mechanism of Visual Hallucinations' may have employed a cautious title, but
the accounts of twenty-three experiments with subcutaneous injections of the
drug gave every evidence of profound and disturbing experiences.

Having begun their article by insisting on the impossibility of verifying
another person's account of his inner world, Maloney and Knauer proceeded
to describe patterns of coloured fine wires moving like the hands of clock,
followed by images of 'illuminated ground glass'. By implication, the article
describes the authors' own experiences with mescalin, augmented perhaps by
the testimony of others whose statements, however, lie beyond verification.
When a moment is compared to 'the blue of the mosque of Omar in Jerusalem
but [without any] trace of Arabic script on the mosaics' it is difficult to avoid
some recollection of Maloney's sojourn in Egypt and the excursions he may
have made to the Holy Land. Six hours later 'a beautiful palace, filled with
rare tapestries, pictures, and Louis Quinze furniture' was peacefully unfolding
itself. In certain rooms ladies appeared but 'they were as a series of portraits,
or of statue groups, which I was observing in a picture gallery'. Some twenty-
four hours later still, 'green outlines suggesting crocodiles and other reptiles
had replaced the ladies'. The account, which has dropped into the first person
singular, now adopts a plural narrative to pursue images of increasing disturbance. 'While watching a panorama of a danseuse on a stage, one of us attempted
to picture a shoe. He repeated to himself all the separate parts of a shoe . . .
then suddenly and unexpectedly there appeared a gigantic misshapen shoe.'

The simultaneous existence of consciousness as an agent and as an object
of attention gradually focuses on questions of bodily movement. In one
person, 'the feeling arose that the body was cut in halves transversely at the

2   See *Journal of Nervous and Mental Disease* (JNMD), vol. 40 no. 9 (Sept. 1913), p. 572. In this
presentation he was joined by Dr Wachsmann.

3   JNMD, vol. 40 no. 6 (June 1913), pp. 395–7.

waist. Presently he saw the lower half of the body before him, and somewhat to the right . . . He danced vigorously in an effort to restore his former integrity. In this person also other visual hallucinations occurred. Thus, he saw a French soldier and had to be forcibly restrained from attacking his delusion.'

With this motion of violence, at once prophetic and displaced, the future self-proclaimed Mons Star draws his co-authored paper towards closure. But before the final word is reached, one is informed how 'it is noteworthy that we found no indication of the fundamental importance of sexual experience in the content of our artificial hallucinations and delusions, even when special means were taken to elicit it'. These special means are not described. The 'we', 'they', 'I' and 'he' of the article's narrative retreat into impersonal professionalism, empty pinstripe trousers.

Among those present when the paper was read were Foster Kennedy (later so tight-lipped on the subject of Maloney) and William Steinach. Knauer and Maloney's inspiration evidently stemmed from Kraepelin's efforts at 'experimentally induced psychoses', which they deemed too remote from the fabrication of madness, for all that Marianne Weber could style the Munich professor the founder of pharmaco-psychology.[4] Something more than experimentation was required. While the testimony remains anonymous within the article, it seems reasonable to conclude that much of it derived from the experience of the authors themselves, who unquestionably had participated. References to French culture, and occasional words of German, in the maelstrom of psychedelic images strongly suggest Maloney himself as a primary source. In late 1912 or early 1913 he was blazing a trail for Aldous Huxley and Tim O'Leary, while a tributary boreen was trodden by Yeats. The Society for Psychical Research and the taking of drugs crop up in the poet's CV at much the same time.[5]

Maloney, then, should not be written off as a brilliant provincial. Quite apart from the tradition of Edinburgh medicine which reaches back to the Scottish Enlightenment, the *Review of Neurology and Psychiatry* (founded 1902), in which his mescalin research was briefly reported, pioneered sympathetic comment on psycho-analysis. Ernest Jones, later Freud's biographer, was a

4   Marianne Weber, *Max Weber: A Biography*, trans. Harry Zohn (New Brunswick: Transaction, 1988), pp. 330, 394. Max Weber read Kraepelin in connection with his study of intensive industrial labour.

5   See JNMD, vol. 40 no. 7 (July 1913), pp. 425–36; the paper had been read in March, and so one may assign the experiments to a date several months earlier still.

contributor. But no seamless dynamic should be assumed in Maloney's case. Coyness on the topic of sex can hardly have been professionally motivated, given the role of the *Journal of Nervous and Mental Disease* as American publisher of work by Freud, Jung, Otto Rank, and A. A. Brill (one of Freud's translators). Indeed, the Edinburgh graduate and junior associate of Kraepelin had quickly inserted himself in a formidable intellectual milieu. Anthropology and Shakespearean criticism jostled with neurosurgery and Viennese speculation in the pages of the journal, presided over by Smith Ely Jelliffe. Shrewdly recognising Freud's early contributions to clinical neurology, Jelliffe after the War became a warm supporter of mature psycho-analysis in theory and practice, even undergoing analysis by the master himself.[6] While Maloney's articles were appearing, Jelliffe's translation of Rank's *Myth of the Hero* was serialised alongside, with detailed references to Greek drama, the life of Jesus, Germanic mythology, and comparative religion. Contemporary political or cultural issues featured also, especially the mental health of minorities such as Jews and American Blacks. In the same issue of the journal which paraded the utility of Krauer and Maloney's pneumograph, Brill and M. J. Karpas asked the question 'Is the Jew Disproportionately Insane?'[7]

Maloney's mescalin jabs did not excite prolonged discussion, nor did he involve himself in the soon-to-be-dangerous debates about race. His central research interest could be summarised in the dullest of terms – movement. Ataxia, or the loss of muscular co-ordination, features in most of his published papers, and is prominent in his 1918 monograph. The causes of this condition were and are manifold – brain haemorrhage, poliomyelitis, severe folic acid deficiency, tertiary syphilic infection, and (more grossly) warfare. In simulating traumatic psychosis by the use of mescalin, Maloney noted difficulty in walking as a hallucinatory experience, and proceeded to link this to a patient under his care at that time – 'a gentleman who is suing a Traction Company because his ataxia began immediately after he fell down a subway stairs'. Accidents are so to speak the protocols of ataxia.

This was his professional concern in 1912–13: indeed, one of his papers in the journal appeared after he had enlisted in the RAMC. It took some time

---

6   See Norman Kiell, *Freud Without Hindsight: Reviews of His Work (1893–1939)* (Madison, Conn.: International Universities Press, 1988). Ernest Jones, *The Life and Work of Sigmund Freud* (London, New York, 3 vols, 1952–7). Paul Roazen, *Freud and His Followers* (London: Allen Lane, 1976).

7   The Brill/Karpas paper had been read to the New York Neurological Society without any evidence of Maloney or Knauer being present; see JNMD, vol. 41 no. 9 (Sept. 1914), p. 512.

for the learned journals to reflect war's impact on medicine, but one quite quickly finds D. K. Henderson (who reviewed Maloney's American papers for Edinburgh's *Review of Neurology and Psychiatry*) transferred to the staff at Nettley (best known of the war hospitals in Britain) and later writing extensively on war psychoses. By contrast, Maloney's transition was brutally short. From the publication of academic research in September 1914 to severe wounds at Krithia in June 1915 amounted to a mere nine months, in which diminished mobility became a personal trauma, not a clinical problem in others. There is abundant testimony to the nature or effect of the wounds Maloney suffered – his use of crutches, his limp, references to a shattered leg. The lower body, swinging from supports under the armpits, moves as if it were detached and autonomous like the hallucinatory figure seen through mescalin in more peaceful times. Though the damage may have been inflicted upon the bone rather than the muscles, injury to the leg raised diminution of mobility to the power 2 – the leg could only be moved with difficulty, the entire body could only be mobilised to the extent the leg could carry it. Hence, it seems reasonable to call Maloney's injury a traumatic one, quite apart from the psychological damage he suffered through feelings of betrayal, official incompetence, or political dishonesty. As late as the mid-1920s, Freud had to admit that 'not a single analysis of a traumatic neurosis of any value is extant'.[8]

Maloney's monograph of 1918, which draws together much pre-war research, opened with a preface already quoted as evidence of the author's capacity for claptrap. Perhaps it might be reconsidered more sympathetically – 'perfect moving is the outward sign of perfect thinking'. For if Maloney became disabled by the war it is clear that the quality of his published thought no longer earned him a place alongside A. A. Brill or S. E. Jelliffe. The post-war writings can be readily classified as propaganda, even brilliant propaganda at times. But success was now measured by cruder standards than those of the *Journal for Nervous and Mental Disease* – the ability to mimic official bombast as in *The Re-Conquest of America*, or to reduce complex political, historical and constitutional issues into the stuff of popular pamphleteering.

8   S. Freud, 'Inhibitions, Symptoms, and Anxiety', in *The Penguin Freud Library*, vol. 10 (On Psychopathology) (London: Penguin, 1987), p. 285.

OVERDETERMINED INCOMPETENCE

There's something wrong with life when men can walk.
SEAN O'CASEY, HARRY HEEGAN
in *The Silver Tassie* (1929)

A measure of Dr Maloney's inner condition might be taken among the conflicting dates given for his return to professional life in New York from the battlefields of Europe. Did he travel with Shane Leslie some time late in 1915 as implied in Leslie's *Long Shadows*? Did he arrive on 13 August 1916, to a fanfare of Casement publicity? Or did he divert through Jamaica and reach his adopted home on 19 April 1917? These irreconcilable claims have their political implications, linked as they to Maloney's shadowy relationships with the British Embassy, with the recruiting of American doctors for the RAMC, with the United Fruit Company.

But if Maloney's (unproven) task was to mess things up among the Irish Americans in the aftermath of 1916, why should he persist in his activities for so long as to become the Great Theorist of 1936? By 1919, his name featured on the masthead of the *Journal*, among twenty-eight collaborators with the editor, Jelliffe. No longer a contributor, he had become a name. 'The Maloney Method of Re-education in the Treatment of Chorea' was written up in the *New York Medical Journal* in May of that year. Maloney had clearly opted for patients rather than publications, a choice above suspicion in itself.[9] After all, he did enjoy a degree of social eminence in New York. There is no reason to doubt McCartan's statement that his admired friend counted the wife of Alfred E. Smith (US presidential candidate in 1928) among his clients, together with Nicholas Brady, a utilities financier. From this position, a gradual retirement from ideological warfare was the easiest thing in the world.

His (presumably) unintended embroilment in a US Senate committee late in 1929 may have forced a reconsideration. World disarmament, with specific reference to naval affairs (and hence British–US relations at the time of the Great War), formed the broad agenda. The obscure and anonymous pamphlet of 1919, *The Re-Conquest of America* was unexpectedly cited, and a hue and cry arose as to its authorship. Maloney owned up, claiming to have written it to

---

9   See Mabel Webster Brown (ed.), *Neuropsychiatry and the War: A Bibliography with Abstracts* (New York: National Committee for Mental Hygiene, 1918) (292 pp.), which indexes no reference to Maloney.

scupper ideas of a League of Nations, and boasting that up to half a million copies had been circulated. In January 1930, he appeared before Senator Shortbridge's committee and – to judge from the newspaper reports – he gave a sprightly account of himself. He had modelled his pamphlet on the work of Ben Franklin (1706–90), the great journalist-cum-scientist of the American Revolution. He had targeted the Dublin-born newspaper baron, Alfred Harmsworth (Lord Northcliffe, 1865–1922), in devising the contents. He and some friends had lugged suitcases of the stuff by ferry to New Jersey, evading New York's attempt to suppress his pamphlet.

Until we know the full extent of Maloney's journalistic activities, it is impossible to say whether the Shortbridge hearings drew him out of retirement. The following year the invalid was even more active. For whatever reason, and notwithstanding his own disabilities and his wife's cancer, Maloney sailed on the SS *Albert Ballin* from New York to Hamburg in April 1931. The shipping line subsequently confirmed to Joe McGarrity in Philadelphia that, on his arrival on 24 April, Maloney had been paid $4,000.[10] While there is no reason to suppose that Maloney met or made any Irish contacts while he was in Germany, the printer Colm O Lochlainn was also there in 1930, and returned several times, even after Hitler's triumph.[11] Quite apart from the transfer of money by non-banking means, there must be continuing doubt about Maloney's (im)mobility. On 28 July 1933, he wrote to Gertrude Parry, recording that he had been ill – 'and had to go to Europe for an operation in May last'. His disability kept him out of Ireland but did not prevent travel to other places. Exactly where he meant by 'Europe' in May 1933 is unclear.

The abrupt termination of correspondence between him and Patrick McCartan, as represented in the NLI archives, might suggest that, after 1924, Maloney had been disengaged from propaganda work. Nothing survives of a large-scale Casement project until we encounter Ben S. Allen as the recipient of a typescript late in 1932. In May of that year, he was in touch with Mrs Parry. Complaining of renewed economic difficulties in the United States, he declared it was 'like being in the trenches again, without the exhilaration of an enemy to fight'.[12] This may have been designed to impress Casement's cousin, in whom he perhaps suspected a residual, or renewed, British loyalty.

10 Letter dated 13 May 1931 (NLI, MS 17, 556).
11 See Desmond MacGuinne, 'Colm O Lochlainn and the Sign of Three Candles: The Early Decades', *Long Room*, no. 41 (1966), pp. 43–51.
12 W. Maloney to Mrs Gertrude Parry, 1 May 1932 (NLI, MS 13,075 (2)).

Deteriorating conditions in Germany called for renewed attention to Irish republicanism and its links with Britain's historic enemy.

The Forged Casement Diaries appeared at the end of 1936, from the decidedly provincial Talbot Press of Dublin. One or two medical publications excepted, all of Maloney's not inconsiderable output sprang from obscure presses in which the practice of self-publication may be suspected where it isn't openly admitted. Given that Denis Gwynn's London publishers had succeeded in finding an American co-publisher for his biography of Casement, it is striking that Maloney with his more dramatic tale could not follow the same path. The reluctance of London firms to issue a ringing indictment of the British Foreign Office – and raise the question of German support for Irish independence – can be exaggerated; more crucially, one is entitled to query why no New York company took up the cause. Was there some subconscious desire among the Forgery Theorists that the resurrection should ideally take place at home in Ireland? Or, to take one last look at the notion that Maloney was himself a forgery, a British agent masquerading as a convert to Ireland's cause, was there a need to 're-patriate' his activities in the era of renewed German militarism, to provide a viewing platform within the Irish Free State?

The resultant publication was odd in many ways, not least its combination of vehemence and authorial remoteness. There is little or nothing of the gifted linguist to be found in its pages, even less of the sensitive neurologist. The experiments in simulating psychosis with Alwynd Knauer provide no insight into the issue of Casement's own mental state. The aspirant pioneer in neuro-psychiatry had been left on the far side of the trenches and shell-holes, beyond a landscape in which the hallucinatory splitting of bodies had found its natural habitat. Research had anticipated the war for this ambitious Scottish Catholic loyal officer, and War distorted the past in the eyes of a traumatised survivor. Paraded as an academic and a medical man in the *Irish Press*, the author had no professional memory.

Even more surprising was Maloney's sudden loss of interest in Casement after 1936. But, as he conceded, he was no investigator, no analyst. In an undated letter to Hobson, the author of *The Forged Casement Diaries* admitted the limited nature of his own role in the publication, and promised better:

> I could improve it considerably so far as my part is concerned if it comes to a second edition. There are a number of repetitions and irrelevances that should come out . . .

[T]hen the book and the lie should not be referred to again and we should set ourselves to building Roger up. It will be a hard job. The 1916 shrines have all been pre-empted. The favored martyrs have established a sort of property right to their high places. What is needed is some sort of formal canonisation.[13]

Perhaps the crank is audible here again. Certainly the religious, or mythopoeic, framework in which Maloney and his management team work is acknowledged, together with a surprisingly casual attitude to further nailing of 'the lie'. (Or – is it possible that the Forgery Theory is itself described here as a lie, Maloney's lie?) In practice, he transferred the larger Casement project to H. S. Dickey, an even less competent investigator than himself. It is true that financial considerations weighed heavily, for by this time he was employing three nurses to look after his wife. Margaret (McKim) Maloney died in the late summer of 1946, after more than twenty-five years of serious illness.[14] Dickey, who had been groomed as an older successor in authorship, (or who may have been spotted as the ideal no-hoper with whom the project would die) died aged seventy-two of a heart attack at his home in Huiga, Ecuador in 1948. In their different ways, these losses contribute to the altered context in which Maloney dropped Casement. A vague reference to a 'third version' of a diary circulated by the British occurs on the second-last page of his text, 'which I hope to deal with later'.[15]

This was not to be. Maloney's publications after 1936 were a preface to someone else's book about rheumatic fever, and two enquiries into Scottish medical history.[16] On the surface, these latter represent a wholly new departure, though both he and John Armstrong (1709–79) had written on syphilis.[17] In the shorter version of this recuperative project, Maloney devoted

---

13 NLI, MS 17,604.

14 See *New York Times*, 2 Sept. 1946, p. 17. The Margaret Sarah McKim Maloney Memorial Collection, in the New York Public Library, presumably dates from this moment or later. Its contents deserve analysis as a complement to the present work.

15 W. J. Maloney, *The Forged Casement Diaries* (Dublin: Talbot Press, 1936), p. 217.

16 See Foreword to Leopold Lichtwitz, *Pathology and Therapy of Rheumatic Fever* (London: Heinemann, 1944), pp. vii–xiv; W. J. Maloney, 'Michael Underwood: A Surgeon Practising Midwifery from 1764 to 1784', *Journal of the History of Medicine and Allied Sciences*, vol. 5 (1950), pp. 289–314; also W. J. Maloney, *George and John Armstrong of Castleton: Two Eighteenth-century Medical Pioneers* (Edinburgh, London: Livingstone, 1954), pp. xii, 115.

17 'A Bibliography of the First Editions of John Armstrong', in Iolo A. Williams, *Seven XVIIIth Century Bibliographies* (London: Dulau, 1924), pp. 17–38.

a disproportion of time and ink to Scottish seventeenth-century history, determined to fix his subject in the actualities of a religious tradition at violent odds with his own. To outline Calvinist and Covenanter backgrounds for the Armstrong family, Maloney quaintly built on a definition of 'exercise' which here does not denote the deliberate practice of physical movement, but broadly means a religious ceremony or discourse – 'Exercise is a critical explication of a passage of scripture, at a meeting of Presbytery, succeeded by the specification of doctrines contained in it, by another.'[18] Why is this incorporated into an essay on medical history? Does it echo and re-orientate that wild remark of 1918 when the author of *Locomotor Ataxia* used the definition of sacraments to compare 'perfect moving' with 'perfect thinking' while lambasting his religious foes among Christian Scientists and the Emanuel Movement? A stage in the reorientation of Maloney's thought can be recognised in the method which he developed for the treatment of Huntington's Chorea, where spasmodic movement (head jerks etc.) could be reduced by the very process of measuring it. This reorientation in 1919 coincides with his political commitment to Irish independence and his opting for patients rather than publications.

Further stages of a post-war assymetry of adjustment and digression, acknowledgement on the title page of the *Journal of Nervous and Mental Disease* matched by excursions into the journalistic underworld, can be traced through the 1920s and into the low decade of the Casement project. But there was to be a clear watershed, or great barrier reef behind which the traitor/patriot disappeared. The ageing Maloney's commitment to the reputation of John Armstrong's brother, George Armstrong (1715–89), led him to present a plaque in honour of the Scottish paediatrician to his native village of Newcastleton. One obituarist recalled Maloney's regular summer trips to the British Isles on medico-historical research, without so much as mentioning Casement or Ireland.

An intriguing feature of the eighteenth-century research, however, is Maloney's allegation of plagiarism committed by one of the doctors (by name Underwood) against another of those whose careers he examined. There is a subterranean continuity here, not only with the Casement controversy, but also with the manner in which Maloney's 'exposé' of the British 'reconquest' of America had been communicated to the public in the form of a bogus letter.

18 W. J. Maloney, 'John and George Armstrong at Edinburgh', *Edinburgh Medical Journal*, vol. 57 no. 12 (Dec. 1950), p. 614 n1.

The common denominator is indirect- or mis-writing, a matter of considerable psychological interest. Perhaps his health contributed to the shift away from Ireland, linked to a renewed commitment to the country of his birth. Maloney died in Edinburgh on 3 September 1952. Already a widower, he left three sisters in Edinburgh. The body was returned to America for burial at Rosedale Cemetery, Orange, New Jersey.[19] His last, posthumous, publication was prepared for the press by F. N. L. Poynter, who was given Maloney's largely unnumbered and unorganised notes by Rose Maloney, the author's sister.[20] No obituary appeared in *The Lancet*, nor in the *Journal of the Royal Army Medical Corps*, while the *New York Times* recorded his post-1916 service to the RAMC.

Maloney's death uncannily disinters the topic of his early research. According to one obituary, he died in an Edinburgh hospital as the consequence of an accident. But, in the short memoir by Poynter, Maloney in the previous few weeks had been diagnosed as suffering from an incurable disease (not specified). Finally, there are obituaries which record his death without reference to any accident or disease. These not very numerous accounts of his last end do not contradict each other, but each manages to omit some detail of significance. The relationship between accidents – falls, for example – and psychosomatic illness had been at the root of an implicit research programme curtailed by the 'accident' at Krithia. In the final weeks, Maloney returned to the city where he had received his medical training, suffered an accident, and died (not at the site of the accident but) in a hospital familiar since his youth. Did he at some level of unconsciousness retrace the stages of his life so as to make his exit at the point of entrance?

CRIMES AGAINST EUROPE

Those last unknowable events took place in a world totally different from the one in which Maloney had launched himself on his Casement crusade. And there had been political analogues to the retraction in bio-space which

---

19 *Who Was Who in America*, vol. 3 (1951–61).

20 G. L. Annan, 'William J. M. A. Maloney, M.D.', *Bulletin of the Medical Library Association*, vol. 41 (Jan. 1953), pp. 100–1; an anonymous notice in *The British Medical Journal* (13 Sept. 1952, p. 619) was augmented in a subsequent issue (1 Nov. 1952, p. 1000) by F. N. L. Poynter in which he claimed that Maloney left his book on the Armstrongs 'almost ready for the printer'. See also *New York Times*, 5 Sept. 1952, p. 27. The sisters are named as Mary Agnes, Rose and Isabella [Maloney], suggesting that they were unmarried.

brought him home. Whereas the trajectory of one man's life can be reversed so that his end is in his beginning, the social world enjoys no privilege to undo a generation's folly or its suffering. The Casement Committee in London pursued its objective of repatriation, more for its nuisance value in the eyes of the British authorities than with faith in the Dublin government's support for the cause. At a large meeting in Conway Hall, Red Lion Square on 21 January 1938 which Desmond Ryan addressed, the faithful Special Branch noted that 'Throughout the whole of the proceedings no mention was made of Mr De Valera.'[21] These renewed meetings took place as Sean Russell was establishing himself as Chief of Staff of the IRA, and planning the bombing campaign in England which erupted the following January.

Long before Mrs Maloney's happy release, and Dickey the intrepid explorer's final departure, the outbreak of war in September 1939 had changed everything. While the cause to which Dr Maloney had dedicated twenty years might seem puny on the world stage, the Casement issue was inextricably bound into the conflict. There was, for example, a vigorous pro-German faction within Irish republicanism and its American support base. Joseph McGarrity took his family on annual holidays to Nazi Germany in the late 1930s, and they were in Berlin on the day the Second World War began.[22] Early in 1940, Britain executed two IRA men for an explosion in Coventry. The campaign, killing five bystanders, had been financed by the Nazis through McGarrity's good offices.[23] These factors not only complicated the Irish Government's attitude to Germany's democratic opponents (especially Britain), but also affected relations within the United States (especially before Pearl Harbour concentrated the American mind wonderfully). Maloney, who was fifty-eight years old, appears to have closed down the Casement inquiry. His former employer, McGarrity, banked on Nazi victory, as did Sean Russell with whom McCartan had threatened J. W. Bigger two years earlier. Liam Gogan's boss in the National Museum, Adolf Mahr, departed for the Reich on 19 July 1939, where he joined the Irish desk in Ribbentrop's Foreign Ministry.

21 PRO, MEPO 2/10675. When a further meeting took place at Limehouse Town Hall, in southeast London, on 25 Mar. 1938, the Special Branch detected that a local Catholic priest, Fr Vincent Rochford, was among the organisers.

22 See *The Irish Times*, 4 Sept. 1999 for an obituary of Mary McGarrity Shore (1912–99), the eldest daughter.

23 Eunan O'Halpin, *Defending Ireland: The Irish State and its Enemies Since 1922* (Oxford: Oxford University Press, 1999), pp. 148–9.

The novelist Francis Stuart, who like Gogan supported Maloney in the *Irish Press*, followed within months. Though Stuart's principal employment in Nazi Germany took the form of lecturing and broadcasting, he sought Maloney's permission to translate *The Forged Casement Diaries*. Unsuccessful in this, Stuart wrote *Der Fall Casement* (1940) which, however, probably owed as much to its translator (Ruth Weiland) as it did to the novelist.[24] German wartime interest in Casement not only served to maintain a dialogue with the dominant fascistic element within the IRA, it also created internal problems for the British authorities. Forgery Theorists have mocked – with justification – the inability or unwillingness of each successive London government to explain what happened to the documents circulated in 1916. But they too had their embarrassments. The living Casement had confronted rubber bosses and their sadistic functionaries; the dead Casement was allied to SS commanders and prophets of extermination, becoming even more of a conundrum than he had been thirty years earlier. His posthumous cause became fused or confused with that of the Coventry bombers, even after the Second World War had ended.[25] Could anyone in Whitehall remember with accuracy what had been circulated in 1916, what had been forged, what had (by other means) been misrepresented? The invasion of Poland rendered these questions more important, and less pressing, than they had been in 1936 when Maloney's supporters demanded an inquiry.

Radio propaganda was a new kind of phoney war by means of which Nazi Germany could 'invade' neutral countries with impunity. While recent work on this topic concentrates on European target audiences, the United States also featured in Adolf Mahr's plans. Irish-American opinion was to be mobilised against entry into the war and, after the Japanese attack, in opposition to the Democrat Party.[26] Maloney had contributed to IRA–German relations, and

24 Information from the late Francis Stuart, provided when the present writer compiled a checklist of his publications – see W. J. Mc Cormack (ed.), *A Festschrift for Francis Stuart* (Dublin: Dolmen, 1972), pp. 46–62. For a more recent treatment, see Karin Wolf, *Sir Roger Casement und die deutsch-irisch Beziehungen* (Berlin: Duncker & Humboldt, 1972), pp. 84–5, 135.

25 In 1949, the Scottish Communist MP, William Gallagher, once again appealed for the repatriation of Casement's remains along with those of Peter Barnes and James McCormack, the Coventry bombers: see PRO, HO 144/23448 and DO 35/3946B. Letitia Fairfield, a friend of Casement's who came to accept the Black Diaries as authentic, published a report of the Barnes and McCormack trial in the same series which had originally issued George Knott's account of Casement's.

26 David O'Donoghue, *Hitler's Irish Voices* (Belfast: Beyond the Pale, 1998), p. 144 etc.

even brought into focus a symbolic figure whose role in 1914–16 might be emulated in the war for a Thousand Year Reich. If Celts in Brittany and Aryans in Norway were to respond, there could be no room in this reconstructed Casement for a doubtful sexuality. Yet it is at this crucial moment in the serial fabrication of Casements that the Great Forgery Theorist quits the Irish scene. His refusal of Stuart's request signalled a more comprehensive remaking of himself.

'THE NATION', ONCE AGAIN

Maloney's last throw of the dice was aimed in a quite new direction. A short news article, 'Eire and the Atlantic Sea-Lanes', slipping into a late edition of the London *Times* on 31 January 1942, summarised his views of the altered international situation. Here was a change of heart, at least on the sleeve. 'Dr. Maloney writes that Eire had awakened from a nightmare of Nazi vengeance "to find that its official neutrality, defensible no longer than it could be reasonably pleaded as essential to its very existence, had grown somehow into a fearful yet comfortable habit which 28 months of practice had made hard to give up".'[27] *The Times* sub-editor gave no reason for singling out Maloney's opinion, implicitly granting him the status of expert.

'Eire and the Atlantic Sea-Lanes' probably had appeared in *The Times* unknown to Maloney, as the paper acknowledged its source in a special 'Ireland and America' supplement to a venerable New York magazine to which he had contributed a longer article.[28] Here was a major effort to shift public opinion in such a way as to persuade Ireland to co-operate with her old enemy in the fight against Nazism, and to dissolve the compact between Irish America and Germany, which reached back to Casement's mission of 1914. Contributors included George W. Norris, a veteran senator for Nebraska, and William L. Shirer, the journalist whose *Berlin Diary* had done so much to alert America to the nature of Hitler's regime. The supplement had been assembled by Maxwell S. Stewart, whose annual contributions on Ireland to *The National Encyclopaedia Yearbook* gave him a historical perspective in which to design an essentially political dossier.

27 *The Times* (4th edn), 31 Jan. 1942, p. 3 col. 2. I am grateful to Eamon Dyas for excavating this article from the archives of News International.
28 See *The Nation*, vol. 154 no. 5 part 2 (31 Jan. 1942), p. 141.

Maloney's inclusion signalled the Allies' need to woo hard-line Irish-American opinion away from traditions which had been laid down by Casement's departure from New York for Berlin in 1914. The death in 1940 of Joe McGarrity – Irish republican, American retailer of drinks, and Nazi collaborator – may have facilitated Maloney's conversion to the war effort. The United States's declaration of war in December 1941 provided the immediate stimulus to the redeployment of his propagandist skills. But did these circumstances, with their implications of a truly global conflict, prompt something more than just a late career move? Or was the Maloney, who wrote in *The Nation* about Ireland's obligation to Canada and the United States, emerging as the British agent whom John Devoy had suspected decades earlier?

In 1942, as the United States threw itself into the European war, Margaret Sarah McKim Maloney was still alive. Her grandfather had been among the founders of *The Nation*, which regarded itself as 'America's Leading Liberal Weekly Since 1865'. In 1920, it had embraced the Sinn Féin cause in revulsion from the means employed by Britain to suppress Irish discontent. Twenty years later, it issued the supplement which concluded with Maloney's article on 'De Valera's Neutrality'. This took the form of a potted history, commencing with the Treaty of 1921, tracing de Valera's serpentine career, and summarising the early stages of the Second Word War. Maloney's ingenuity as a propagandist was to argue that, after the fall of France, de Valeran neutrality was dividing Ireland and rendering it more vulnerable to foreign interference. Having slyly undermined the Taoiseach's authority as wartime national leader, Maloney closed his case by quoting a minister in de Valera's government: on 10 January 1942 as the Battle of the Atlantic lay in doubt, Dr James Ryan declared 'When the position becomes acute there will be some who will favor departure from neutrality . . . There may possibly be a stampede.'[29]

Viewed cynically, this might be regarded as an attempt to destabilise de Valera by promoting one of his most intelligent younger ministers. As if to mitigate any such suggestion, the supplement was augmented with copious quotations from speeches made by the Taoiseach during his American tour. Maloney's strategic analysis went beyond party politics. Seaports had featured in the Treaty arrangements, but access to air facilities was of increasing importance. The steady stream of southern Irishmen crossing the border to

29   William J. M. A. Maloney, 'De Valera's Neutrality', *The Nation*, vol. 154 no. 2 (31 Jan. 1942), pp. 141–5.

assist the British war effort made nonsense of partition, an anachronism in the era of Realpolitik. The Irish in America demanded a political response which transcended insular boundaries. It was time for Ireland to assist Britain. 'The democratic way of life', for which America ultimately would fight, demanded as much.

ELEVEN

TEXTUAL CORRUPTION

OR, THE DIARIES IN TODAY'S RETROSPECT

There could be no honour in a sure success, but much might be wrested from
a sure defeat. Omnipotence and the Infinite were our two worthiest foemen,
indeed the only ones for a full man to meet, they being monsters of his own
spirit's making; and the stoutest enemies were always of the household.

T. E. LAWRENCE

——

Maloney's true allegiances may never be known. There are so many available explanations for his relative incompetence on the Casement question – his war neurosis, his covert allegiance to Britain, his lack of historical training – that, in classic Freudian terms, they cancel out or throw each other into radical doubt. It would be presumptuous to expect constancy and consistency in someone whose psyche evidently suffered grievous damage in the Great War. But the very short passage of time elapsing between *The Forged Casement Diaries* and the reigniting of World War requires some consideration of the motives lying behind its publication in 1936. Despite the high stakes, Maloney's book is a tissue of confusions and misrepresentations, steered into print by managers who entertained murder and blackmail to enforce their theory. Was it at some subterranean level intended to sow confusion and encourage misrepresentation? Did some remote controller in Whitehall approve this 'tale of a tub' thrown among Irish republicans who might otherwise follow in greater numbers the hard left initiatives of the Gilmore brothers in the Republican Congress? Could one read Peadar O'Donnell's response as evidence of success in that kind of diversionary and dirty trick?

Its success in convincing a sizeable public opinion in Ireland that forged diaries had been used to blacken Casement's name is itself a tribute to the power of black propaganda. Herein lies its dangerous 'un-dead' power. Figures like Lord Birkenhead and Sir Ernley Blackwell may have been hateful, but that itself does not prove forgery in the Black Diaries. A. J. P. Taylor may also have been right in declaring that two members of the Cabinet which rejected clemency were homosexuals like Casement. But that again alters nothing as to the material status of documents. Eighty-year-old hatred is no basis for scholarship. Nor is *The Forged Casement Diaries*, whose continued use by Forgery Theorists can only be lamented.

In the same spirit, it should be recognised that the exposure of Maloney's book as deeply flawed in both execution and intention does not in itself prove that the material used by the British authorities in 1916 was authentic. Some of course may wonder why *The Forged Casement Diaries* was ushered into the public domain in so unhappy a state. O. G. Esmonde had his suspicions in 1921. John Devoy's theory would cast Hobson, McCartan and O'Hegarty as stooges (willing or otherwise), Irish instances of what Stalin called 'objective traitors'. The work of a mole or not, Maloney's book is best read as a product of 'the low dishonest decade'.

Contrary to the view established in 1936 and consolidated in the isolated years which followed, there had been no general consensus on the issue before Maloney and Company got to work. Casement's faithful and Fenian sister, Nina (Mrs Newman), understandably believed what the authorities circulated in 1916 to be a fabrication, because she did not believe that her brother was a person of the kind depicted. His cousin Gertrude (Mrs Sydney Parry) acted on the same assumptions, but inwardly seems to have harboured certain reservations, that is, admitted certain possibilities. This is the only way to interpret the letter which Charlotte Shaw wrote to her in 1935 about T. E. Lawrence's interest in a biography of Casement:

> Yes: about Lawrence. It is as you say he 'understood' & I remember what a bound my heart gave when he said he would like to write about Roger. Perhaps he would have – who knows! But I think it was a passing inspiration. But I feel he 'understood'. Perhaps T. E. is better where he is – his life was not happy lately.[1]

That this view of Lawrence's attitude originated with Mrs Parry should not be forgotten in the better known context of the Shaws' liberal attitudes towards sexuality. Equally, one should not jump to the conclusion that she privately endorsed everything which is now embodied in 'The Black Diaries'. Her earlier efforts to recover documentation from the British authorities

1 C. Shaw to G. Parry, 24 June 1935 (NLI, MS 13,075); quoted in B. L. Reid, *The Lives of Roger Casement* (New Haven: Yale University Press, 1976), p. 466.

had been clearly designed to end in its destruction, not its publication. Nevertheless, the notion that Lawrence (1888–1935) – himself a homosexual but not a happy one – 'understood' Casement takes her out of the category of simple deniers. Lawrence's abandonment of his plans for a biography stemmed from his failure to gain access to the very diaries which might have enhanced understanding.

Against these latter, an impressive array of people had seen something of the documentation and accepted it as genuine, or on other grounds accepted Casement's homosexuality. Leaving aside the outraged bishops and disgusted diplomats, these included Michael Collins, Eamonn Duggan, Alice Stopford Green, John Redmond, Shaw, and possibly Yeats – formidable witnesses. To these, the names of John Quinn and Shane Leslie can be added with, perhaps, a diminished significance. De Valera, as we have seen, was keen to repatriate Casement's lime-corroded remains, but fought shy of asking about the diaries. Whatever Pentonville might unearth, it could be relied upon to be unrecognisable, posing no challenge to the iconic, idealising photographs and portraits.

Other figures maintained a calculated neutrality, at least in their public utterances. Take H. W. Nevinson, for example, frequently invoked by the Forgery Theorists. In a first volume of autobiography, *Changes and Chances*, he had nothing to say on this topic except to note that J. H. Morgan was 'a barrister distinguished for courage in defence of my friend Roger Casement at the State Trial'. In a sequel, Nevinson devoted more than a page to Alice Stopford Green's cheerful resilience during the Anglo-Irish War and mocked 'ex-gentlemen known as "Auxiliaries"'; in the course of his tribute to Mrs Green he referred to excerpts from the diary 'whether genuine or forgeries'. A third volume adds details about London editors assembled by 'a member of the Government' in June 1916 for briefing on a diary allegedly found among Casement's papers, incriminating him in 'unnatural vice'. This account has been used to throw doubt – as if further doubt were needed – on the reliability of Sir Basil Thomson's several versions of the discovery. Though lying outside Nevinson's trilogy, yet a further volume (appearing in the same year as Maloney's *Forged Casement Diaries*) had absolutely nothing to add.

Nevinson died during the Second World War. A second edition of his *Last Changes Last Chances* was published posthumously in the late 1950s. The Wolfenden Report (1957) already reflected a liberalisation of public opinion in the UK (excluding Northern Ireland!) on the issue of homosexuality. Its recommendations related to private acts between consenting adults, thus tending to redirect legal focus on to ancillary issues: prostitution and consent, the nature of a 'public act' and – in due course – the whole realm of paedophilia. More immediately and specifically, the Casement diaries were about to enter the public domain the following year, and soon there was little need for arch neutrality on the part of Nevinson's literary executors. Angus Mitchell quotes extensively from *Last Changes* but neglects to cite *More Charges* which had commented even-handedly on the forgery issue.[2]

HOW WHITE IS THE WHITE DIARY?

In Casement's diaries one comes across references to his diaries which contribute to the notion that one compilation was sometimes used to comment on, or as a source for, another.[3] These allusions have attracted rival interpretations, especially with reference to the so-called Black Diary and White Diary of 1910. The latter – now preserved in NLI – was handed over by Casement to assist the Foreign Office in preparing a public text of his findings in the Putumayo. For Charles Roberts, the MP charged with collating much of this material, Casement provided a curiously low-key assessment of its worth:

> I am afraid the Diary wont be of much help. Much of it is redundant & it was really a sort of Supplementary note to the long depositions of the Barbados men which in truth were often my whole day's work. I had no clerical help of any kind & the writing down of so much of the prolonged questioning & reexamining and often confronting witnesses took nearly all my time – so that the Diary represents a very fagged hand & mind simply.[4]

2   H. W. Nevinson, *Changes and Chances* (London: Nisbet, 1923), p. 196; *More Changes, More Chances* (London: Nisbet, 1925), p. 296; *Last Charges, Last Chances* (London: Nisbet, 1928), pp. 114–16. *Running Accompaniments* (London: Routledge, 1936). Nevinson also published a one-volume version of his trilogy under the title *Fire of Life* (London: Nisbet, with Gollancz, 1935: on Casement see pp. 328–39, though there is nothing added). See also Angus Mitchell (ed.), *The Amazon Journal of Roger Casement* (Dublin: Lilliput; London: Anaconda, 1997), pp. 31–2n. Nevinson's papers in the Bodley Library can shed further light on European travellers' interest in African sexual practices.

3   See, for example, Mitchell (ed.), *Amazon Journal*, p. 324.

4   Casement to Charles Roberts, 13 Mar. 1913, writing from Cape Town (Rhodes House, MSS Brit. Emp. s22, Anti-Slavery Society file G344c).

One reading of this description would claim that the so-called diary was written after all the depositions which took up so much time, and might be better thought of as a deliberately constructed retrospect in need of considerable further work before it might be of any value as evidence. An entry, apparently made on 14 October 1910, strongly suggests a pre-planned agenda: 'I have a theory which will be developed later on when I come to deal more closely with the Indians and their customs.'[5] The more one recovers from Casement's own description of it at the time the less it conforms to the authoritative record required by the Forgery Theory to show up 'black' imposters:

> less a diary than a reflection – a series of daily and weekly reflections.
>
> As a diary it must be read in conjunction with the evidence of the Barbados men, which ran concurrently with most of it. Also I have two notebooks in which are other portions of the diary and sometimes letters are to go in when I have left blanks.[6]

This then is the document upon which Mitchell and others have staked their view that the Black rival must be a forgery, constructed to defame Casement as a promiscuous homosexual.

Yet the White document has its own opacity. Responding to an execution-by-drowning, Casement in his early days in the Putumayo made this odd contrast, 'And so the fearful tale goes so, when I was merely talking of the dangers of sleeping <u>en garçon</u> in these hells of Circe!' While ignoring the temptation to inquire about the dangers he feared, we can note that the allusion to Homer's cave of foul enchantment and shape-changing finds its practical enactment in Casement's own text. Even earlier in the White document, one finds his characteristic amalgam of observation and behaviour: 'This very afternoon at teatime, while Sr. Macedo's little boy of 3 years was at my bedroom door, playing with me, with his Indian nursegirl, and another little girl, not a nurse, but evidently the child of a Peruvian – a pretty child, a

5   NLI, MS 13,087 (25) f. 54/40; cf. Mitchell (ed.), *Amazon Journal*, p. 242. The manuscript of the so-called White Diary carries two internal numbering systems – top left and top right corners of the leaf. Why this should be remains unexplained by its editor. These certainly raise questions about the history of the manuscript. For example, the single sheet numbered 40 on its right corner was previously numbered 41, and no number appears on the top left corner: the text opens with some comments about cannibalism in the Congo which reinforces one's sense of the document as less a direct day-by-day account of the Putumayo inquiry than a work-in-progress-towards-publication.

6   Rhodes House, MSS Brit. Emp. s22.

girl of 5 or 6 – Bishop [one of the labourers] seeing me pet the boy and glance at the girl whose hand he was holding, said to Barnes and myself, "That girl's father, Sir, was killed by his own muchachos a few months ago."[7]

A certain unease among the Theorists was discernible even in the 1930s. The examination of Patrick McCartan's correspondence with Maloney and other activists in the 1920s and 1930s provides some support for the view that, even amongst them, there was no fully declared and unambiguous faith in Casement's heterosexual conventionality. As B. L. Reid and others have pointed out, his solicitor Gavan Duffy never went so far as assert this faith, instead chiding Maloney for advancing a thesis which he (Gavan Duffy) could not endorse. Finally, there was the pointed observation of Frank MacDermot in 1937 that the Irish government's refusal to seek an independent examination of documentation led one to unavoidable conclusions.

More recently, Montgomery Hyde, Brian Inglis, Geoffrey Parmiter, B. L. Reid, and Roger Sawyer have all examined the diaries and accepted them as genuinely Casement's.[8] Various attempts to discredit some or all of these biographers have been made. In the case of Hyde, it has been suggested that he was compromised by his links with British Intelligence, his role as a Unionist MP, or even (possibly) by his own sexuality. Two seminars organised by the present writer at Goldsmiths College, London (February 1998) and the Public Record Office, Kew (December 2000) have given sharper definition to the issues at stake. As a third event (at the Royal Irish Academy, Dublin, in May 2000) revealed, there are supporters still of the Forgery Theory: a year later, at the annual Casement Foundation symposium in Dublin (September 2001), the attendance numbered thirteen, just like the Last Supper. But one finds few of them willing to endorse the process of forensic examination. In their case, MacDermot's comments of 1937 remain particularly relevant.

As a third London Casement Colloquium is in preparation, a shadow suddenly falls over the White Diary, long regarded as the gold standard against which spurious mintings were to be tested and found wanting. This is the document, preserved in NLI in a manuscript and in typed-copy form, which forms the centrepiece of what Angus Mitchell has called Casement's *Amazon Journal*. On every recent occasion when forensic examination of the

---

7   NLI, MS, 1622 ff 74 and 24; cf. Mitchell, *Amazon Journal*, pp. 175, 136; Roger Sawyer (ed.), *Roger Casement's Diaries: 1910, the Black and the White* (London: Pimlico, 1997), p. 153.

8   For Parmiter's retraction of his tacit acceptance of the Normand Defence in 1936, see *Quarterly Review* (Apr. 1960).

Black Diaries was proposed, true believers insisted that the White Diary must be used as a 'control' in a comparative analysis of handwriting in the manuscripts. This insistence was strikingly passive; that is, the true believers never intended to act upon their own advice or opinion, never acted to subject the Black Diaries to any examination which might vindicate their belief or shatter it. Tests might be conducted by a lesser breed, vulgar scientists or crypto-antinationalists, friends of Fintan O'Toole, or tools of the FO.

The parallel between Black and White diaries is more apparent than real. The only period covered by both is late 1910 when Casement was in the Putumayo region in pursuit of the rubber extortionists. The document preserved in NLI – unlike those at Kew – has the appearance of a planned narrative, written as it is on 128 sheets of paper of uniform size.[9] It is now stated that the manuscript White Diary was presented to NLI by Mrs Sydney Parry with other material on 30 September 1950, at which date Maloney had ceased to concern himself with her brother's reputation.[10] According to Angus Mitchell, however, the White Diary 'eventually reached the National Library of Ireland in 1951 after the death of Gavan Duffy (1882–1951)'.[11] Mitchell's imputation – that the White Diary had been in the possession of Casement's solicitor until the time of his death – blurs the real provenance of the document. The most reasonable summary is B. L. Reid's, which traces the diary from the time of Casement's (indirect) handing it over to Charles Roberts of the Foreign Office early in 1913 to back up his Putumayo report, to its return from Roberts to Casement on (it is deduced) 7 August of the same year.[12] From this it is

---

9   The MS also has a deliberately planned area of margin, in which the diarist has occasionally entered additional or explanatory material. While it basically adopts a day-by-day order, the diary also accommodates retrospectives; for example, the entry on 26 Sept. 1910 had a marginal note 'Begins Friday 23 Sept.' Certain cancelled material, e.g. a note on Peruvian control of the Putumayo region in 1910, with a subsequent direction 'Begins here' in blue crayon, further suggests that the MS was in a state of modification for further use or publication.

10   I am grateful to Dr Noel Kissane, Keeper of Manuscripts, at NLI, for a letter of 12 Oct. 2001, making these facts plain. The material is generally classified as NLI, MSS 13,073–92: the manuscript diary is MS 13,087 (25). However, Mrs Parry had died on 23 Sept. 1950: a copy of her will (dated 12 Feb. 1944) establishes that, after a small number of monetary legacies, she left all her estate to two cousins of her late husband. From this we may deduce that the material in the NLI was deposited by her in her lifetime or, at latest, by her lawyer immediately after her death.

11   Mitchell (ed.), *Amazon Journal*, pp. 38–9.

12   From Roberts's letter to Casement, acknowledging receipt of the diary, it is clear that he arranged for a typed copy to be prepared 'by an expert' (quoted in B. L. Reid, *The Lives of Roger Casement* (New Haven, London: Yale University Press, 1976), pp. 160–1 n (c)).

reasonable to suppose that it was seized by the British authorities at some point before Casement's arrest and during the period when they were anxious to curtail his Irish political activities. Despite Mrs Parry's belief to the contrary, the manuscript was returned with Casement's effects after the execution, and indeed the manner of its final arrival in NLI tends to confirm this provenance.[13]

But in *The Forged Casement Diaries*, Maloney recorded George Gavan Duffy's gift to him in 1921 of a typescript Casement diary for the same period. Furthermore, in November 1923, Patrick McCartan had claimed that 'the British Gov. has Casement's diaries & photographs of the Putumayo but won't give them up'. Was McCartan relying here on a conscientious, but mistaken, belief of Mrs Parry's, that she had not been given the Putumayo diary for 1910 – mistaken in that she was expecting a print-form, commercial diary, and not a bundle of foolscap? It has now been established that the typescript in NLI was presented by George Gavan Duffy, who had either (post 1936) recovered the copy given to Maloney in 1921 or handed over a second copy retained since Casement's death.[14]

Two factors thus affect the suitability of the White Diary manuscript for any part in a comparative study of handwriting in the Black Diaries. First, its provenance does not exclude temporary possession by the British security authorities (in addition to Roberts of the Foreign Office), where it may have served as a model for the alleged forger of other documents or may itself have been tinkered with; second, its physical and scribal format does not in practice match that of the commercially printed diaries at Kew. In terms of scribal practice – use of both pencil and pen, untidy appearance – Casement's letters to his Congo Reform associate E. D. Morel (1873–1924) are closer to the Kew diaries than the White Diary is. For the purposes of a comparative forensic examination of the White and Black Diaries, the LSE's chief archivist made available some two hundred sheets of Casement's correspondence with Morel, for the years 1903, 1910 and 1911. The Trustees of NLI authorised a loan of the White Diary for the same exercise, but in the event only a small portion of the manuscript was made available to the Giles Document Laboratory.

---

13 Reid, *Lives of Roger Casement*, pp. 160–1.

14 We can be sure that Maloney did in fact receive the typescript (MSS 1622–3) from Gavan Duffy who was alive in 1936 and alert to the deficiencies in Maloney's procedures: any false claim in this connection would have been publicly repudiated. When it arrived in Kildare Street, the document was not accessed in the normal manner, but in February 2002 Mr Tom Desmond of NLI unearthed evidence establishing Gavan Duffy as the source.

TESTING, TESTING . . .

The intention of the essay from which the present book grew was not to prove a case about the authenticity or otherwise of the diaries associated with Casement's name, preserved in the Public Record Office at Kew. On the contrary, its objectives were limited to an analysis of the case made for forgery in the 1930s. Readers will differ in their interpretation of the evidence assembled alongside the analysis. Certain aspects of the matter require further investigation. Nevertheless, much has been illuminated – the complex framework in which *The Forged Casement Diaries* was brought to publication, the elusive yet ebullient character of the author, his position in transatlantic Irish propaganda and politics. Aspects of the Irish newspaper world, also of the mentality of Irish officialdom, emerge in unexpected detail. Meanwhile, Casement remains in the shadows.

As I wrote, specifications were being drawn up for the first comprehensive forensic examination of the contested documents.[15] Were the scientists to be directed to test for forgery or authenticity in each of the five documents? Or, to put it another way, should one begin with a hypothesis that the documents are forged or are authentic? Answers to these questions are inevitably affected by what one now knows about the Forgery Theory's emergence.

What, then, should an examination attempt? The hypothesis to be tested must surely be that the diaries are genuinely Casement's. As a consequence, an examination is to be comprehensively, systematically and rigorously conducted to establish the extent of any forgery, interpolation, excision, or other interference. These involve both an internal examination of the documents, and a comparison with others indisputably written in Casement's hand and (as far as possible) uncontaminated by third parties. The physical components of the documents at Kew are to be subjected to examination – binding, paper (including blotting paper), ink, and any attachments. The handwriting is to be examined both with regard to its agent (Casement or some other/s), its consistency as to time of inscription, its consistency with reference to the time-frame of the print-form diaries (three only, of the five documents), its relationship by way of transferred indentation to pages adjacent to that on which it is inscribed.

15 On 26 Apr. 2001, Sir Richard Wilson, of the Cabinet Office, was advised that 'Casement remains highly sensitive to this day'.

There may be a case for either DNA or pollen analysis, or both. These latter indicate how forensic testing has developed since the 1930s when Noyes, Maud Gonne and others called for an independent tribunal. By the same token, the ponderous structure of a tribunal, as envisaged at the time of Maloney's publication, is obviated by improvements in telecommunications, computer technology etc., not to mention greater sensitivity to the complexities of Anglo-Irish politics, including sexual politics. Finally, one should note the easing of distrust in both Dublin and London on the Casement issue, as indicated by the two Prime Ministers in 1999.[16] As a consequence, the methodology of the Mc Cormack Tests is historical and forensic rather than political and jurisprudential.

It would be a mistake, however, for anyone to assume that such procedures can come up with a simple 100 per cent verdict, one way or the other. Almost certainly, some issues will be indeterminable. For example, the army-issue field notebook (HO 161/1) which Casement used for notes mainly in pencil was made up of pages with a perforation to the top binding: many pages have been torn out, but it may not be possible to establish whether these were removed all in one fell swoop, or individually. Other imponderables are predictable. The application of DNA analysis could (at best) only result in certain kinds of one-dimensional result. The presence of Casement's genetic code would certainly establish that he handled the object in question, but it would not rule out its being also handled by a forger. (Each item has, by now, been handled by hundreds of people, including the present writer.) Secondly, the absence of Casement's genetic code (if it could be identified and isolated) could not be interpreted as establishing (after eighty-five or more years) that he had not handled the item in question. Similar problems arise with regard to pollen traces distinctive to – say – the Amazon region.

The physical examination takes us towards psychological or (in the neutral sense) mental issues. In this regard, we look back to 1916 rather than 1936, to Dryhurst and Conan Doyle rather than William Joseph [Marie Alois] Maloney. An examination of handwriting may establish that Roger Casement was its agent. But this should be distinguished from the conclusion that he was its author. Mrs Dryhurst appears to be the earliest traceable advocate of such a view. However, her appeal to Basil Thomson (as it comes down to us) is not without its own problems. Did Casement take notes in 'Spanish or Portuguese'

16 See Angus Mitchell, 'The Casement "Black Diaries" Debate: The Story So Far', *History Ireland*, vol. 9 no. 2 (summer 2001), pp. 42–5.

(she is not sure which) and then translate them himself into English? These notes could not simply be the evidence he could not employ a woman secretary 'to take it down', for there was no woman among his party in the Putumayo. The Dryhurst Defence, emanating from Downshire Hill in Hampstead (where Casement's public supporter Lynd later maintained a sociable house for artists, radicals and writers) makes a vital distinction but is otherwise confusing. Was Nannie Dryhurst the unknown name through whom more targetable supporters of Casement attempted a rescue operation? Within a few years her husband was decorated by the state, in marked contrast to the treatment meted out to Casement's sister.[17]

The Normand Defence, flawed though it seems in terms of its own emergence, usefully reinforces her basic distinction. If, as Dr Dickey claimed, Casement took notes from dictation on the topic of sexual practices in the Amazon basin, then the resulting manuscript would have

1   Casement as its agent, *and*

2   Dickey as its author.

As to the forensic issue, physical examination could establish the first, but never (on its own) the second. If, as Hobson and O'Hegarty submitted, Casement copied a diary written by Armando Normand, then the copy would likewise have Casement as its agent. The suggestion has been made that some parts of the documentation may be translated from French pornographic fiction; here too the distinction between agent and author is important.

Beyond it, there arise others no less important. The diary-form which the documents generally take imposes a schematic representation of time to which the diarist can adopt a flexible attitude – or indeed a variety of attitudes. That is, on a specific day s/he may write within the page-space assigned to that date, or may write elsewhere on that day, or may write on another date within that page-space. Most people are familiar with situations in which a diary is used as an emergency notebook, with an address hastily entered (by a colleague, a chance acquaintance, or by the owner) on a dated page to which it has no intrinsic time-connection. Others will recognise the practice of retrospective diary-reading-and-annotation as, for example, when an entry for last week is 'updated' with comment about persons subsequently met or actions completed.

17   For the award of a DSO to A. R. Dryhurst, see *The Times*, 3 June 1918, p. 10 col. 4.

The role of time in material undergoing editorial reflection can be further refined with reference to the distinction between intention and commission. The diarist enters some words which record his intention to do a certain thing – buy a wedding present, for example. But the commission of this thing remains quite distinct; perhaps it never happened, due to financial embarrassment, forgetfulness, a change of mind about the persons involved, major distractions from quite a different world, non-availability of the item in the shops. While it seems natural to regard diaries as records, one must take care to discriminate between the different mental acts they may record – intentions unfulfilled, acknowledgements of actions completed, intentions met by some third party which are thus both unfulfilled and fulfilled, desires, regrets, mistaken beliefs, fantasies . . . In connection with the last category, the Freudian concept of the unconscious becomes relevant.

In other words, the interpretation of diaries is never a simple matter. The documents preserved at Kew as HO 161/1–5 possess their own distinctive complexities. Forensic examination is a necessary first stage in their analysis, but it is far from being a full or sufficient mode of approach. While bearing in mind the possibility of mixed or incomplete findings, we can briefly consider two contrasting outcomes. If the diaries are adjudged not to be Casement's, or adjudged to contain a significant amount of writing which is demonstrably not his, then the issue of official British interference or forgery acquires a degree of compelling authority it has never possessed before. From such an outcome would arise questions about the conduct of the Foreign Office, the Home Office, the military, the police and 'the secret service' during the Great War (and after), questions which would not be limited solely to the Casement trial, the campaign for a reprieve, and the execution. The document seen by Ben S. Allen in 1916 and described by him in some detail – now to be called the Buff Diary – would be sought with the greatest determination. Forensic examination would be superseded by historical and archival inquiry.

But if the diaries are adjudged to be Casement's in their entirety, or adjudged to contain only an insignificant amount of writing which is demonstrably not his, then the issue of his homosexuality beats upon the door. Those who have thought such an orientation incompatible with patriotism or philanthropy will be obliged to revise at least some of their prejudices. In the longer term, a textual analysis of the diaries may enable us to distinguish between Casement's reported actions, his desires, his observations of others, and his fantasies (if any). In a broader context, his writings may lead us into a more sensitive understanding of transgression, whether its manifest vocabulary be – in crude terms – political or sexual. If Casement runs the risk of ejection from the National Pantheon, he may find alternative accommodation on the American Campus.

Will the last state of that man be better than the first?

SOCIAL PSYCHOSIS AND THE EGO'S ERA

The scientific demonstration that the Black Diaries are Roger Casement's through and through opens up new possibilities for scholarship in this area. Some will wish to pursue what is at times called linguistic analysis, though the prospect of reversing, qualifying or embarrassing the Giles Report can scarcely be regarded as bright. The claim (which has been made) that word-frequency counts could demonstrate that the White and Black diaries for the same period were not composed by the same mind depends (so far) on a number of inadequacies. First, the computer programme employed by Ó Maille and Co. was a very elementary one, unfitted for the complex task they were undertaking. Second, the distinction between 'mind' and 'hand' (or 'author' and 'agent') remains as valid and as damaging for linguistic analysts as it was for upholders of the Normand Defence. Third, the assumption that radically different states of mind cannot co-exist in the same personality acts as a censoring mechanism of unfalsifiability; that is, a rhetorical manoeuvre by which an assumption protects itself in advance from the risk of its contrary being admitted. Finally, the Giles Report's comments on the White Diary go some way towards substantiating the view that it was not a strict day-by-day diary, and as such only partly suitable for comparison with the Black. Perhaps a forensic examination of the White Diary in its entirety might shed further light on this issue, in which case the typescript copy should be included in the materials to be examined.

With the end of forensics in sight for Roger Casement, his literary remains may soon rest in physical, if not interpretative, peace. Beyond the desirability of clarifying the status of certain documents in NLI – and here one looks beyond Casement's own manuscripts to some of those deposited by Maloney and his managers – there is little to be gained by turning to German or American archives for ESDA fodder. Already certain theoretical questions have thrust themselves forward. The Freudian concept of the unconscious has been invoked, with reference to the possible presence in the diaries of writing linked to desires rather than acts or reports. This is not simply a matter of naming some mode of interpretation available in relation to texts of any age; Freud and Casement share a historical context, which could be characterised in terms of positivism in the scientific discourses it inherited, in terms of crisis in the imperial economies which drove it, and in terms of accentuated racism in the accounts it generated of global activities and internally oppressed minorities.

Drawing on the work of Jacques Lacan, Teresa Brennan has identified what she calls 'the ego's era'. What is suggestive here is Brennan's ability to link altered attitudes to the physical environment with the growth of 'social psychosis'. In an early paper, Lacan had described aggression as projecting 'the predations of Victorian Society and the economic euphoria that sanctioned for that society the social devastation that it initiated on a planetary scale'.[18] Quite simply, the Putumayo provided a case study in this historical process, with the financial activities of Julio Cesar Arana doubling up as redesigned national frontiers and contested zones of jurisdiction. The commodity in question – rubber – possessed a dizzying flexibility in its potential for industrial, medical, military and recreational uses. Its relationship to capital is neatly encapsulated in the notion of 'the bouncing cheque'. Marx believed that commodities with the potential to 'fetishise' themselves exerted magical influence over their user/victims: rubber, though not yet a commodity in itself, took that pseudo-Circean metamorphosis several stages back into the realm of natural resources. Revolutionary in its impact on the manufacture of goods, rubber was also primality itself, the free-flowing juice of nature.

Writing in far more general terms, Brennan characterises the period in which these innovations flourished, in terms of *velocity* as well as substance, in a manner which challenges the traditional relations of time and space. The ever-intensifying extraction of profit from labour and materials has taken on a specific and new form: 'Capital will live or die according to the speed of acquisition, but to live by the speed of acquisition is to live under a fantasmic law. Natural entities and substances will live or die depending on how far their reproduction is permitted, and it is permitted less and less under the law of speed.'[19] Writing as a feminist, she relates reproduction to the role of women

18 Quoted in Teresa Brennan, *History After Lacan* (London: Routledge, 1993), p. 41. It is not possible here to explore the breathless complexity of Brennan's argument as it bears upon environmentalism, feminism and theology.

19 *Ibid.*, p. 133.

and woman in the new dispensation of *circa* 1900. But it is clear that other applications of her general theory of relativity may be essayed.

Just as the elaboration of a full psychological biography of Casement must be postponed for another, more bountiful occasion, so the economic and symbolic context in which he acted awaits other explorers. Nevertheless, a strikingly succinct correlation can be articulated even from the as yet inadequately edited diaries, both black and white.

The production of rubber involved the breaking (or penetration) and scarring of tree-bark, resulting in the extrusion of the white sticky substance.

The punishment of insufficiently speedy rubber producers involved the breaking and scarring of their skin and, in numerous extreme cases, the mutilation of their organs of reproduction.

The recording of these proto-industrial activities, interfiled in the production process with these other barbarous practices, involved additionally the recording of same-sex (i.e. non-reproductive) practices in which the diarist details the extrusion of a different white sticky substance (namely semen).

Finally, the inscription of all these records involved the application of black (or, yes, blue and grey) ink or carbon on white (or, yes, buff) paper.

The stages of a process, which resembles a line stretching from action in the illiterate jungle to inscription in a London (or Dublin) housed diary, should, however, be recognised as partly simultaneous as well as sequential. This at least would be the ideal required under the law of speed. While this is at one important and practical level an impossibility, its attraction in the blinkered view of investors leads to a paradox. (After all, beauty is in the eye of the shareholder.) Casement, searing critic of the rubber industry, practises a form of sexual writing which mimics both the primitive production and the brutal punishment he condemns. This mimicry can be read as at once the response of a personality disorientated by the horrors he has witnessed and also the response of a witness who actively deconstructs the social psychosis by refusing to play the part of a dominant, rigidly defined ego. Here, the condition of being at once actor and observer takes on a positive ethical coloration which might be impossible were it not for those attendant violations implicit in Casement's account of petting the boy, an account which unconsciously distracts itself into a focus upon the female, but only through the announcement of violent death inflicted on her absent father.

I am aware that much of this may be dismissed by seasoned readers of Casement material as psychobabble, generated by an amateur relying on generalisations. The closed shop of Freudian analysis does not prevent one acquiring (over four or five years of first-remove engagement) at least as much competence as the average amateur historian boasts of in his or her own discipline. And the coming together of history and psycho-analysis – even for just these few pages – has its well-established propriety, for both disciplines are concerned essentially with the interpretation of texts.[20] As for the common-sensible distrust of generalisations, there is no need in the present context to avoid a specific textual analysis. With it, we return to the Normand Defence and thus to the arguments of Maloney and his managers.

THE RENEWED QUEST FOR ARMANDO

In chapter 8, we pursued a line of inquiry – inconclusive – about the family of Normand, especially in *fin de siècle* London. A different kind of pursuit should now be considered. An examination of early leaves in the document known as the White Diary shows Casement's gradual focusing on the man initially registered in the text through the surname Norman. There is some confusion about the names which emerge to denote the figure ultimately accused of the grossest crimes perpetrated on behalf of the Peruvian Amazon Company. In the Black Diary entry for 13 October 1910, Casement records the murder of a man by Armando King. In the White entry for Tuesday 11 October, he refers to Armando Blondel and, further down the same page, refers also to Norman. Shortly afterward he places at the top of the 'principal criminals' list the name 'Armando or Felipe Norman'.[21] In the typescript version of this 'diary', one finds the early appearance of the name Normand amended in pencil with an

20 The standard work in this area is Peter Gay, *Freud for Historians* (New York: Oxford University Press, 1985).
21 NLI, MS 13,087 (25) f. 45/31 side 3; f. 47/33 side 4. In the Black Diary, the name appears to be consistently spelled Normand. This detail may contribute to the debate about the order in which Casement wrote the two accounts of the time in Putumayo.

additional final letter 'd' that has Casement's distinctive left-leaning upright
stroke. The quest leads from Norman to Normand.

On 17 October 1910, Casement and his party of investigators got thoroughly
drenched in torrential rain as they made their way to another outpost of the
Peruvian Amazon Company. In Casement's case, even his Dublin brolly – 'the
first, I'll wager, ever seen in these forests' – proved useless against the
downpour. Because of the weather or some other factor, he became detached
from the rest of the party and made his way ahead of them. The narrative
provided in the White Diary has something of the psychological complexity
found in a Conrad novel – with the difference that the dangers Casement
faced were real and the villains unrestrained by the conventions of fiction:

> I found myself at the verge of a clearing and saw the roof of Matanzas or Andokes
> Station, and the Peruvian flag flying. I decided to wait for the others, rather than go
> on to meet alone and be civil to this evil reputationed [sic] man, Armando Normand,
> with whom I wish to have as little and as brief intercourse as possible. The
> Commission and Tizon arrived about 3.30., perfectly soaked, and we all went
> on over a knoll into the Station in the midst of the tail of the storm. Found
> Mr. Normand at the other Station, where he lives, La China, named capriciously
> like 'Indostan,' or Abisinia – which is 10 hours away . . .[22]

This last incidental confirmation of an 'orientalism' in the Peruvian Amazon
Company's naming policy leads Casement to recall that, in Walter Hardenburg's
wake-up account of the atrocities, 'Normand's name [occurred] probably
more often than that of any other [person].'[23] For the reader, if Casement
indeed intended there to be a reader other than himself, the imminent
encounter with the villainous mass murderer has been carefully prepared. A
further stage in the evolving narrative delays the moment of confrontation by
looking back to reconsider the testimony of other employees in the Company,
'Bishop . . . firmly believes the stories related of Normand dashing children's
brains out against tree stumps and burning them alive. He declares that Donal
Francis who was here for nearly two years with Normand at the beginning, has
told him more than once of these things'.[24] It is worth noting in passing, that
Casement usually prefers to render Mr Francis's forename in the Gaelic form
(Donal) than the more usual (Donald).

22   NLI, MS 1622 f. 154; cf. Mitchell (ed.), *Amazon Diary*, p. 254.
23   NLI, MS 1622 f. 155; cf. Mitchell (ed.), *Amazon Diary*, p. 255.
24   NLI, MS 1622 f. 155; cf. Mitchell (ed.), *Amazon Diary*, p. 255.

Though Normand is not present when the investigators arrive, but is at the station where he normally dwells, Casement is nonetheless assigned to or chooses 'Normand's sitting room' as his own accommodation while at Matanzas. One can assume that the allocation was made on the basis of his seniority as the Foreign Office's representative, for other members of the party have to share a room (on one occasion identified as Normand's bedroom). These arrangements allow him to detail and reflect upon the decor of the sadist's parlour – 'it is pasted round with pictures from the "Graphic", largely dealing with the Russo-Japanese War of 1904. There are also a lot of ~~female midettes~~ [*sic*] cocottes taken from some low-class Paris paper, and several photos of brutal faced South American people'.[25] If the Graphics in question included that of 20 February 1904, then Normand would have read of Casement's Congo report (p. 230) and the mutilations which had gone hand in hand with rubber production for Leopold II. The effect of this domestic interior survey must be to dilute any sense the reader (including Casement, perhaps including only Casement) may have of Normand as a unique and isolated monster: he is very specifically linked to recent world events, to popular European recreation, and even to a gallery of acquaintances represented by personal photographs rather than newspaper cuttings.

Casement's narrative closes in on these images, for one of them he imagines 'to be Normand himself "when a boy"', and this reflection opens up the possibility of a history for the man who has been more often presented as a contextless brute or murder machine. Oddly choosing the impersonal pronoun, Casement continues 'it looks like a low typed [*sic*] East-end Jew, with fat greasy lips and circular eyes'. Leaving aside the all-too-conventional anti-Semitism of this, we should recall that the diarist uses a good deal of physiognomical description to characterise both villainous adults and the charm of native children. Returning to Normand, he notes 'certificates from The London School of Book-keepers of 1904, giving him a certificate as "Book-keeper" and a certificate from some senior school of earlier date'.[26]

The murderer whose entrance is awaited has been equipped with a personal dossier directly linked to the imperial capital, and it will be no

25 NLI, MS 1622 ff. 155–6. The cancellation of two words, and substitution of a third, is in effect in pencil; in French a midinette [*sic*] is a work girl, a humble milliner etc.; Mitchell, *Amazon Diary*, pp. 255–6; Sawyer (ed.), *Roger Casement's Diaries*, p. 185.
26 I have yet to trace an address for this academy, the London Post Office Directories for the years round 1904 having failed to deliver one.

surprise to discover that he speaks both English and Spanish. Certain other apparently minor details further link him to Casement himself, for Gielgud (one of the Company's travelling representatives) advises Casement that Normand is 'quite a remarkable walker'. As if on cue of a rifle-shot heard from the woods, Normand enters the narrative and prompts the diarist into a preliminary assessment:

> He came up, I must say, to all one had read or thought of him, a little being, slim, thin and quite short, say, 5' 7" and with a face truly the most repulsive I have ever seen. It was perfectly devilish in its cruelty and evil. I felt as if I were being introduced to a serpent. All through dinner he spoke Spanish, but whenever by chance a word came to me, I answered in English.[27]

This linguistic stand-off could be regarded as a crucial stage in Normand's taking on uncanny [*unheimlich*] features in the narrative: he is both familiar and unfamiliar, 'one of us' and a monster. From this point Casement begins to manoeuvre. He turns in early to avoid a further meeting but is woken by the arrival of his host's harem – 'tiny little things . . . Poor little creatures . . .'. It is not entirely clear whether Normand is or is not on the premises at this moment, for Casement records that 'some voices shouted down the passage and they all bolted to the room Normand is sleeping in . . .', but continues that the women were 'making for the room where they presumed [*sic*] their sleeping lord was lying'. This uncertainty is inscribed in the diary as part of Casement's alternating relationship with the monster.

The next day the FO's man declared that he 'could not stand another hour of Normand' for it made him sick to look at the 'absolute monster'. Instead, he interviews a man named James Lane, leaving his fellow investigators to interview Normand in the next room. 'The double inquiry going on within earshot with only these thin palm-bark screens between, will be interesting.'[28] All in all Casement inscribes an intermittent, broken fascination with the chief perpetrator of the atrocities under investigation, while also maintaining narrative drive.

The next headed section of the typescript commences with an account of Lane's testimony, but gradually it is clear that Casement can hear both Normand's voice and Lane's simultaneously, the former through a partition

27 NLI, MS 1622 f. 156; cf. Mitchell (ed.), *Amazon Diary*, p. 256
28 NLI, MS 1622 f. 158; cf. Mitchell (ed.), *Amazon Diary*, pp. 257–8.

separating the rooms. The certified bookkeeper denies having flogged Indians within three years: 'as Normand was actually stating this in my hearing, Lane was declaring – unwillingly declaring – that within a month he had seen a man beaten to death, beside five others, three of them women, by the very orders of this man, and giving me the name of the employé . . . who had laid on the lash'.[29] These horrific accounts of sadistic butchery are accompanied in the larger narrative by the arrival of native porters carrying Normand's 'fabrico' of rubber from the forest.

> Their bodies were slim and graceful, and their bodily strength remarkable. I tried to carry one load of rubber. Made Chase lift it and put it on my shoulder, Normand standing on. I could not walk three paces with it – literally and truly. My knees gave way and to save my life, I don't think I could have gone 50 yards. . . The little boys, some of them 5 or 6, without even a 'fono', stark naked, dear little things with soft gentle eyes and long eyelashes were coming along too, often with 30 lbs or more on their tiny backs. I saw one lad, looked about 15, with a boy's frank voice, with a load of fully 75 to 80 lbs. I asked N[ormand] for his balance to weigh some of them. He said he had none there . . .[30]

By this point, the latter-day reader is aware of 'interference' in the official narrative by a seemingly unconscious sub-narrative devoted to the appearance of the boys, their nakedness and their trust in him. By trying out the weight of their burdens, Casement on the ground gathers valuable information against the Peruvian Amazon Company. By his placing of this account, Casement on the page relates himself to the victims. For those who regard the White Diary as unblemished by the 'contentious' matter in the Black ones, these accounts may seem wholly innocuous. But the status of the parallel records is also unclear. If it is held that the White Diary is Casement's day-by-day account at length of what he did during these weeks in the Putumayo, how is one to explain his remark that on 20 October, 'I am trying in the quiet of a day off to

29 NLI, MS 1622 f. 161; cf. Mitchell (ed.), *Amazon Diary*, p. 259.
30 NLI, MS 1622 f. 165; cf. Mitchell (ed.), *Amazon Diary*, p. 263–4, where an intrusive editorial sub-heading has been placed between the penultimate and final sentences quoted here. The presence of Casement's section headings in the original manuscript strongly suggests that he envisaged a reader other than himself – though at the moment of writing, no commitment to publication had been made. The addition of further editorial sub-headings in the text as finally published by Mitchell confuses the matter.

write up the happenings of the last three days' or explain the non-report of an 'interview with Normand yesterday afternoon'?[31] There is, it is true, a short character assessment: 'Most of these criminals I have met here are fools. This man is not. He realises to the full, I can see, the position he is in. He was partly brought up in England and, no doubt, wishes again to go there.'

Casement's account of Normand gradually adopts a perspective of irony. Reflecting on the chances of the monster catching up on an ailing labourer, he notes 'That beauty was still behind.' Glimpsing the harem (as he had earlier termed it), he notes 'The Mrs Normands appeared to be travelling fast, all were skurrying [*sic*].' Normand, for his part, is presented full of assurance and style. He 'came out dressed and cleaned to tea and made up to me with a sweeping bow'.[32] Whatever Normand may have thought of Casement, the diary reveals more clearly than can have been intended the extent to which the battle of wits was tipping in Normand's favour. When he hypocritically uses the phrase 'a good time' about the life of the labourer, the Foreign Office man can only record it scornfully in parentheses. 'His last touch was perhaps the funniest of all – it was a volunteered explanation of why he had not come directly up to the house at Entre Rios, but had tried to slip past through the chocara. His rubber people, it seems, always robbed Mr. O'Donnell's fields, so he had given orders that none of his people were ever to pass through this station, but to go round it without spoiling anything.'[33] Disarmed for the moment by Normand's blatant lying, Casement reverts to physiognomy, 'It is a perfectly atrocious face – but there is no doubt the brute has courage – a horrid, fearful courage, and endurance, and a cunning mind too. He is the ablest of these scoundrels we have met yet, and I should say far the most dangerous. The others were murderous maniacs mostly, or rough cruel ignorant men . . . This is an educated man of a sort, who has lived long in London, knows the meaning of his crimes'.[34] When the two men parted, Normand 'again bowed elaborately and shook hands all round'.[35] What did he know, guess, or imagine about Casement?

31 NLI, MS 1622 ff. 175, 182, 183; cf. Mitchell (ed.), *Amazon Diary*, p. 278–80. The date of the interview was Friday 21 Oct. 1910.

32 NLI, MS 1622 ff. 188, 189; cf. Mitchell (ed.), *Amazon Diary*, p. 285–6.

33 NLI, MS 1622 f. 191; cf. Mitchell (ed.), *Amazon Diary*, p. 287.

34 NLI, MS 1622 ff. 192–3; cf. Mitchell (ed.), *Amazon Diary*, p. 289.

35 NLI, MS 1622 f. 195; cf. Mitchell (ed.), *Amazon Diary*, p. 291. The two men met subsequently, when Normand tried to present Casement with a native boy as a parting gift: the same (one suspects) mocking effusion of gesture was performed – see NLI, MS 1623 f. 238; see also f. 229.

TWELVE

ECONOMIES OF WRITING

Aschenbach did not enjoy enjoying himself.
THOMAS MANN

—

Thus the first bound volume concludes, and the second begins in a different key, with calculations of profit, commission etc.[1] The division of the typescript into two volumes appears to have been effected while it was still in Gavan Duffy's possession but, in the present context, what is significant is Maloney's possession of it (or a copy of it) at the time he wrote *The Forged Casement Diaries*. It is true that he quoted some brief passages, ordering them in much the same way that he treated quotations from Ben S. Allen's correspondence.[2] Yet his treatment of the White Typescript is curiously isolated within the argument, and never admits any of the material about Casement's admiration of native boys, his description of their nakedness and their injuries, and the affection shown by some of them to him. An irresistible question must be – why did Maloney not publish the White Typescript in the 1930s? Surely, such a publication would have been a more effective response to the British Government's refusal to say 'yes, aye or nay' than the cumbersome argument eventually issued through the Talbot Press. This proposition never seems to have been seriously considered by those who were best placed (not always on the same side) to judge the matter – George Gavan Duffy, Patrick McCartan, Shane Leslie, Gertrude Parry, the Shaws, W. B. Yeats. If, as Maloney expressed it, 'the transcript reveals a Casement to whom indecency could not rationally be attributed', why not give this extensive document to the world?[3]

1   NLI, MS 1623. This volume also poses problems for the bibliographer, as it includes some pages of top-copy typing (e.g. f. 197) and a greater number of corrections by typewriter. There are also tipped-in replacement leaves – e.g. ff. 243, 290–305.
2   W. J. Maloney, *The Forged Casement Diaries* (Dublin: Talbot Press, 1936), pp. 184–93, constituting chapter 13.
3   *Ibid.*, p. 185, where the length of the typescript is specified as evidence of its authority.

Though lacking the distinctive literary qualities of T. E. Lawrence's master-piece, it could have been a diminished eighth pillar of wisdom.[4]

Copyright was vested in Mrs Parry who (though she may not yet have realised the fact) was in possession of the manuscript – no insuperable problem there. The typescript carried quite a number of typing errors, but these mainly related to proper names easily verified or amended through reference books. In many ways, the document was ready for the copy-editor.[5] One obstacle to publication may have been feared (wrongly, as we now know) in the Foreign Office's exclusive retention of the manuscript. This fear could best be explained in terms of a further anxiety – that the diary in Casement's own hand might differ somewhat from the typescript, an anxiety which takes us straight to the Normand narrative with its anticipations and delayed decodings, the 'inter-polations' of seemingly homoerotic description, and the pattern of confrontation/ avoidance with regard to Normand, itself a minor exercise in Conradian plotting. This might have been Casement's heart of darkness.

Some may think this a matter best resolved through recourse to classic Freudian (or more fashionable Lacanian) psycho-analysis, in search of cultural-historical understanding.[6] Others will insist on emphasising the extraordinarily traumatic quality of Casement's experience in the Putumayo, experience – the sight of many hundreds mutilated bodies, of disregarded human remains, the encounter with administrators and perpetrators of gross violence, etc. etc. – in which sexuality plays only a secondary and occasional role (as with the killing of some men by beating them repeatedly on the testicles, and the free-booting fornication of the leading executioners). For the latter group of readers, the Traumatic Stress Foundation might be able to provide greater illumination than the several schools of psycho-analysis. Yet, as Casement himself eloquently testified, he was the observer of brutality and torture *at one remove*, neither its immediate victim nor its direct witness.

---

4   Lawrence's *Seven Pillars of Wisdom* was published commercially in 1935, having previously appeared in a highly limited edition. The Shaws had been instrumental in seeing Lawrence's work into posthumous publication.

5   A comparison of the White documents – manuscript and typescript – makes it plain that modifications of the name Norman to read Normand were made by Casement himself –his distinctive 'd' has a left-flying upright stroke, especially when it features as the last letter of a word.

6   Of Casement's biographers to date only B. L. Reid has ventured into tentative psychological accounts of his subject's behaviour ('just short of real pathology'), political as well as sexual, see *The Lives of Roger Casement* (New Haven: Yale University Press, 1976), pp. 453–4.

At once passive and active, almost in the professional style of an anthropologist, Casement was an observer of his own diaries as well as their author. The interpolations suspected by Forgery Theorists in the 1960s are now established as Casement's own additions to writing which he read, observed and – in a strictly philological sense – corrupted. That is, the corruption lies not in the sexual nature of some of the material but in the processes of writing itself. We reach the crux of Casement's desperate sexual economies – the concentration on writing, the use of sundry writing implements (pen, pencil etc.) within an inscription, the duplication of this writing in White and Black texts, the interrelation of these texts through copying from one to another, the annotation of texts after initial inscription and – though this is difficult to prove *in extenso* – the reading of this writing with or without further inscription as the accompaniment of reading. In this last practice one encounters that further eroticisation of the text, which is paralleled in Casement's photographing young male Amerindians – the text as visible object. Yet the diaries exist, whereas it is Casement who is seen to dissolve through his philological corrupting of his own text.

The Forgery Theory had insisted on the *oneness* of Casement, but this was an entirely futile endeavour, reducing him to a mere illustrative piety, while casting its own task into the realm of hagiography. Maloney had even attempted to insist that only one diary had been manufactured or circulated in 1915–16, and failed to edit out completely this initial view when the evidence of Eamonn Duggan drew unwelcome attention to two volumes upon a table in the House of Lords. By condemning whatever was circulated in 1916 as a forgery, the unsullied diary was to be uniquely genuine, even though McCartan and Gwynn gave the game away by pointing to evidence of mental disturbance in a German diary.

Diary/diaries – this too was a verbal problem of oneness masking plurality. Possessing the White Diary (in typescript), Maloney felt unable to issue it, perhaps fearing in merely practical terms that its account of Normand might result in the emergence of that individual as a second recorder of events in the Putumayo. And if not Armando, then some other member of the Normand family might well step forward to disown all responsibility for the 'little being' and, in doing so, throw more light on Casement's familiarity with the name than was desirable. Alternatively, the New York neurologist recognised in the White Diary a dual narrative which – if it were to be in any degree confirmed, echoed or augmented by a newly released and previously unknown diary (call it Normand's) – would itself present Casement in an ambiguous light. Read at length, the White Diary was not univocal; read together with the mere threat

of Black Diaries, its whiteness darkened. And so the diary they declared
genuine had to be held in perpetual reserve by the Forgery Theorists. Angus
Mitchell was the first to break the deadlock in 1997, though in doing so he
found it necessary to maintain the forgery theory with reference to the
material in the Public Record Office.

Now that the Giles Report has established the material preserved at Kew
also to be genuine, we are confronted with prolific dual texts. In Dr Giles's
terminology, the Black Diaries contain 'contentious' and 'non-contentious'
entries and passages. These diaries are paralleled (for one period) by 'white'
writings which – in 1910 at least – are found to contain their own dual narrative.
Editors, historians, and any other commentators who turn to deal with Casement
in the aftermath of the Giles Report will be obliged gradually to reintegrate
this body of work while at the same time acknowledging that it may record a
process of personal disintegration.[7] The contentious entries are written by the
same hand which inscribed the non-contentious, and it will be no longer
possible to isolate just one group as the work of a true Casement. The bonus
added to this procedure will be, of course, that the Black Diaries will emerge
as only partly 'black'. They too will be accepted – as indeed Roger Sawyer has
already demonstrated in 1997 – as evidence of their author's humanitarianism.

It is important to distinguish between the prospects of greater simpli-
fication and the need for greater sophistication as work in this area proceeds.
The Giles Report simplifies matters by proving beyond all reasonable doubt
that Casement wrote all of the material in PRO, HO 161/1–5. But this is a
finding with reference to penmanship, not necessarily reportive authorship, or –
to be more exact – not necessarily as to authorship reporting acts committed
as described. It is too simplistic to conclude that Casement wrote about a blow
job on such-and-such-a-day because he experienced one then. (The crudeness
of my language is designed to reflect the crudeness of such conclusions.) The
issues of desire, of voyeurism, of recollection, day-dream, fantasy and delusion
cannot be eclipsed by a notion of diary-as-report. Nor can unease about
Casement's sanity in his last years be wholly forgotten. The task of editing the
diaries will be a delicate one, again not simply because of the material in some
passages, but because diaries are by *their* nature complex documents. And
Casement's are doubly complex because of the way in which he acted as a
copyist or annotator of his own writing.

7   On Casement's medical condition in 1916, see PRO, HO 144/1636/311643/40; see also Roger
Sawyer (ed.), *Roger Casement's Diaries: 1910, the Black and the White* (London: Pimlico, 1997), pp. 6–7.

The copyist is a venerable figure in the history of texts. Through his labours, classical, biblical and (important for Ireland) Gaelic documents were disseminated down the centuries. If the Gaelic instance could be matched by reference to a dozen other cultures, it remains important for the late date at which texts continued to be produced by hand (certainly in the nineteenth century, and possibly later). While the copyist aimed for fidelity *literatim*, even the most careful manuscript reproduction of texts was susceptible to corruption. Some of the causes of textual corruption may lie in erroneous copying deliberately committed in good faith, where the copyist believes himself to be correcting a feature he wrongly deems to be wrong. Other causes arise from human frailty – as when a line of text is skipped (paralipsis) or duplicated (dittography) by mistake.[8] The Philadelphia-based Institute for Biblical and Scientific Studies lists a dozen or so other types of textual corruption. Some prolonged and reflective consideration of the many ways in which texts are 'corrupted' should precede any attempt to edit Casement's diaries.

It will be pointed out, of course, that the kinds of copying and corruption with which biblical or classical scholars are concerned took place over long periods of time, involving generations of manuscript production. Casement, in stark contrast, was writing up his black and white diaries within days or at most weeks of each other. A second difference lies in the very loose way in which he can be described as a copyist: his scribal activities might be said to produce different versions of an elusive true diary, rather than anything approaching *literatim* copies. And a final objection would rightly focus on the identity of author and copyist in the Casementalist instance, an identity rarely if ever encountered in the larger fields of manuscript production referred to.

The concept of identity employed here is essentially forensic – that is, the hand of Roger Casement wrote both the contentious and non-contentious accounts of certain days, meetings. No psychological identity or unity is implied. Psychoanalytical biography of figures from the past has produced some notable results – for example, Erik H. Erikson's *Young Man Luther* (1962) and Jean-Paul Sartre's multi-volume study of Gustave Flaubert, *The Idiot of the Family* (1971 onwards), to which might be added the complex of work devoted

8   An interesting instance of this can be found in the Olympia Press text of Casement's ledger for 1911 where under 6 Aug. the Dublin location 'Hatch St' is repeated immediately: the offending copyist was either a police typist in 1916 or a French compositor in 1959.

to the strange inner life of Max Weber.[9] Where these subjects differ from Casement one finds problematic writing – Luther, Flaubert, and Weber may have been psychologically wracked by anxiety and even greater demons, but each produced a body of published work of exceptional quality, revolutionary contributions to the thought of his age. While Casement's two official reports deserve more attention than they currently receive, his most enthusiastic supporter could scarcely classify them with the foundational texts of German Protestantism, realist fiction or academic sociology. In all his broken complexity, Casement might be better approached through the work of Bruno Bettelheim who, in addition to treating disturbed children, refugees and the survivors of concentration camps, also advised an appreciation of Freud as less than dogmatically scientific. None of this should be regarded as a covert insistence on a psychoanalytical approach to Casement and his writings, though the implication must surely be that a study of Casement will not resemble a study of – say – James Connolly or Constance Gore-Booth, except in its inessentials. The Irish biographical paradigm can be a snare as often as it is the means towards understanding.

Now confirmed as authentically Casement's, where shall we place the Black Diaries? The nickname needs reconsideration, though not before the symbolism it has encoded is fully appreciated. Casement's life was in many ways dominated by oppressive symbolic systems, some of which excluded him, while others absorbed him with a like indifference. His destiny, as the official appointed twice to investigate the tropical rubber trade, might have been very different had the industry in question been tin mining or the region temperate. A human slaughterhouse rarely makes for refinement. Certain encounters generate a response which exceeds what one's psychic economy can provide for, and the cause of this may lie not only in the physical but also and more tellingly in a symbolic domain.[10] What, for sufficient example, is to be made of the discovery that a man in whose parlour one slept, and at whose

9   Erik H. Erikson, *Young Man Luther: A Study in Psycho-analysis and History* (New York: Norton, 1962); Jean-Paul Sartre, *The Family Idiot*, trans. Carol Cosman (Chicago: University of Chicago Press, 1981); Marianne Weber, *Max Weber: A Biography*, trans. Harry Zohn (New Brunswick: Transaction), 1988; Fredric Jameson, 'The Vanishing Mediator: Max Weber as Storyteller', in *The Ideologies of Theory: Essays 1971–1986* (London: Routledge, 1988), vol. 1.

10   What follows is based primarily on the Putumayo inquiry, and may require modification if the Congo experiences (in which amputation rather than flogging was inflicted) were to be assimilated. No general application is suggested.

table one took meat, had baked a small Indian boy in an oven, merely dismissing the (non-Indian) servant who witnessed the deed?[11] The experience is not conducive to *l'amour propre*.

From the four-part schema relating rubber to semen and ink in the previous chapter, one might generate a less coarse-grained diagram:

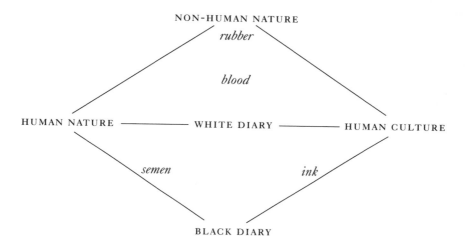

First let us examine the diagram as indicated in CAPITALS. In this abstract representation, the central position is occupied by the diary which keeps apart sexuality and writing, never (consciously) allowing one to corrupt the other. Interpreted architectonically, the central line bears the stress of separating the right and left poles, when that line is removed (or it collapses) the result is the bottom single point of the diagram and, as Nature and Culture become congruent the Diary turns Black. The central line can also be read as the base of a triangle, with – (*a*) Nature occupying two corners, or (*b*) the Human occupying two corners. These alternate designations can generate a series of dynamic relations between the three terms.

However, the triangle is also reflected below the line in another triangle in which there is only one set of designators – the two Human terms, plus an anomalous DIARY which is the single inscription of those two. This lower mirror- or reverse-triangle is a preliminary psychic map of Casement's private world, with the WHITE DIARY serving as its intended but never fully issued frontier to a public world.

11 See the preliminary 'memoranda' page in Casement's 1911 Diary (PRO, HO 161/4).

The co-ordinates given in *italics* constitute another representation, less abstract yet still dependent on a metonymy of liquid/solid distinctions rather than on so-called things-in-themselves. The apex of the diagram is designated *rubber*. For this newly valuable commodity one might have to reach back to Milton's Garden of Eden in search of a suitably mixed description: like the fruit on God's tree of life it was 'vegetable gold' and fallen Man pursued it with devilish energy.[12] Less grandly, rubber was a commodity tapped as a liquid extracted in the penetration of tree-bark and then rendered valuably (semi) solid by being fired. Elasticity of the material constitutes its value both in the market and in the psychic map of Casement's career. In his Putumayo experience, the extraction of profitable rubber cannot be effected without the spilling (extraction) of blood from the labour force. This is not just a cause-and-effect economy; it enacts a sardonic irony, for the flogging of labourers mimes the cutting of tree-bark to release potential value. The element of mimicry is chillingly endorsed when we note that Normand's gamut of atrocities located the burning of children close to the flogging of adults, just as rubber had its generational valorisation from seminal release through purification/concretisation by fire. In such an industrial inferno, Hegel's remark (as reported by Marx without a shred of verification) that history repeats itself twice, first as tragedy then as farce, achieves a remarkable endorsement.

The left-hand polar point is labelled *semen* as a metonymic for male sexuality located almost exclusively in a field of action from which females have been elided. It is largely a concealed field of action. When the Book of Genesis records Onan's offence – spilling his seed on the ground – the Lord killed him though Onan's intention was to avoid conceiving a child by his sister-in-law. The biblical prohibitions against premature ejaculation and masturbation take their place in a hierarchy, which also condemns homosexuality and bestiality. The fifth chapter of Leviticus is devoted to unseen offences, things done unwittingly, and one must wait until chapter 15 before discovering that 'if any man's seed of copulation go out from him', then he is unclean until nightfall, even after washing his flesh. These are arcane injunctions observed nowadays by very few except Orthodox Jews, but they were part of the biblical Protestantism in which Casement (and most of

---

12 *Paradise Lost*, Book IV, line 220. Again Hardenburg's *The Devil's Paradise* demonstrates the aptness of its title.

his generation) was versed.[13] Youthful sexual guilt is frequently encountered first in nocturnal emissions and masturbation. In the Putumayo, Casement was appalled by the laughter of servants while 'three boys played with each other'.[14] The laughter, not the physical behaviour, provoked his response. It is ironical, and thus a source of further guilty feeling, that the white seed of semen is blanked out from the White Diary, only to find sanctuary in the darkness of the Black Diary and its anal 'other temple'. Casement's horror at the consequences of rubber-tapping is matched/compensated by his sexual practice, a differentiating resemblance. Between the two – but never precisely locatable – lies human *blood*, which flows as a consequence of a punishment which in turn resembles the cutting of tree-bark. In the diagram it is placed above the WHITE DIARY, which intervenes between it and the more seminal BLACK DIARY.[15] That *semen* is essential to Human Nature is acknowledged by the unparalleled rigour with which it is policed in the Bible and in other constitutive texts of HUMAN CULTURE.

The right-hand pole – *ink* – seems the least contentious of these devices; after all, we have an everyday acquaintance with it (unlike raw rubber) and we do so without the discretions required in the case of semen. Such a presupposition would be entirely unjustified. Leaving aside the now-pervasive contact we have with treated or synthetic rubber, one must emphasise the limitations of any use of ink as a metonym for HUMAN CULTURE. Even today, there are old non-literate communities, while ink-literacy as such may diminish in new e-economies of knowledge. Casement in his day was exactly placed on the contact-line between western literacy and tribesmen whose culture was oral and iconographic – they painted their bodies as a distinctive custom much commented upon by him. Yet ink distinctly signals Casement's

---

13 Leviticus 5 was prescribed reading at Church of Ireland services in the week beginning with the 22nd Sunday after Trinity. On the relationship between biblical injunctions and psychoanalytical concepts, see Janine Chasseguet-Smirgel, 'Devil's Religions: Some Reflections on the Historical and Social Meaning of the Perversions', in Nancy and Roy Ginsburg (eds), *Psychoanalysis and Culture at the Millennium* (New Haven, London: Yale University Press, 1999), pp. 313–36.

14 Sawyer (ed.), *Roger Casement's Diaries*, p. 91 (4 Oct. 1910).

15 Though there is scarcely enough material for a satisfactory analysis, it seems that the Black Diary may record less about punishments and flogging than the White, a comparison difficult to confirm given the relative size of each document. The implication, however, is that the compensatory recording of sexual acts is achieved by a mitigation of the violence which called forth the need for compensation. In this mechanism, one can see how a downward spiral of psychic disintegration can accelerate.

culture – as private diarist and as the author of published reports on the bloodshed inflicted on rubber-gatherers. He was not an orator like G. B. Shaw in the borough of St Pancras or Patrick Pearse at the grave of O'Donovan Rossa. Nor could he respond to the non-European 'Other' in the manner of Paul Gauguin who arrived in Tahiti while Casement was building railways in the Congo basin. Casement's relationship with the visual remains problematic, partly because the most obvious images diverge into two distinct collections – those portraying Casement himself, and those photographs of natives which he took in West Africa and South America.

The diagram requires reconsideration, for its right-side polar term signals a limitation and a frontier. Yet this is balanced by earlier observations of the extent to which *semen* acted metonymically for HUMAN CULTURE only if one presupposed a field from which the female has been largely evacuated. If the apex of the diagram were to be similarly re-examined, one discovers its distinctively historical character. For the flow of rubber-juice enters into contact with literate human culture only through intensively exploitative farming under European or 'white' direction. The lash, the bloodshed, is its photographic negative, with photography equally an industrial intrusion. To move back beyond this ego's-era social psychosis is in one sense pointless, for the Incas on whom Dickey and Casement both doted are extinct. Yet if one was to imagine such a pre-history then, together with the erasure of ink and the non-violation of the rubber tree, we would have to imagine a HUMAN NATURE without semen.

While it is unlikely that William Joseph [Marie Alois] Maloney ever gave the reins to such thoughts, even during his mescalin experiments, it has a place in the classics of structural anthropology. More exactly, in analysing the Oedipus myth, Claude Lévi-Strauss postulates a conflict between two cognitive systems in ancient Greek culture – one based on kinship, the other on cosmology. Within this, the biological origin of man in sexual intercourse is countered by a belief in his chthonic origin – that is, direct generation from the earth. Ill-fated Oedipus' name – meaning swell-foot – encoded his treatment at birth, when he was exposed on a mountain and staked through the foot, that is, reattached to the earth from which it was thus indicated that he had sprung unwelcome. The theme is far more pervasive than the reference to Oedipus might suggest.[16]

16   For a sophisticated analysis of the chthonic myth in the foundations of Greek democracy, see Nicole Loraux, *The Invention of Athens: The Funeral Oration in the Classical City* (Cambridge, Mass.: Harvard University Press, 1986). Arlene W. Saxonhouse examines a literary exploration in 'Myths

If such a regressive reading of the diagram is justified then we have indeed discovered a structure of relentless disintegration in Casement. What its causes may be remains to be seen, possibly. Those who resist psychoanalytical claims to bring all home to infancy may prefer the notion of a collapse resulting from the dreadful scenes encountered repeatedly in Africa and South America. Wilfred Owen's poem 'Mental Cases' may result from a different conflict and refer to numberless victims, but its opening line seems apt for Casement – 'These are men whose minds the Dead have ravished.'[17] The Dead and, one might add, the uncanny monsters. To regard Casement as a casualty of the Great War is entirely accurate, if one looks to the trial in 1916. Indeed, the covert and homeopathic circulation of bits from his sexual diaries could be read as an attempt by the collective executive to deal with the more inchoate and elusive homoeroticism implicit in war rhetoric. Nowhere is Casement more thoroughly enmeshed in symbolic systems than in the seemingly crude blackguardism of G. H. Mair's machinations or Basil Thomson's interviews.

To consider him as a pre-war casualty may seem to fly in the face of chronology. There is a longer history of this critical period in western civilisation than that configured between the words 4 August 1914 and the eleventh hour, of the eleventh day, of the eleventh month, 1918. The conditions *for* war were long in place; perhaps they should be re-labelled conditions *of* war, as the arms race and industrial competition built up over decades. If Casement did fall in some obscure psychic prologue to the war, some jungle of the mind, he was doubly unfortunate falling in death into the hands of Dr Maloney, a decorated casualty of the Great War.

Maloney's activities in the 1930s contributed a little to the isolationist public policy adopted by de Valera as the Second World War approached. His discreet volte-face in the pages of *The Nation*, while unflattering to the Taoiseach personally, was in tune with attitudes of indirect compliance with the needs of the Allies.[18] The mood of inward self-censorship generally, but not exclusively, adopted during the Emergency led to the perpetuation of Maloney's claims against the British. When repatriation of Casement's remains was nimbly executed in 1965, the effect on public consciousness in Ireland

---

16 *cont.* and the Origins of Cities: Reflections on the Autochthony Theme in Euripides' *Ion*', in J. Peter Euben (ed.), *Greek Tragedy and Political Theory* (Berkeley: University of California Press, 1986), pp. 252–73.

17 *The Collected Poems of Wilfred Owen* (London: Chatto, 1967), p. 69.

18 See Dónal Ó Drisceoil, *Censorship in Ireland 1939–1945* (Cork: Cork University Press, 1996).

was to confirm a sense of guilt in the British, and that too was rather simplistically taken as evidence of forgery. Nearly forty years later, the diaries must be accepted in all their prolix impoverishment, because for too long denial claimed the moral high ground.

It is quite a leap from Casement's writing practices to the theories of German scholarly editors.[19] Yet, if a proper response is to be made to the Giles Report and the exposé of Dr Maloney's machinations, then the question of editing his diaries and other texts deserves measured consideration. While Angus Mitchell and Roger Sawyer have advanced our awareness of the 1910 writings, the largely unadorned transcript technique they adopted has at times simplified things where recognition of their complexity was urgently needed. Realising the authenticity of the material in advance of any forensic examination, Sawyer was the more generous of the two editors in giving the reader access to cancellations and anomalies; unfortunately, his publisher permitted only the inclusion of selections from the White Diary. The at-first bewildering co-existence in the Black Diary of diagonal inscriptions, red inscriptions, ink and pencil inscriptions, big and small hands, blue crayon marks, gaps and crowded lines, intrusive X marks and exclamation marks deserves closer attention than the levelling use of a single typeface and font-size permitted. The old-fashioned concept of an 'editio diplomatica' – so appropriate for a Consul's secret record of demeanour and misdemeanour – has largely been replaced by electronic possibilities. Yet no decision as to how Casement's work might be edited should be hastily taken. The question might properly be pondered if a text-centred edition is the right objective, and not some complex German-style apparatus – again appropriate in Casement's case as the advocate of European rather than Anglophone allegiances for independent Ireland.

Until those issues can be fully explored, alternatives debated, and decisions made in the context of Casement's total corpus of writing, Roger Sawyer must surely be commended as the one editor who resisted Forgery Theory.

19   The essays gathered in George Bornstein et al. (eds), *Contemporary German Editorial Theory* (Ann Arbor: University of Michigan Press, 1995), offer a variety of challenging approaches.

Appendix 1

An Amateur on Forensics –
Dropped 'a' in a letter by Ben S. Allen

It is almost certain that Allen personally typed the two letters (for clarity referred to here as documents) to W. J. Maloney preserved in NLI. This contention is made despite the use of office stationery, and the presumed availability of a professional typist. The principal argument in favour of considering the third page of Allen's letter of 2 December 1932 suspect, as not being proven to be his work, continues to lie in the nature of its contents. Two observations summarise this issue:

> 1 page three returns to the issue of Casement and the encounter with Captain Hall, though these matters have been effectively dealt with in the previous pages.

> 2 though page three adds some impressive circumstantial detail of value to the Forgery Theorist, it consists largely of repetition and what might been deemed 'padding' sufficient to occupy an entire page.

One might therefore suspect that Maloney or one of his managers effected a substitution of page three in order to possess a page of impressive testimony from Allen, which did not draw in embarrassing additional material. Further pursuit of this hypothesis must take into account any evidence of forgery to be observed in the form rather than the content, and this despite the difficulty of our having page three only as a photostat copy.[1]

A distinctive feature of the typing is a misaligned or dropped lower case 'a', generated occasionally by mode of typing rather than invariably by a badly damaged key. (A somewhat damaged key may have contributed to the effect.) In the two-page document of 20 October 1932, this characteristic appears on

---

1 For an account of photostat copies and their variable size (due to the use of a lens), see Wilson R. Harrison, *Suspect Documents: Their Scientific Examination* (London: Sweet & Maxwell, 1958), pp. 144–5.

five occasions, the words being – asset, Casement (three times), and McCartan. As the name Casement also appears once without the dropped 'a', it is clear that the effect is not an invariable product of the machine.

In the four-page document of 2 December 1932, this characteristic appears on ten occasions – a closely comparable frequency. The words affected are Casement (six times), Naval (once), and Sacramento (three times).

If one concentrates on page 3 of the second document, the page which is under suspicion of being a substitute (for only photostat copies survive), then a distinctive pattern is visible. Here only the word Casement displays the dropped lower case 'a', though there is also a raised lower case 'a' (in the word Managing) unique to either document, and a similarly unique dropped upper case 'A'.

Finally, there is one instance of a dropped letter which is not 'a/A'. This is a dropped lower case 'e' in Revelation (page two of the second document, i.e. in a non-suspect part of the correspondence).

In all, eighteen instances of a misaligned letter can be analysed. The vast majority of these occur where 'a' is preceded by an upper case letter – Cartan (once), Casement (nine times), Managing (once), Naval (once), Sacramento (three times) – fifteen in all, or *83.3 per cent. And if one eliminates the solitary instance of a raised lower case 'a', then the result is *77.7 per cent. This second-letter after an upper-case predominance suggests a distinctive personal trait in the typist which, of course, is open to imitation.

Viewed in one perspective Numbered Page Three Copy is consistent with the rest of the documentation in that it has two occurrences of Casement with a dropped lower case 'a' (and none without this feature). Pages compare as follows

Document 1 – page 1 (two instances of Casement with dropped 'a'; none perfect)

Document 1 – page 2 (two instances of Casement with dropped 'a'; none perfect)

Document 2 – page 1 (two instances of Casement with dropped 'a'; none perfect)

Document 2 – page 2 (two instances of Casement with dropped 'a'; *one* perfect)

*Document 2 – page 3 (two instances of Casement with dropped 'a'; none perfect)

Document 2 – page 4 (no use of Casement)

In this perspective, the suspect page is consistent with the others and might be regarded as above suspicion.

However, a different analysis emerges if one considers the hypothesis of forgery. In this perspective, Numbered Page Three Copy is inconsistent in that

(*a*) it does not display a dropped letter other than 'a/A' though there is an instance of this on page two of the same document;

(*b*) it displays the characteristic dropped lower case 'a' only in the word Casement and in no other word;

(*c*) it displays a dropped upper case 'A' which appears nowhere else in the two documents;

(*d*) it displays a raised lower case 'a' which appears nowhere else in the two documents, both (*c*) and (*d*) suggesting that the forger-typist experienced difficulty in reproducing Allen's distinctive practice.

These typographical features, together with the evidence of superfluous repetition in the text of the same page, might invite further forensic inquiry. If the Theorists have declined to force an examination of the material in Kew which they declare to be forged – indeed, they have poured scorn on the idea of forensic authentication – will they prove any more adventurous in testing the reliability of Dr Maloney's archive?

Appendix II

How not to do history
W. J. Mc Cormack

In December 1936 a New York doctor, W. J. Maloney, published in Dublin a book with the provocative title, *The Forged Casement Diaries*. Ever since, there has been an amorphous public opinion in Ireland that the material circulated by the British in 1916 to discredit Roger Casement was indeed forged. The release of five ('Black') diaries in 1959 convinced many scholars to the contrary, but the older view has lingered on in certain quarters. Herbert O. Mackey, Roger McHugh and – more recently Angus Mitchell, Eoin Ó Maille, Michael Payne and Máire uí Callanán – have maintained Maloney's basic position, while modifying their tactics as occasion has demanded.

Consider, for example, two points raised in their 1995 pamphlet, *The Vindication of Roger Casement* by Ó Maille, uí Callanán [*sic*] and Payne (henceforth The Vindicators.)

THE 1903 DIARY

It is their view that the 1903 'Black' diary must be a forgery because it erroneously records the election to parliament of James Craig who, as history does indeed confirm, was not elected until 1906. In this they echo, and perhaps plagiarise, Roger McHugh.[1] Rightly certain of that success, the Vindicators never think it possible that Craig might have stood for parliament on some earlier occasion. Or, to focus the matter precisely on their assumptions, they presume forgery in the 'Black' and never look further.

What in fact the 1903 diary records is the process of Craig's *defeat* in a by-election. Given the impermeable nature of Forgery Theory, we may want to add some factual details. For the sake of consistency with Casement's reading matter, these are derived from the London *Times*, though it is unlikely that the other newspapers differ to the extent of three years in the report of events.

Reprinted from the Dublin-based magazine, *Times Change* (no. 22 autumn/winter 2001), with modifications.

1   Roger McHugh, 'Casement: The Public Record Office Manuscripts', *Threshold* (Belfast) (summer, 1960), pp. 38–57, esp. p. 34.

Edward Mitchell (born 1859) was mentioned (page 8) as early as 5 March 1903 as a likely candidate in the division (or constituency) of North Fermanagh, in the event of a by-election. This was a period of considerable activity in electoral politics, and the note about North Fermanagh was immediately followed by another dealing with Woolwich, where the local issue was rates of pay in the British Army's arsensal. On 7 March (page 12) *The Times* reported the interest of J. L. Green (secretary of the Rural Labourers' League) in the politics of Sussex (Rye Division); the succeeding article kept readers up to date on developments in North Fermanagh where the sitting member was expected to resign. He duly did so. On Saturday 21 March (page 13), the paper was able to report heavy polling in North Fermanagh, and followed this up with an account of affairs in Chertsey.

In *The Times* of 23 March 1903, the by-election results appear on page 10. There one reads that Mitchell (Independent Conservative and Land Purchase candidate) beat James Craig (Conservative) by 2,407 votes to 2,255 votes – a majority of 152 achieved mainly by strategic voting among nationalists. The successful candidate remarked in his victory speech that he hoped 'any unpleasantness on either side would be forgotten'. Craig replied in kind. As *The Times* saw it, 'The great bulk of the Unionist farmers voted for Captain Craig, whose friends believe he would have won had there been more time to canvass the division.'

Turning to the 'Black' diary, we discover that the relevant entry appears on 28 March, the delay attributable to the diarist's lying off the West African coast, not in North Fermanagh:

> Rye has followed Woolwich giving Liberal huge majority. Now Chertsey has to Poll. North Fermanagh too may give Russellite, and then Camborn where Caine has died – his majority was only 108, so the Torys have a chance there. A. C. seat. N. Fermanagh polled Sat. 21st. Craig (U)* Mitchell (L). A. C. seat by big majority. Chertsey polled 26 Thursday. Fyler (C). Longman (L).

As references to Chertsey, Rye and Woolwich indicate, Casement had been following the course of several elections, not just that in Fermanagh. While it seems that he misread the result (and thus confused his Vindicators), in fact he has shrewdly calculated that the 1903 contest was something of a freak. Mitchell was a 'Russellite', a follower of Thomas Wallace Russell (1841–1920), an erstwhile Tory who had adopted Compulsory Land Purchase. In the event, both candidates called themselves Conservatives, and no nationalist stood against them. A clear Conservative majority existed in the constituency, despite the eventual defeat of the official Conservative candidate. Mitchell formally joined the Liberals in February 1904. At the general election in 1906, he was defeated, though not by Craig who had taken himself off to East Down.

Casement was mistaken in some particulars – Mitchell was not yet a Liberal, though in local terms he was liberal. He also anticipated Craig's victory, which was frustrated by a small majority (3.26 per cent). Nothing in the above could be honestly mistaken for the 1906 election. I have quoted here from the Olympia Press edition of Casement's diaries rather than from the manuscripts in the Public Record Office. My reason is that the Parisian editor's footnote (indicated with the asterisk) alludes to James Craig's career, pointing out that he did not win the 1903 seat and was first returned to the House of Commons in 1906. The Vindicators, who regard the Parisian Black Diaries as the most contemptible fabrication and a gross libel upon their hero, have actually relied on this devil's edition in order to fabricate their own rubbish about a forger's blunder. Nobody working from the original manuscript in Kew could dream up their theory. What's more they blithely ignore Letitia Fairfield's pointing out this error about 1903 and 1906 to Roger McHugh back in 1960.[2] This is either wilful ignorance or *suppressio veri*.

THE 1911 DIARY

The Vindicators are even less attentive and more scornful when they focus on the 1911 'Black' diary. Here, they aver, the forger has exposed himself by getting the date of George V's coronation wrong. They transcribe the 'Black' diary entries for 22–23 June 1911 to show that the document states an historical impossibility, Casement marking 22 June as 'Coronation Day!'. By way of comparison, they reproduce the June 1911 entry from some popular 'encyclopaedia of the twentieth century', the central feature of which displays a report 'June 23. In ceremonies lasting no less than seven hours at Westminster Abbey, amid sumptuous church and state pageantry, King George V was today crowned'.

Fortunately, Casement was a better reader of newspapers than his Vindicators. Even a casual acquaintance with the history of the period will

2   See *Threshold* (Belfast), vol. 4 no. 2 (autumn/winter 1960), pp. [91]–3.

establish, as a preliminary point, that the cororation of George V was marked by several days' pageantry and ceremonial in London. Thus *The Times* for Thursday 22 June carried (page 6) a map of 'The Royal Progress To-Morrow', but also (page 7) 'To-day's Processions: Order of Carriages'. On page 8 we read 'CORONATION DAY – The Royal Procession to the Abbey – Today's Ceremony and Pageant'. Examining the establishment's own newspaper for the day the 'Black' diary declares to be Coronation Day, we discover that – it was coronation day!

But the Vindicators are entitled to a sympathetic second hearing. Let us therefore attend to *The Times*'s account of Friday 23 June 1911 which, on their authority, was the big day. It is true that we find (page 4) 'The Royal Progress To-day' with a map similar to the previous day's. We also find articles headed 'London After the Coronation – The Break-up of the Crowd' (p. 6) and 'Country Celebrations' (page 9): this latter reports 'In the country, as in London, yesterday was devoted to festive celebrations of the crowning of the King and Queen.' We can conclude that 23 June was the day after Coronation Day, though the pageantry lingered on.

All of this could have been avoided if the Vindicators had simply referred to a decent work of reference – the *Dictionary of National Biography*, for example. Instead, they reacted presumptuously to a slackly edited popular compendium of pretend journalism. The editors of this vividly wrote up their story of long ago with a date line for the day of publication (23 June), a story narrated as from the day of composition (22 June, the Coronation Day, 'today'). Flying from this god-given error to check their transcripts or copies of the 'Black' diary for 1911, the Vindicators presumed the forgery and never looked further.

This is to take a charitable view of the Vindicators. They do not always practise that Christian virtue, though they preach a travesty of Catholicism at every turn, and trade in miraculous muddles at every opportunity. They refer contemptuously to the presumed forger of the 'Black' diaries – 'degenerate and moron that he was' – in a psychic mechanism of transferring on to him the very allegations they fear may be proven in their hero.

As a cultural phenomenon in late-twentieth-century Ireland – alongside clerical child abuse, prime-ministerial corruption, and paramilitary terror (not to mention even-handed sectarianism) – Casement Vindication transcends its pretext. It is an abrogation of history, a rejection of verifiable knowledge, a very Irish instance of fideism. Comparisons with Holocaust Denial may seem strained, but the philo-nazis among W. J. Maloney's backers in 1936 provide some justification. Regrettably, a more recent invocation of the *Barnes Review* as an authority confirms the trend. According to Eoin Neeson, by reference to *Barnes* and its touching faith in a Gestapo officer we can name the forger of Casement's diaries. Mr Neeson once presided over the Irish government's Information Bureau.[3]

Not unlike that hard-core of Irish politics – 'ordinary decent members of Fianna Fáil' – intelligent and honest people who regard the Black Diaries with suspicion are deeply embarrassed. The late Professor McHugh would be mortified at this compounding of his oversight, while his own critique of the Diaries' authenticity still deserves serious re-reading. And the explosion of Vindicator Chronology in the careers of James Craig and George V does not in itself prove the diaries authentic.

The bad faith of Vindicators has culminated in a situation where those who believe the Black Diaries are forged refuse to test them. It is thus left to someone whose interests are not centred on Casement to act in their place. The commissioned scientists cannot be expected to produce some single unanimous judgment, covering all of the documents and all of the tests. Some results will perhaps be indeterminate; others may be expressed as a 'majority' verdict. But what we get will be human knowledge, not faith.

POSTSCRIPT

In the aftermath of the Giles Report, Eoin Neeson has courageously declared that he is now inclined to accept the diaries as genuine – see his article in *The Irish Times*, 4 April 2002.

---

3   See Eoin Neeson, *Birth of a Republic* (Dublin: Prestige, 1998). The Swiss forger was supposedly named Zwingelmann. An earlier 'suspect' was Maurice Magnus, who committed suicide in 1920; see an article in the (Dublin) *Sunday Press*, 4 Aug. 1957 by Clarence H. Norman. If one adds the names of Frank Ezra Adcock (accused by Owen Dudley Edwards) and Donald im Thurm (suspected by Kevin Mannerings), the proposed forgers outnumber the diaries.

Appendix III

The Secondary Literature

*I never travel without my diary. One should always have
something sensational to read in the train.*

OSCAR WILDE, THE HON. GWENDOLEN FAIRFAX
in *The Importance of Being Earnest* (1895)

I ABOUT ROGER CASEMENT

The presence of Roger Casement in recent work by three decidedly non-Irish
writers – the Australian anthropologist, Michael Taussig; the German poetic
novelist, W. G. Sebald (died December 2001); and the Oxford-based critic of
postcolonialism, Robert Young – testifies to a widespread enduring interest.[1]
For each of them, Casement is in some way exemplary, and strangely inaccessible. Yet, allegedly, more has been written about Roger Casement than
any other contributor to the Irish 'revolution'.

Measurement of these matters is an imprecise art, and one wonders if
scholars of Collins (moved to London at age sixteen), Connolly (born in
Edinburgh) or de Valera (born New York) do not rival the productivity of those
devoted to the Ulsterman from Sandycove, County Dublin. The question of
distance between origin and action may help to make precise some of these
measurements, for nationalism is characterised by a desire – and concomitant
incapacity – to abolish the historical actuality of socio-geographic movement.
In Joyce's *Ulysses* (1922), Jewish Leopold Bloom clumsily defines a nation as
'the same people living in the same place', for his own presence in Dublin
testified to the wandering imposed on his people. Incapacity to overcome
these historical realities was no absolute: the English origins of Cathal Brugha
and Patrick Pearse were to a significant degree accommodated in the evolving
protocols of Irish separatism.

---

1   See Michael Taussig, *Shamanism, Colonialism and the Wild Man* (Chicago, 1987); W. G. Sebald,
Die Ringe des Saturn (Frankfurt, 1995) and in English as *The Rings of Saturn* (London, 1998); Robert
J. C. Young, *Postcolonialism: An Historical Introduction* (Oxford, 2001).

Despite self-delusion, the 'actually existing' United Kingdom did not circumscribe the entire sentient world. In Casement's case, there was a German sphere of discussion and publication unmatched in the other cases instanced. Nor does the Casement literature in France or (before the fascist period) Italy exist on anything like the scale of Germany. The bibliography listed below makes no sense if one regards as marginal those publications emanating from Augsburg, Berlin, Hamburg, Munich etc. In contrast, nobody (so far as I am aware) was publishing books about Collins or Connolly under the imprint of the Kaiser, though Carl Schmidt would in due course (1923) sympathetically attend to Pearse's 'interventionism'. Encouraged or otherwise by Schmidt, Nazi interest in Casement was self-interest, without reference to native rights in the Putumayo or Congo basins, but with its own racialist perspective on Celtic European peripheries as primitivist ally-victims.

It should not be assumed that all German authors of the 1930s who wrote about Casement were fascistically inclined. Balder Olden was of a very different sort, and his early life of Casement was republished in the German Democratic Republic in 1977. Notwithstanding Olden's survival, his generation was shaped and defined by the politics of the 1930s. A very different post-war German scholarship has contributed much to a proper historical understanding of the Great War context of Casement's vision, even if the manipulations of his legacy in the 1930s remain to be fully analysed. The archival work of Reinhard Doerries has opened up a vast panorama for future research.

English historians have paid little attention to the only leader of the 1916 Rebellion tried in England.[2] Despite the latter-day embarrassment, there is a legal dimension to the literature which emerged even before sentence of death was carried out. While some of this very early material was produced in Ireland, Casement's fate was the intimate concern of writers who were not Irish, among them H. W. Nevinson (as we have seen) and Clement Shorter (1857–1926). Published transcripts of the trial (Knott 1917, and onwards) testify to a public interest not readily summarised as complacent acceptance of rumour and innuendo. Montgomery Hyde's repackaging of this material, together with his own inquiries into the mystery of the diaries, served to keep the Casement issue alive. In 1961, the English poet and mountaineer, Ronnie

2   The rule-proving exception is A. J. P. Taylor, who reviewed Inglis's biography in the *Times Literary Supplement*; see his *Essays in English History* (London: Penguin, 1976) where the review is reprinted.

3   R. J. Wathen, 'Letter to the Editor', *Threshold* (Belfast), vol. 5 no. 1 (spring/summer 1961), pp. 70–2.

Wathen, took issue with his friend Hyde and made a neglected contribution to the debate in which he kept alive the Normand Defence.[3] It is striking that, in the golden age of biography which followed, only one (Brian Inglis) of those who have turned their hand to writing Casement's life has been Irish. It seems very likely that Séamus Ó Siocháin will shortly adjust the balance by publishing a new and extensive life.

Adam Hochschild's *King Leopold's Ghost* (New York, 1998) has revived interest in the west African context of Casement's first major inquiry, and has the merit of treating him *en passant* rather than as an object of vindication or revisionist muck-raking. Its inclusion below may strike some readers as anomalous – why not Sebald or Taussig? – but the effect is salutary. No absolutely consistent criteria have been adhered to in drawing up this list of separate publications about Casement. (It is likely that a thorough search of French and Belgian sources would result in substantial discoveries.) Editions of the diaries have been included because they are accompanied by substantial commentary. On the other hand, editions of Casement's other writings – poems, journalism, wartime propaganda, the official reports – are excluded. While there is undoubtedly a new wave of interest in the man, nobody seems keen to reissue his non-diary work.

An Annotated Checklist of (Mainly) Separate Publications

BEFORE 1916

Charles Sarolea, *A propos du rapport Casement sur l'administration du Congo*. Bruxelles: Weissenbruch, 1904. 14 pp. In the imprint Weissenbruch is styled 'Imprimeur du Roi'. The text had previously appeared in the *Revue de Belgique*.

1916 AND AFTER

Arthur Conan Doyle, *A Petition to the Prime Minister on Behalf of Roger Casement*. [London, 1916]. ('Of this leaflet 12 copies only have been privately printed in this form.')

L. G. Redmond Howard, *Sir Roger Casement: A Character Sketch without Prejudice*. Dublin: Hodges Figgis, 1916.

Antonie Meyer (ed.), *Der Casement-Prozess und Seine Ursachen*. Berlin: Karl Curtius, [1916]. (With a foreword by Professor Theodor Schiemann, and a poem 'Den Manen' von Ruairi Mac Asmuind (p. [5]). The British Library copy ('Dritte Auflage') was accessed on 23 March 1917.)

George H. Knott (ed.), *Trial of Roger Casement*. Edinburgh, London: Hodge, 1917. (Dedicated to the judges who presided at the trial and appeal.)

Franz Rothenfelder, *Casement in Deutschland*. Augsburg: Reichel, 1917.

Agatha M. Bullet, *Roger Casement och Indien*. Stockholm: Dahlberg, 1917. 24 pp. (Two further editions in 1918, one of 26 pp, the other of 32 pp.)

Agatha M. Bullet, *Roger Casement and India*. Stockholm: Dahlberg, 1917.

Karl Spindler, *Das Geheimnisvolle Schiff; Die Fahrt der 'Libau' zur irischen Revolution*. Berlin: Scherl, 1921 [recte 1920?]. (The author later referred to Russian, French, Italian and Spanish translations.)

Karl Spindler, *Gun Running for Roger Casement in the Easter Rebellion 1916*. London: Collins, 1921. (A translation of the German text published by Scherl.)

Charles Emerson Curry (ed.) 'The Diary of Sir Roger Casement', *The Nation* (New York) vol. 113 (30 Nov. 1921) pp. 615–17; vol. 113 (7 Dec. 1921) pp. 644–5; vol. 113 (14 Dec. 1921) pp. 698–700; vol. 113 (21 Dec. 1921) pp. 717–28; vol. 113 (28 Dec.1921) pp. 754–6; vol. 114 (4 Jan. 1922) pp. 13–14; vol. 114 (11 Jan. 1922) pp. 40–1; vol. 114 (18 Jan. 1922) pp. 67–8; vol. 114 (25 Jan. 1922) pp. 94–5; vol. 114 (1 Feb. 1922) pp. 120–1; vol. 114 (8 Feb. 1922) pp. 150–1.

Though this is not a separate publication, it is of significance partly because of its timing – the Treaty Debates were in full swing – and partly for the editorial comment of Curry (in whom the Diary is copyrighted) and (less palpably) Maloney. See below for Curry's publications in Germany.

George Bernard Shaw, *A Discarded Defence of Roger Casement Suggested by Bernard Shaw with an Appendix of Comments by Roger Casement*. London: privately printed by Clement Shorter, February 1922. (A footnote on p. 19 by Shorter comments that the comments (reprinted here) 'are in Roger Casement's handwriting, which does not tally with the handwriting of the notorious "diaries" shown to me at Scotland Yard by Sir Basil Thomson'.)

Charles Emerson Curry [ed.], *Sir Roger Casement's Diaries: His Mission to Germany and the Findlay Affair*. München: Arche, 1922.

Robert McCahan, *Life of Sir Roger David Casement, Knt, CMG*. [Coleraine: Northern Constitution, 1923.] A pamphlet published under the local newspaper's imprint.

Charles Emerson Curry [ed.], Sir Roger Casement; *Meine Mission nach Deutschland während des Krieges und die Findlay-Affaire, auf Grund der tagebücher und Korrespondenz dargestellt von Dr. Charles E. Curry*. Altenburg: Geibel, 1925. (This is essentially a German language version of Curry's 1922 publication.)

1926–

Karl Spindler, *Le Vaisseau fantôme; épisode du complot de Sir Roger Casement et de la révolte irlandaise de Pâques 1916*; traduit de l'allemand par R. Jouan. Paris: Payot, 1928. (The translator was evidently one of Spindler's crew in 1916.)

Karl Spindler, *The Phantom Ship*. London: London Book Company, [1929?] Translated by W. Montgomery (MA, late lieutenant RNVR) and E. H. McGrath (MA) – a variety of footnotes, some not written by Spindler. The spine assigns this to 'The Novel Library'.

Denis Gwynn, *The Life and Death of Roger Casement*. London: Cape, 1930.

Denis Gwynn, *Traitor or Patriot; The Life and Death of Roger Casement*. New York: Cape and Smith, 1931. This is the American version of the book published by Cape in London a year earlier.

Karl Spindler, *The Mystery of the Casement Ship*. Berlin: Kribe, 1931.

Mario Borsa, *La Tragica Imprese di Sir Roger Casement*. Verona: Mondadori, 1932.

Robert Monteith, *Casement's Last Adventure*. Chicago: [privately printed for the *Irish People Monthly*,] 1932. Textually, the most significant detail is the Preface's dating to 'New York City, 1917', though the presentation of the author as a member of an IRA regiment is questionable: the IRA was not regiment-based and in 1917 the term 'Irish Republican Army' was not in currency. As a physical object, this is an elaborate production with a title-page using red ink, a front cover with 'gold' ornamentation, and fifteen photograph illustrations in the text. These latter include pages from a diary allegedly found in Casement's bag at Banna Strand. Ideologically, Monteith opts for a 'workers' republic' which is closer to James Connolly's politics than those of Casement, Pearse or Plunkett.

Balder Olden, *Paradiese des Teufels: Das Leben Sir Roger Casements*. Berlin: Universitas, 1933.

1936–

Denis Gwynn, *The Life and Death of Roger Casement*. London: Newnes, [1936]. (Omits material about the diaries, included in the first edition of 1930.)

Geoffrey de C. Parmiter, *Roger Casement*. London: Barker, 1936.

William Joseph Maloney, *The Forged Casement Diaries*. Dublin: Talbot Press, 1936. (Illustrated.)

Walter Guenter Schrenckenback, *Von England Verraten: Roger Casement, ein Leben für Irlands Freiheit* (by H. W. Günter-Franken, pseud.). Berlin: Friedrich Osmer, [1940]. A prefatory note is datelined February 1940; illustrations include two photographs taken in Germany.

Francis Stuart, *Der Fall Casement; Das Leben Sir Roger Casements und der Verleumdungsfeldzug des Secret Service*. Hamburg: Der hanseatische Verlag, 1940.

Hanns [*sic*] Walther, *Gewitter über Irland: Roger Casements Opfergang*. Leipzig: Bohn, 1942.

1946–

P. S. O'Hegarty, *Bibliographies of 1916 and the Irish Revolution. No. XVII Roger Casement*. Dublin: privately printed by Alex. Thom, 1949. (40 copies off-printed from *The Dublin Magazine*.)

Passages Taken from the Manuscript Written by Roger Casement in the Condemned Cell at Pentonville Prison. [1950.] [8]pp. 'For private circulation only.' Preface by Herbert O. Mackey.

Robert Monteith, *Casement's Last Adventure* [revised and expanded edition, with a foreword by Franz von Papen]. Dublin: Moynihan, 1952. (As in the first edition, dedicated to Casement, 'The Man Who Eliminated Self'.)

Herbert O. Mackey, *The Life and Times of Roger Casement.* Dublin: Fallon, 1954.

1956–

René MacColl, *Roger Casement, a New Judgment.* London: Hamish Hamilton, 1956.

René MacColl, *Roger Casement, a New Judgment.* New York: Norton, 1957.

Alfred Noyes, *The Accusing Ghost, or Justice for Casement.* London: Gollancz, 1957.

René MacColl, *Roger Casement.* London: Landsborough Publications, 1960. This is McColl's 1956 study, issued now in paperback with an 'Author's Foreword' dated October 1959.

Peter Singleton-Gates and Maurice Girodias, *The Black Diaries: An Account of Roger Casement's Life and Times with a Collection of his Diaries and Public Writings.* Paris: Olympia Press, 1959. 'This special edition of The Black Diaries (the only one to contain Roger Casement's diary for the year 1911), is limited to 1,500 numbered copies.' Printed in France. (626 pp.) What is referred to here as Casement's 1911 diary is in fact a ledger for that year, rather than the print-form diary also preserved in the PRO.

Peter Singleton-Gates and Maurice Girodias, *The Black Diaries: An Account of Roger Casement's Life and Times with a Collection of his Diaries and Public Writings.* London: Sidgwick & Jackson, 1959. (536 pp.) Special edition limited to 2,000 numbered copies. The British Library copy carries an errata slip.

Peter Singleton-Gates and Maurice Girodias, *The Black Diaries: An Account of Roger Casement's Life and Times with a Collection of his Diaries and Public Writings.*

New York: Grove Press Inc., 1959. 536 pp. Printed by offset in the United States, distributed in Canada by McClelland and Stewart Ltd (Toronto). No statement of limitation.

H. Montgomery Hyde (ed.) *Trial of Sir Roger Casement*. London, Edinburgh, Glasgow: Hodge, 1960. This is the Knott text of 1926, with a lengthy introduction by Hyde added (pp. xv–lix) and two additional appendices.

Herbert O. Mackey, *'I Accuse!' One of the Most Celebrated Cases of a Miscarriage of Justice; A Monstrous Fraud that Deceived Two Continents*. [Dublin: the author, n.d. *c.* 1960]

Herbert O. Mackey, *Roger Casement: A Guide to the Forged Diaries*. Dublin: Apollo, 1962. (I have also seen reference to a work of Mackey's of this date with the sub-title 'The Secret History of the Forged Diaries'. Mackey recycled material through his many apparently different publications.)

H. Montgomery Hyde (ed.), *Famous Trials 9 – Roger Casement*. Harmondsworth: Penguin, 1964. A shortened version of Hyde's 1960 edition, reissued periodically since 1963 without apparent alteration. It is notable, however, for Appendix 4 which reprints an extract covering two weeks from Casement's diary for 1911, previously unpublished.

Karl Spindler, *The Mystery of the Casement Ship*. Tralee: Anvil Books, 1965. (2nd edition of the 1931 publication, with a new foreword by Florence O'Donoghue.)

René MacColl, *Roger Casement*. London: Four Square, 1965. A reprint of the 1960 paperback, adding a further Author's Foreword dated April 1965.

1966–

Herbert O. Mackey, *Roger Casement: The Truth about the Forged Diaries*. Dublin: Fallon, 1966.

Gearóid Ó Cuinneagáin, Séamus Ó Cléirigh, and Eoin Ó Máille, *Casement Slanders Refuted*. Áth Claith: Nuactáin Teoranta, [1966]. Ó Cuinneagáin's 'Cúpla Focal' (pp. 2–4) is in Gaelic, the other two articles in English. The bibliography includes A. Noyes's *Two Worms* [*sic*] *for Memory*.

Karin Wolf, *Sir Roger Casement und die deutsch-irischen Beziehungen*. Berlin: Duncker & Humboldt, 1972.

Brian Inglis, *Roger Casement*. London: Hodder & Stoughton, 1973.

Brian Inglis, *Roger Casement*. New York: Harcourt Brace, 1973.

Brian Inglis, *Roger Casement*. London: Coronet Books, 1974. (Paperback edition of the 1973 biography, with some additional material.)

David Rudkin, *Cries from Casement as His Bones are Brought to Dublin*: London: BBC, 1974. A play.

Eoin Ó Maille (*et al.*), *The Vindication of Roger Casement: Computer Analysis and Comparisons of The Dublin 1910 Diary and The London 1903 and 1910 Diaries, and The 1913 "Nation" Letter*. [Dublin:] The Authors, 1975.

1976–

B. L. Reid, *The Lives of Roger Casement*. New Haven, London: Yale University Press, 1976.

Séamus Ó Cléirigh, *Casement and the Irish Language, Culture and History*. Dublin: Clodhanna Teo., 1977.

Balder Olden, *Paradiese des Teufels: Biographisches und Autobiographisches; Schriften und Briefe aus dem Exil*. Berlin: Rütten & Loening, 1977. (Includes his 1933 life of Casement; see pp. 81–215 of this East German publication.)

Roger Sawyer, *Casement, the Flawed Hero*. London: Routledge, 1984.

Michael Steinman, *Yeats's Heroic Figures: Wilde, Parnell, Swift, Casement*. London: Macmillan; Albany: State University of New York Press, 1984.

Daniel Vangroenweghe, 'Le Repport Casement', *Enquetes et Documents d'Histoire africaine*, vol. 6 (1985) pp. 1–174.

Daniel Vangroenweghe, *Rood Rubber; Leopold II en zijn Kongo*. Brussels: Elsevier-Librico, 1985.

1986–

Daniel Vangroenweghe, *Du sang sur les lianes; Léopold II et son Congo*. Paris: Didier-Hatier, 1986.

Eoin Ó Maille *(et al.)*, *The Vindication of Roger Casement: Computer Analyses & Comparisons of The Dublin 1910 Diary & The London 1903 and 1910 Diaries, and The 1913 "Nation" Letter*. Revised edition. [Dublin:] The Authors, Feast of All Saints 1995.

1996–

Angus Mitchell (ed.), *The Amazon Journal of Roger Casement*. Dublin: Lilliput Press, 1997. (Also issued under the imprint London: Anaconda, 1997.)

Roger Sawyer (ed.), *Roger Casement's Diaries: 1910, the Black and the White*. London: Pimlico, 1997.

Adam Hochschild, *King Leopold's Ghost; A Story of Greed, Terror, and Heroism in Colonial Africa*. New York: Houghton Mifflin, 1998. (This is not centrally concerned with Casement, though he features prominently.)

Adam Hochschild, *King Leopold's Ghost; A Story of Greed, Terror, and Heroism in Colonial Africa*. London: Macmillan 1999. (Subsequently issued in Papermac, 2000.)

Reinhard R. Doerries, *Prelude to the Easter Rising: Sir Roger Casement in Imperial Germany*. London: Cass, 2000.

Andrew Weale, *Patriot Traitors: Roger Casement, John Amery and the Real Meaning of Treason*. London: Viking, 2001.

Brian Inglis, *Roger Casement*. London: Penguin, 2002. New edition of Inglis 1973/4.

2 A PRELIMINARY CHECKLIST OF WRITINGS
BY W. J. [M. A.] MALONEY

It is clear that Maloney was a prolific journalist, using several pseudonyms. A full listing of his publications in Irish-American newspapers might never repay the effort required to construct it. Nevertheless, some sense of his output is essential if his oddly shaped career as doctor and propagandist is to be understood. What follows is intended as a starting point for more dedicated theorists.

The List

Pierre Budin, *The Nursling. The Feeding and Hygiene of Premature and Full-term Infants* (authorised translation by Maloney). London: Caxton, 1907. xxiv, 199 pp.

'On the Reckoning Test and its Uses in Psychiatry', *Review of Neurology and Psychiatry*, vol. 9 no. 7 (July 1911), pp. 366–77. The journal was published in Edinburgh by Otto Schulze.

(with – or by? – Foster Kennedy) 'The Pressure Sense in the Face, Eye, and Tongue', *Brain* (Sept. 1911), p. 1 et ff.

Kraepelin's Reckoning Test as used in the Crichton Royal Institution, Dumfries (key by Maloney). Edinburgh: 2 pt. John F. MacKenzie; London: Simpkin, Marshall & Co.: [1911] unpaged 4° & obl 8°.

'The Treatment of the Meningitides' (i.e. chapter 7 of) W. A. White and S. E. Jelliffe, *The Modern Treatment of Nervous and Mental Diseases*. Philadelphia: Lea & Febiger; London: Kimpton, 1913, vol. 2, pp. 274–303.

(with A. Knauer) 'The Psychic Action of Mescalin, With Special Reference to the Mechanism of Visual Hallucinations', *Journal of Nervous and Mental Disease*, vol. 40 no. 7 (July 1913), pp. 425–36

'Blindness and Tabes; an Introduction to a New Method of Curing Ataxia', *Journal of Nervous and Mental Disease*, vol. 40 no. 9 (Sept. 1913), p. 553 et ff.

'Fear and Ataxia', *Journal of Nervous and Mental Disease*, vol. 40 no. 11 (1913).

'The Cure of Ataxia', *New York Medical Journal*, 29 Nov. 1913.

Ivar Wickmann, *Acute Poliomyelitis (Heine-Medin's Disease)* (translated by Maloney) New York: The Journal of Nervous and Mental Disease Publishing Company, 1913. 135 pp., illus. (The original was published in Berlin: Springer, 1911.) This was still being advertised in the mid-1920s.

(with A. Knauer) 'The Cephalograph, a New Instrument for Recording and Controlling Head Movements', *Journal of Nervous and Mental Disease*, vol. 41 no. 2 (Feb. 1914), pp. 75–80.

'The Mechanism of Mental Processes as Revealed in Reckoning', *Psychology Review* (Baltimore), Apr. 1914.

'The Co-ordination of Movement', *Journal of Nervous and Mental Disease*, vol. 41 no. 5 (May 1914), pp. 273–85.

(with V. E. Sorapure) 'Note on the Mechanical Support for the Feet in Locomotor Ataxia', *Medical Record*, May 1914.

'Relief of States of Vascular, Muscular and Mental Tension', *New York Medical Journal*, May 1914.

(with A. Knauer) 'The Pneumograph, a New Instrument for Recording Respiratory Movements Graphically', *Journal of Nervous and Mental Disease*, vol. 41 no. 9 (Sept. 1914), pp. 567–74.

Locomotor Ataxia – Tabes Dorsalis: an Introduction to the Study and Treatment of Nervous Diseases for Students and Practitioners . . . Illustrated. New York, London: Appleton, 1918.

'Earl Reading as Ambassador', *New York Evening Post*, 18 Jan. 1918. Assesses Isaac Rufus's abilities as Britain's ambassador, begins with high praise, moves through Rufus's role in the Casement trial, and develops a highly repetitive argument about Jews in public life and endorses a quasi-Zionist 'solution'.

'Dr William J Maloney, late captain in the British Army declares proposed British measure may be losing of the war by allies.' NLI: ILB 300 p. 6 (item 44).

Ireland's Plea for Freedom. New York: The America Press, 1919. 48 pp.

The Irish Issue. New York: Donnelly, 1919. 32 pp.

[Maloney, as editor/author] *The Re-Conquest of America: full text of the most astounding document ever discovered in the history of international intrigue* . . . [New York]: Published by the Statesman Press 164 East 37th Street, New York, 1919. [1–2] 3–29, [3] pp. Some effort appears to have been made to create the impression in Dublin that Maloney's book had been previously published in America, doubtless with the intention of inflating its reputation. As late as December 1942, J. J. McManus of the *Irish Press* assured Richard Hayes of NLI that *The Forged Casement Diaries* had appeared in the USA in 1935, at the same time McManus opened negotiations to sell (for his own benefit) the file of letters by Yeats, Shaw, Noyes etc. which he had received in his business capacity (NLI, MS 5,460). McCartan wrote to Hobson on 13 Jan. 1937 indicating that no US edition had materialised, despite McGrath's support to the tune of $1,000 (NLI, MS 17,604(3)).

The Recognised Irish Republic. [New York:] Statesman Press, [?1920]. 30 pp. (This may be the item referred to by F. M. Carroll as *We Must Recognise the Irish Republic*, otherwise untraced.)

The Forged Casement Diaries. [With plates.] Dublin, Cork: Talbot Press, 1936. xi, 275 pp.

Foreword to Leopold Lichtwitz, *Pathology and Therapy of Rheumatic Fever*. London: Heinemann, 1944, pp. vii–xiv.

'De Valera's Neutrality', *The Nation*, vol. 154 part 2 (31 Jan. 1942), pp. 141–5.

'John and George Armstrong at Edinburgh' *Edinburgh Medical Journal*, vol. 57 (1950), pp. 600–16.

George and John Armstrong of Castleton. Two Eighteenth-century Medical Pioneers. [With portraits.] Edinburgh, London: Livingstone, 1954. xii, 115 pp., illustrated.

Biographical Register

ADCOCK, SIR FRANK EZRA (1886–1968), classicist; employed in the Admiralty Intelligence Division 1915–19; Fellow (1911) King's College, Cambridge. One of numerous individuals alleged to have forged the Black Diaries.

ALLEN, BENJAMIN SHANNON (born 1882), a Californian educated at Stanford University (1903–7), he worked as a journalist with the Associated Press before joining Herbert Hoover's staff. In the summer of 1916, Allen was shown the Buff Diary by Captain Reginald Hall, and was denied access to Casement. Later inspected the Black Diaries in the PRO and did not declare them forged.

BIGGER, FRANCIS JOSEPH (1863–1926), Belfast born antiquarian and cultural-revivalist; Casement frequently stayed at his home, Ardrigh.

BIGGER, JOSEPH WARWICK (1891–1951), professor of bacteriology at Trinity College, Dublin; nephew of F. J. Bigger.

BLACKWELL, SIR ERNLEY HAY (1868–1941), legal adviser to the Home Office, a man of arrogant demeanour and profoundly hostile to Casement.

COLLINS, MICHAEL (1890–1922), member of the Supreme Council of the Irish Republican Brotherhood; mastermind of the Irish War of Independence; killed by republican forces during the Irish Civil War.

DE VALERA, EAMON (1882–1975), American born; fought in 1916; political leader of the Republicans in the Civil War; became President of the Executive Council of the Irish Free State in 1932; thereafter, the dominant figure in Irish politics.

DEVOY, JOHN (1842–1928), powerful leader of Clan na Gael in the USA.

DICKEY, HERBERT SPENCER (1876–1948), American doctor and explorer, born Highland Falls, NY; his *Misadventures of a Tropical Medico* (1929) imputed near-insanity in Casement, later aligned himself with Maloney; a chancer.

DILLON, JOHN (1851–1927), leader of the Irish Parliamentary Party in 1916; supported the British war effort.

DRYHURST, MRS NANNIE (*née* Robinson; died October 1930), Dublin born, honorary secretary of the Nationalities and Subject Races Committee; translated (1909) Kropotkin's *The Great French Revolution 1789–1793*.

DUFFY, GEORGE GAVAN (1882–1951), Casement's solicitor in 1916; Sinn Féin member of Commons and Dáil Éireann; the last signatory to the Treaty in adding his name; became a judge in 1936, and president of the High Court in 1946; for his measured sagacity, he became the butt of Myles na Gopaleen's humour. ·

DUGGAN, EAMONN (1874–1936), sometime IRA intelligence officer; as a solicitor by training, he was included among the Irish negotiators of the 1921 Treaty; became Minister for Home Affairs in the post-Treaty Irish government.

FAIRFIELD, LETITIA (1885–1978), friend of Casement; doctor and barrister; organised a short forensic examination of the 1911 diary; a Catholic convert, she upsets pious unanimity on the forgery issue.

GONNE (MACBRIDE), MAUD (1865–1953), Aldershot born to a family with roots in County Meath; fell in love with Lucien Millevoye, a right-wing French adventurer; took up Irish good causes and became the beloved of W. B. Yeats; married John MacBride by whom she had a son, Seán.

GREEN, MRS ALICE (*née* Stopford, 1847–1929), daughter of a liberal Church of Ireland cleric; married the English historian J. R. Green in 1877, and became an ardent Home Ruler; published extensively on British and Irish history; a close friend of Casement.

GWYNN, DENIS ROLLESTON (1893–1972), son of the nationalist MP and writer, Stephen Gwynn; converted to Catholicism (as did his brother Aubrey, the Jesuit mediaevalist scholar); wrote extensively on Irish and French historical topics.

HACKETT, FRANCIS (1883–1962), Kilkenny-born journalist and novelist who spent his early manhood in the United States; married a Danish writer and travelled extensively in Europe; having settled in Ireland, quit the country after the banning of *The Green Lion* in 1937.

HALL, SIR [WILLIAM] REGINALD (1870–1943), director of the Admiralty Intelligence Division 1914–18; planned the capture of Casement.

HOBSON, BULMER (1883–1969), Belfast-born Quaker; joined the IRB; close associate of Casement; like him, opposed the timing of the 1916 rising.

LESLIE, SIR SHANE (1885–1971), British diplomat and Irish writer, edited the English-based *Dublin Review*.

MCCARTAN, PATRICK (1878–1963), Ulster-born Irish Volunteer and medical doctor; elected to the House of Commons (1916) and later to Dáil Eireann; member of the Irish Senate 1948–51; published *With De Valera in America* (1932); corresponded with W. B. Yeats, and later stood as a presidential candidate in the Irish Republic.

MACDERMOT, FRANK (1886–1975), educated at Downside and Oxford; rose to the rank of major in the British Army during the Great War and spent some years afterwards in New York banking; was elected to Dáil Éireann in 1932, but found the party system irksome. Later became a *Sunday Times* journalist, but published a biography of Wolfe Tone in 1939.

MCGARRITY, JOSEPH (1874–1940), Irish revolutionary and wealthy American retailer; dominated the Philadelphia chapter of Irish-American opinion through his paper, the *Irish Press*.

MCGRATH, JOSEPH (1887–1966), politician and businessman; held various ministries in the early post-treaty administrations, but resigned from politics in 1924; established the Irish Hospitals Sweepstake in 1930.

MCHUGH, ROGER (1908–1987), playwright and university teacher; professor of Anglo-Irish Literature, 1967–78, at University College Dublin.

MACKEY, HERBERT O. (1894–1966), published a valuable edition of Casement's miscellaneous writings, *The Crime Against Europe*.

MAGENNIS, REV. PETER E., a Carmelite attached to the priory at 338 East 29th Street, NY, in 1918 when money was being raised for Mrs Pearse; by this date he certainly knew Maloney with whom he subsequently travelled to Ireland to broker (unsuccessfully) a truce in the Civil War; National President of the American Friends of Irish Freedom; reviewed *The Forged Casement Diaries* with promptitude in the *Catholic Bulletin* of December 1936.

MAIR, GEORGE HERBERT (1887–1926), graduate of Aberdeen and Oxford; engaged in intelligence work during the Great War, and attended the Versailles Peace Conference; later employed with the League of Nations.

MALONEY, WILLIAM JOSEPH (1882–1952), Edinburgh-born neurologist; served in the Royal Army Medical Corps; injured at Krithia in 1915; married Sarah Margaret McKim in 1913; published Irish propaganda in USA.

MITCHELL, ANGUS (born 1962), postgraduate student at the College of Saint Mary Immaculate, Limerick; edited Casement's White Diary in 1997.

NEESON, EOIN (born Cork, 1927), author, and former head of the Irish Government Information Bureau.

NEVINSON, H. W. (1856–1941), English war correspondent of liberal views, and prolific author; exposed slavery in Portugal's African colonies, 1904–5; covered the Dardanelles campaign for the *Manchester Guardian*, and was wounded in August 1915; attended Casement's trial in a personal capacity.

NORMAND, ARMANDO, named by Casement as a particularly sadistic manager for the Peruvian Amazon Rubber Company. Few other details known.

NOYES, ALFRED (1880–1958), English poet and miscellaneous writer; undertook lecturing tour in the United States, at the behest of the Foreign Office, with a view to encouraging American entry into the Great War (Noyes's first wife was the daughter of an American army colonel). Devoted part of one lecture to Casement's career and character.

O'HEGARTY, PATRICK SARSFIELD (1879–1955), civil servant and bibliophile.

PARRY, MRS GERTRUDE (*née* Bannister; died 1950), together with her sister, she constituted Casement's closest approximation to a family through which he found employment with the Elder Dempster shipping line; supported her cousin loyally during the trial and execution; later sought to recover diaries from the British authorities.

PEARSE, PATRICK (1879–1916), too well known to require summary, the patron saint of 1916 is strangely absent from *The Forged Casement Diaries*; in February 1936, Maloney insisted that the Pearsean blasphemy 'One man can redeem a nation as One Man redeemed the World' be excised.

RUSSELL, SEÁN (1893–1940), IRA Chief of Staff, who organised the bombing campaign in England 1939–40; never looked anyone in the eye.

SHORTER, CLEMENT (1857–1926), English author and editor; married Dora Sigerson, daughter of Dr George Sigerson, Irish antiquarian and writer.

SMITH, F. E. (1872–1930; Lord Birkenhead), lawyer and supporter of Ulster Unionist armed resistance; as attorney-general prosecuted Casement.

STUART, FRANCIS (1902–2000), Australian born Irish novelist; married Iseult, daughter of Maud Gonne and Lucien Millevoye in 1920; interned for republican activities during the Civil War; spent the Second World War in Berlin; prolific novelist and natural controversialist; best remembered for *Blacklist Section H* (1971).

THOMSON, SIR BASIL (1861–1939), assistant commissioner of the Metropolitan Police 1913, director of intelligence Scotland Yard 1919–21.

WILSON, FIELD MARSHAL SIR HENRY (1864–1922), Born in Edgeworthstown and educated at Marlborough; distinguished military career in the field and in administration; assassinated in London.

WISEMAN, SIR WILLIAM GEORGE EDEN (1885–1962), chief of British intelligence in the United States during the Great War, something of a *bête noire* to Maloney.

ZWINGELMANN – the non-existent forger.

Index

Abbey Theatre, 18, 69
Adcock, Frank Ezra, 210
Allen, B. S., 24, 36–7, 40–1, 53–4, 84–97
    passim, 98, 160, 181, 191
    meets RDC, 84
    and Mrs Dryhurst, 87
    Normand Defence attributed to, 75–6
    in NLI: MSS 5,588 etc., 83–97 *passim*,
        203
    in debt to Maloney, 86
    neglected by Maloney after 1932, 88
    inspects Black Diaries, 89
    description of Buff Diary, 90
    letter of 2 December 1932 analysed,
        91–3
    typographical style, 93
    possible victim of extortion, 97
Allen, Mrs Ben S. (*née* French), 84, 91
Allgood, Molly, 27
Alzheimer, Alois, 154
anarchism, 15, 17, 19
anti-Semitism, 42, 112, 145, 154
Antrim, 8–9, 18, 77, 126, 145
apartheid, 112
Arana, Julius Cesar, 4, 5, 99, 116, 117, 183
Arana Brothers, 4
Armstrong, George, 162–3
Armstrong, John, 162–3
Army Mutiny (1924), 50
Archer, William, 23
archival engineering, 29, 44–5, 52–3
Asquith, Herbert (British prime minister),
    23
Associated Press, 84, 87
Auden, W. H., 25
autochthony, *see* chthonic

Bailey, Pearce, 155
Baldwin, Stanley (British prime minister),
    11, 66, 83

Balfour, Arthur, 149, 150
Bannister family, 23, *see also* Parry, Mrs
Baptist Union, president of, 23
Barbados, 21
Barker, Pat, 141
Barnes, Louis, 175
Barnes, Peter, *see* Coventry (IRA bombers)
Barnes Review, 210
Barry, Tom, 30
Barton, Robert (TD), 30
Bath Club (London), 104
Belgian Congo, *see* Congo
Belgium, 84
Bennett, Arnold, 23
Bennett, Gill, 82
Berlin Photographic Co., 123
Best, R. I., 29, 45, 52
Bettelheim, Bruno, 196
Bewley, Charles, 8
Bigelow, Annie, *see* McKim, Mrs Annie
Bigger, F. J., 98, 126
    Maloney's opinion of, 77, 145
Bigger, J. W., 77, 79, 97, 165
Birkenhead, earl of, *see* Smith, F. E.
Birrell, Augustine, 60
Bishop, Frederick, 175, 186
blackmail, 79, 81
Blackwell, Sir Ernley, 10, 170
Blackwood, F. T. H-T. (marquess of
    Dufferin), 122, 125
Blackwood, Lord Terence, 112, 125, 126
Bliven, Bruce, 86, 88–9
    name misspelled, 89, 92, 96
Blondel, Armando, 185
'Blueshirts', *see* fascism in Ireland
Blythe, Ernest, 75
Boer Wars, 16
bondage, 119, 120, 121
book history, 45
Boole, Ethel Lilian, *see* Voynich, Mrs